FUTURE CITIES

ARCHITECTURE AND THE IMAGINATION

PAUL **DOBRASZCZYK**

REAKTION BOOKS

To my father

Published by Reaktion Books Ltd
Unit 32, Waterside
44–48 Wharf Road
London N1 7UX, UK

www.reaktionbooks.co.uk

First published 2019, reprinted 2019
Copyright © Paul Dobraszczyk 2019

Printed and bound in Great Britain by TJ International, Padstow, Cornwall

A catalogue record for this book is available from the British Library

ISBN 978 1 78914 064 4

Contents

Introduction: Real and Imagined Future Cities

I n January 2013 a photograph of a projected image on a smog-enshrouded high-rise building in Beijing became an Internet sensation because it seemed uncannily reminiscent of the urban landscape seen in the 1982 film *Blade Runner*.[1] Notwithstanding the negative effects of excessive urban pollution on urban residents, *Blade Runner* tours are now being offered to tourists to cash in on this unexpected coming together of life and art, of the real and the imagined – a situation that has only intensified after the 2017 release of the film's much-lauded sequel *Blade Runner 2049*.[2] This phenomenon demonstrates just how attuned we are today to the links between what we experience in real cities and the mental images we carry of imagined ones we have encountered in science fiction films, novels and video games. It seems that in cities like Beijing and Shanghai, with their astonishing rate of growth in recent years, the futuristic visions of the past have already arrived, producing a strange mingling of past, present and future. Indeed, the urban landscape of perhaps the most 'futuristic' city today – Dubai – is already being used as a set for cinematic visions of the future, such as in the very first science fiction film produced in the United Arab Emirates, *The Sons of Two Suns*, released in 2013.[3]

The fundamental way in which we make sense of the future is through the imagination: to think of the future is, by necessity, to imagine it. Yet so much of current thinking on the future of cities is instrumental in its nature, drawing on science-based predictions to

Photograph of a projected image on a high-rise building in Beijing in 2013 (top), compared with a shot from the 1982 film *Blade Runner* (bottom).

map out possible scenarios and separating this empirical data from the rather more subjective predictions stemming from the creative imagination. Cities are always a meld of matter and mind, places that we are rooted in both physically and mentally. Furthermore, in the digital age, the real and the imagined are already thoroughly intertwined – why else, after all, would tourists now be offered *Blade Runner* tours? Rather than cleave the imagination from reason, should we not explore how the two are entangled – how together they can open up rich possibilities in terms of how we think the future?

This book aims to do precisely this, by bringing together visions of future cities from the nineteenth century to the present day in all their many and varied forms: in literature, art, architectural imagery, cinema and video games. The central aim of the book is to ground these imaginary cities in architectural practice, demonstrating just how many connections can be made between the two. It will show that images of the future, no matter how fantastical they may be, are really about the present moment – a way of changing current thinking and practice in order to set them on a different course or courses. The book organizes representations of future cities into three thematic areas – unmoored cities (submerged, floating and flying), vertical cities (skyscrapers and undergrounds) and unmade cities (ruins and salvage) – each of which presents a range of examples that relate to real issues confronting urbanists and architects today. These include flooding generated by climate change, rapid population growth and increasing social division, and technological failure and societal collapse, whether imagined or otherwise. At its heart, the book aims to reveal the vital ways in which the imagination impacts on how we think through urban futures and how those can and do link with how cities are designed and lived in today. This is to bring the imaginary back into contact with the real – or rather to show how embedded the imaginary already is in the real – a futurism grounded in the present and in practices of many kinds.

Imaginary Cities

To imagine is to present in your mind's eye something that is absent. It's a conjuring act – a form of magic – in which new images are revealed to the person who imagines.[4] Although always recognized as an important human faculty, the imagination only became ascendant in the Romantic period, as a reaction against the rise of scientific rationalism in the eighteenth century. As poet Samuel Taylor Coleridge argued, for the Romantics, the imagination was like a 'master current' underlying conscious human experience – a powerful force that always threatened to overflow and disrupt the order of the rational mind.[5] Today, imagination is more readily associated with fantasy – the creation of worlds completely separated from 'real' life. Imagination carries a pejorative meaning of escape – of an unwillingness to accept the world as it is and a flight into fanciful worlds of make-believe; and with this, an association with immaturity and childishness. At best, imagination is viewed as a kind of ornamental embellishment of the real, its products – the creative arts – a valuable, albeit unnecessary, way of softening the hard asperities of real life. Yet the human imagination also carries with it a much more serious intent, namely to overturn and rewrite the rules of what the real actually is, or rather, how it is defined. By moving beyond what is given in the world – the things we perceive – imagination reaches for the unforeseen and for what has not yet been experienced. Thus imagination can be said to prepare the ground for the 'real' and is always at work trying to transform it. Here, what is real and what is imagined are not two separate worlds, but ones that are always informing and transforming each other.[6]

But what has the imagination to do with cities – cities after all being made out of materials that we can sense directly? It is no accident that the explosion of literature *about* cities in the nineteenth century coincided with the rapid growth of cities themselves, particularly those affected by industrialization, such as London, New York and Paris. Once a city becomes so large and complex that it exceeds one's ability to comprehend it in a single mental image, then the imagination has to take over – to fill in the gaps in our mental perception of the vast urban environment.[7] The London described in Charles Dickens's novels is a city that melds imagination and reality – a kind of mental projection of the city superimposed over the real one. And we now experience London as a *product* of Dickens's texts, whether by engaging in walking tours taking in his literary landmarks or by 'feeling' the atmosphere of the city at certain times as somehow Dickensian. A similar transference of imagined to real is now happening in the *Blade Runner* tours currently being offered to tourists visiting Shanghai. For every city we visit, we bring a prior imagination of that city, whether formed through paintings we've seen, films we've watched, novels we've read or, more prosaically, through the guidebooks and maps we consult before setting foot on the ground. Think of Kafka's Prague, New York in the films of Woody Allen or Paris in Victor Hugo's *Les Misérables* and its long-running musical counterpart. Indeed, many cities are dependent on the tourism generated by such texts, films and other images; not just in terms of the popularity of their landmark sites or museums dedicated to literary figures, but in the sense of the whole city infused by an imaginary that *attracts*.

Clearly, then, the imagination is important in how cities are perceived and experienced; but how might it affect those that masterplan cities, namely architects and urban planners? First, both architecture and urban planning begin by seeking to picture what the city might become; that is, they *imagine* new possibilities for cities. Although architectural designs have to negotiate a host of constraints that simply don't apply to authors or film-makers, they are still fundamentally imaginative works in that they visualize something that does not yet exist. Architectural visualization – especially in the digital age – relies upon images as tools of persuasion that effectively present something that is essentially a speculation, a fiction. Yet such images often fail to make us *feel* anything about their possible effects on the city. In the same way as the hyperrealism of CGI effects in blockbuster films often leave us cold, many architectural visualizations try to cover over the gap between fantasy and reality. But it is precisely this gap that allows the imagination to function – it alerts us to the difference between fiction and fact; between the world as we find it and the world as we want it to be. As this book will demonstrate, there are countless ways in which architectural projects can be connected to the stories in novels and films, thus enriching their potential to situate us in the built environment they are imagining.

The imagination is both an active agent – a way of constituting something – and also a transformative faculty. When the imagination is at work, what is produced is not an image that bears no relation to the existing world, but rather a reworking of some image that already exists. In other words, there can be no imagination without a past; no conception of what is to come without what has already been. In this sense, history is critical as to how the imagination projects itself into the future: 'the desire for a good city in the future already exists in the imagination of the past.'[8] Consequently, when considering the relationship between the imagination and future cities, past precedents will always be important because they almost always form the basis for more recent urban plans, no matter how unprecedented the latter may seem. Thus when Dubai's Burj Khalifa was opened in 2010, becoming by a clear margin the world's tallest building, its achievement seemed unprecedented; yet it bore a striking resemblance to a much earlier unrealized design by Frank Lloyd Wright for a fantastical mile-high skyscraper in Chicago,[9] even though the Burj's Chicago-based architects Skidmore, Owings & Merrill denied this was the project that inspired them.[10] Whatever the true model for the Burj Khalifa, its design shows how the architectural imagination builds upon itself in a gradual process of accumulation, rather than through any clear breaks with precedent. Bringing past, present and future together in the imagination of future cities has the potential to significantly enrich how we think about the relationship between the speculative and real, and between what has been, what is, and what is to come.

Future Thinking

As we become increasingly aware of the destructive impact of human activity on the planet, some have called for us to recognize that we have entered a new epoch in the planet's history: the Anthropocene.[11] When one is confronted with the fact that the levels of human-produced carbon dioxide in the Earth's atmosphere are now higher than they were 2.5 million years ago, how are we to think about the spans of deep history that separate us from this pre-human era?[12] And how are we to think about the possible impacts of our collective actions in the far future? Even if the human race were to become extinct today, our legacy will live on for many thousands if not millions of years – not just in terms of the CO_2 we are pumping out in vast quantities into the atmosphere, but also the other deadly wastes we are producing, particularly radioactive ones where the half-life of some materials is tens of thousands of years. Here, cities are particularly implicated in the Anthropocene because they are the main driving force of human activity on the planet today: over half of us currently live in cities; by 2030, that figure will probably rise to 70 per cent.[13] With such unprecedented urbanization in the history of human civilization, the making (and unmaking) of cities today requires ever larger quantities of natural resources, energy-guzzling processes of construction, the destruction and despoliation of nature, and the generation of vast quantities of waste.

Too often, the approach adopted in thinking about the future of our cities is based on instrumental thinking, or the idea that the future can be predicted through the projection of empirically observed facts and tried-and-tested technologies. Much of the literature on future cities tends to focus on pragmatic responses to such threats as climate change, with an emphasis on the mitigation of those threats by creating more resilient, energy-efficient and less wasteful cities. While it is obviously laudable for cities of the future to minimize their dependence on fossil fuels, to reduce their wastes and to establish a more harmonious relationship with the natural environment, the current acceleration of urban growth in the Global South does not suggest that these instrumentalist approaches are up to the job of confronting the challenges presented by the explosive population growth and mass migration to cities that are already underway. Indeed, the awareness that comes with the Anthropocene has the effect of shattering conventional ideas about the relationship between cities and the wider planet.

Historian Dipesh Chakrabarty has forcefully argued that the fact that human activity is already having a profound effect on the future of the planet leads to four primary conclusions. First, that the age-old distinction between cities and nature as two separate domains has collapsed; second, that human activity – and city building in particular – is equivalent to a geological force, the future effects of which we don't yet understand very well; third, that we need to think about our long history and future as a species; and, fourth, that there can be no one who is exempt from the effects that our activity will have on the future world, even though it is the urban poor who are likely to be worst affected.[14] Thinking about the future of our cities means looking at the kinds of timescales involved, the interactions between those players that produce the urban environment, and how cities will interact with the non-human world – and all will need to be radically reimagined in ways that are entirely unforeseen because they are completely unprecedented in human history.

What might help us along the road to this radical new type of imagination of cities of the future? To begin with, the imagination needs to be reinvigorated as a genuinely transformative human faculty. We must recognize that the imagination is key in how we 'pre-experience' alternative futures – how we can prepare ourselves for what might be coming. The sheer uncertainty about the possible effects of human activity on the future of the planet forces us to reach for the imagination in sketching out these alternatives. These will not be primarily predictive – believable outcomes based on what we know already – but rather a range of stories that allow us to *feel* what it might be like to live in the future. Scientists, climatologists and policy-makers may balk at the lack of objectivity in the creation of such stories, but it is clear that, in thinking the future, humans need narrative to make sense of a whole range of possible outcomes that can never be predicted with any degree of certainty. This story-based approach to imagining the future encompasses the metaphorical, the ethical, the aesthetic and the speculative, each contributing to a vision not of a predicted future, but of one that is 'probable, preferred, or hoped for'.[15]

We already have an enormous body of speculative fictions out there to ferment this new kind of imagination – over a century's worth of science fiction novels, films and comics, unbuilt architectural projects and, more recently, video games and digital art. Indeed, architecture, and particularly speculative design, shares the same purpose as science fiction – that of imagining what the future might look like if certain tendencies in the present were played out or exaggerated.[16] Geographer Stephen Graham's recent work on vertical urbanism has argued that science fiction cities are 'pivotal in constituting the materialities of contemporary cities' because 'built projects, material cities, sci-fi texts, imaginary futures, architectural schemes and urban theories mingle and resonate together in complex and unpredictable ways.'[17] As the example of the *Blade Runner* tours in Shanghai demonstrates, this intermingling is crucial to the power of science fiction in that it temporarily takes readers and viewers out of the real world they inhabit into an imagined one which is both alluring in its strangeness but also convincing in its familiarity.[18] Thus, when we read a science fiction text, watch a film or look at an image of a future city, we are not escaping from the real, but rather redefining its parameters by creating links between imagined and real cityscapes that are already the ground of our own urban experience. In Graham's estimation, 'real and imagined sci-fi cities . . . offer powerful opportunities for progressively challenging contemporary urban transformation' because they hold, at their core, 'the value of multiplicity rather than the homogeneity of urbanism under global capitalism, and they emphasise the forging of linkages rather than the cutting of ties in an increasingly fragmented world'.[19]

Nurturing an imagination of the future that takes into account our newfound awareness of the Anthropocene will not be an easy task, even with the wealth of imaginative fictions we already have access to. How can architecture and urbanism evolve in more progressive ways when we have become increasingly aware of their destructive nature? Is it just a question of mitigating those tendencies, or is a more radical transformation required and, if so, is that even possible?[20] Perhaps it is time to recognize more widely that architecture does not exist in the self-referential world it so often seems to. Buildings – and the cities buildings sit in – are always much more than the sum of their parts. Rather than simply being material objects, buildings are in reality a whole series of connections: between makers and users; between spaces and forms; between materials and mind; and between flows of all kinds – people, non-human things, facilities, information, time and so on. In thinking of buildings and cities as primarily about connections, we can open our minds to an almost infinite array of possible futures for them – futures that will be defined by how we connect up all manner of things, both material and immaterial, in the here and now. Such futures can never be predictive, but they can empower us because they will release us out into worlds beyond ourselves. In these strange new worlds – the imagined ones – connections we haven't yet been able to realize will suddenly make themselves apparent.

Mental Ecologies

In arguing for the vital role of the imagination in reckoning with the future of our cities, this book taps into an important current tendency in radical politics. There is no doubt that we live in a world saturated by images, a world in which it seems that it is almost impossible to distinguish truth from fiction, 'fake' news from real news. It is therefore completely understandable that many wish to find a way through this cacophony of competing voices by filtering out those they regard as false. Yet, as we have seen recently in our political life, this desire to contain and control is often reactionary, leading to a politics that turns out to be decidedly ugly. A different approach might be to simply accept that the boundaries between the fictive and the real are irrevocably blurred. Perhaps rather than seeking to uncover the 'real' truth behind all those many false appearances, we should try to imagine other truths in order to reinvent the conditions of what is actually possible in the first place.[21]

Political theorist Fredric Jameson's oft-quoted remark that it is easier to imagine the end of the world than the end of capitalism directly challenges the poverty of the contemporary imagination in its inability to generate genuinely new possibilities that go beyond mere escapist fantasies.[22] Under the intense pressures of an accelerating pace of urban life and an equally accelerating rate of urban development, there is a pressing need to reinvest the imagination with the kind of charge that is necessary for alternative visions to neoliberal capitalism to emerge and gain potency. It is precisely the argument of this book that bringing together the experience and imagination of future cities has the potential to contribute to this process, where the contemplation of the future leads not to paralysis or cynicism but rather to new and hopeful beginnings.

But how can the intensely subjective world of the human imagination cohere into something that is shared? At the outset, it is important to remember that responses to imaginative texts and images of future cities are never entirely subjective. Whenever we watch a film or read a novel, we are already engaging in a two-way conversation with the author or film-maker; and, of course, we often watch films or read books together – whether in the darkened communal space of the cinema or in a local book group. In this already shared context, it is the attitudes of readers or viewers that define what kind of politics will come out of these imaginative engagements. Although collective action always risks diminishing the sheer multiplicity of individual human experience, this can be mitigated if we hold out openness to connections rather than closing them down. With this openness, the imagination can bring into being many new ways of thinking about the future, together with a rich variety of images of what our cities might yet become.[23]

What any image of a future city does is to provide a visualization that forges a link between how we imagine the future city and how we relate to it as a real place. On the one hand, images of future cities are inevitably grounded in the urban environment we can already know and experience; on the other, they also push us to think about new ways of living and being in cities. This melding of matter and mind is important because it chimes with holistic ideas of ecology that are emerging in response to the awareness of our damaging effect on the planet. Ecology, broadly defined, is not just concerned with the relationships between humans and nature, but rather the coming together of individuals, social relations and the environment.[24] In this reading, an ecology of the human mind is just as important as one that embraces the external world, because it is vital in resisting the tendency of contemporary capitalism – or any dominating world-view – to constrain the human imagination. Thus the imagination is already politicized because, as a faculty that only flourishes when set free, it inherently resists such subjugation. At stake is the cultivation of a kind of mental resilience to dominating worldviews that goes far beyond conventional ideas of resilience when applied to cities. Usually, when we talk about resilient cities, we refer to the ways in which the hard infrastructure of the urban environment might adapt to things that threaten it in the future, such as rising sea levels and greater incidence of flooding caused by climate change. Yet there is much more to a resilient city than this; just like its physical infrastructures, the networks of the minds of its citizens need to develop resilience in the face of existing and future threats.

The way this book is organized reflects how the imagination might be empowered to think through the multiple threats that now confront urban life. The first part, 'Unmoored Cities', focuses on how cities might adapt to the threats posed by climate change. Chapter One explores how the imagination of submergence has informed texts and images that envisage a future urban environment inundated by rising sea levels; Chapter Two looks at architectural responses garnered from a wide variety of sources that propose the inhabitation of these flood waters; Chapter Three deals with architecture and cities' relationship to air – an air that is already being transformed by anthropogenic atmospheric warming. In this first section, the relationship between climate change and cities is not articulated as one that requires so many 'solutions' to be put forward in order to prepare our cities for what will undoubtedly be a rough ride in the future; rather, it presents a rich field of alternative fictions that can broaden the overtly instru-mental approach adopted by most climate-related literature. The middle part of the book, 'Vertical Cities', focuses on the threat posed by increasing social division in cities across the world. If the vertical city symbolizes social polarity, with its enclave skyscrapers for the super-wealthy and its underground spaces for the urban poor, then the two chapters in this section seek to suggest alternative ways in which the vertical stratification of future cities might be reworked to foster connections rather than divisions. Finally, part three, 'Unmade Cities', focuses on the threat of the ruination of cities, whether through acts of warfare, terrorism, or decay and abandonment. So, Chapter Six considers how ruins in cities might be accepted and integrated into the urban environment itself and what this might mean for their future development, while Chapter Seven explores how cities might be remade out of their own detritus, whether ruined buildings, informal architectures, or waste and rubbish. Moving far beyond conventional notions of recycling, this book argues that integrating wastes into architecture might produce future cities of rich possibilities, ones that expand how we think about what cities are actually made out of.

Cities are a meld of matter and mind – our 'real' experiences of cities are interwoven with networks of metaphors that come from a whole range of different sources. This undoubtedly makes cities messy places, full of the mingling of so many individual imaginations that play themselves out in the minds and experiences of each of the city's inhabitants. While this book cannot hope to capture the full range of these countless imaginary cities, let alone cohere them into an encyclopaedic account that embraces past, present and future, it does attempt to connect some of these myriad images in order to demonstrate that the imagination is key to pre-experiencing alternative futures, to show that we must fully accept and embrace the limitless ground on which cities are formed. This is not to induce a kind of paralysis of confusion or a detachment from feeling, but rather to encourage us all to forge connections with others in any way that promotes more openness to future cities that are hopeful, vibrant, inclusive and optimistic.

I
UNMOORED CITIES

1

Drowned: Postcards from the Future

I n Kim Stanley Robinson's 2017 science fiction novel *New York 2140*, the city of the future has become a vertical super-Venice, after being flooded by rising seas caused by global warming melting the Arctic ice caps.[1] While the lower storeys of many of Manhattan's skyscrapers have been overtaken by the sea, residents continue to live in those above, accessing them via boathouses and pontoons. A tangle of sky-bridges connect the lofty heights of many of these skyscrapers, the streets beneath now canals traversed by countless boats and gondolas. Ruins litter the intertidal zone, inhabited by the desperate and the poor; while airships agglomerate above the buildings into sky villages. Robinson's imagined New York of the future hasn't succumbed to the ravaging effects of climate change; rather, it has adapted to the changes by radically reshaping its built environment.

Despite the fact that climate change is already affecting vulnerable cities like New York – principally featuring an increased incidence and severity of urban flooding – it remains a phenomenon that is dominated by future predictions. Even by the cautious estimates of the most recent report by the Intergovernmental Panel on Climate Change in 2014, cities are in for a rough ride in the next century. By 2100 the rise in global temperatures is almost certain to exceed 2 degrees Celsius (3.6°F) above pre-industrial levels, and, alarmingly, already reached that level for a short time in early 2016. Sea levels will rise by anything up to a metre, or more if current predictions prove to be over-optimistic (and *New York 2140* is based on an estimated rise of 15 metres, or 49 feet, over the next one hundred years). At the same time, the oceans will also warm and become more acidic; and the turbulence of the atmosphere will intensify, leading to more extreme weather events and a greater risk of flooding.[2] Cities are especially vulnerable to the effects of climate change, particularly coastal or tidal-river-based conurbations – including 22 of the world's major cities according to the Stern Review of 2006.[3]

As much as these climate reports are grounded in empirical evidence, they are nevertheless essentially predictive, laying out a whole host of possible futures that rely on our ability to imagine those futures, even with the help of a welter of facts and figures.[4] The overwhelmingly future-oriented language of climate change is perhaps the principal reason why it has been and continues to be so difficult to find common agreement as to how to act in the face of such fundamental uncertainty.[5] It is no wonder then that the focus of much of the current thinking on climate change and cities is on mitigation rather than adaptation, and this formed the focus of the landmark international climate change agreement in Paris at the end of 2015.[6] Even the emerging body of literature on climate change and urban resilience, which seeks to shift the focus from mitigation to adaptation, remains firmly grounded in instrumental thinking – whether adaptation of the built fabric through long-term strategic planning, or reshaping of urban governance and socio-political life towards sustainable ends.[7] While these objectives are laudable, what is underplayed in much of this work is the role of the creative imagination in thinking through the relationship between urban futures and climate change. As *New York 2140* shows us, the imagination can be a powerful tool for articulating radical new possibilities for urban life in the face of equally radically uncertain futures.

In this chapter, I explore imaginative modes of thinking – both utopian and dystopian – in relation to future cities and climate change, focusing on images of drowning or submergence produced by fiction writers, visual artists and architects as ways of thinking through the range of possibilities for urban life in a world transformed by rising sea levels. The urban centres that ground these imaginative engagements – here the focus is on London, Washington, DC, Melbourne, Bangkok and New York – are undoubtedly global 'landmark' cities, even though more peripheral and impoverished cities will likely be the first to be affected by rising sea levels and more severe and frequent flooding. This reflects the fact that imaginative engagements with climate change – whether in novels, films, art or architectural speculation – have largely emerged from those landmark cities themselves, probably because there is a sense that the threats posed by climate change for the affluent West are still held at bay – a future possibility rather than a clear and present risk. It remains to be seen how the imagination of climate change will evolve as the threat to these cities continues to grow.

Taken together, the themes and works explored here aim to establish resonances between a wide range of imaginative visions of future cities that engage, whether explicitly or obliquely, with the transformed urban environments that will likely be brought about by climate change. The emphasis here on *multiple* imaginaries of climate change – whether in literature, art or the architectonic – is critical in expanding the narrow range of possibilities that currently characterize conventional ways in which we think about the relationship between cities and climate change. To enlarge these possibilities is not merely to add another layer of interpretation onto the scientific or instrumentalist – an aesthetic embellishment of the pragmatic; rather, it redraws the boundaries of the entire field of thinking about climate change, particularly with respect to how it affects our psyches – that is, our thinking and feeling about the subject.

Climate Change Fictions

There is a long history of collective fears of apocalyptic inundations, ones that date back to prehistory in countless stories of devastating deluges that characterize so many of the world's religious and spiritual traditions.[8] These ur-floods may have grown from myths and legends but their almost universal presence in diverse geographical locations and cultural traditions reflect the fact that floods are the most common disasters known to man.[9] The most famous submerged city in history, Atlantis, may have been a mythic assemblage of classical architectures buried under the city's namesake ocean; but it was probably also inspired by real urban drownings in the ancient world, whether cities submerged by flood waters or others buried by Vesuvius's ash and mud.

Throughout history, vulnerable cities have been literally obliterated by the seas – the archaeologists and scuba diver's paradise off the coast of Alexandria is testament to rising sea levels that drowned ancient cities;[10] the city of Saeftinghe in the Netherlands and Dunwich in England are victims of more recent disasters, the former being devastated in the All Saints' Flood of 1750 (never to be recovered), the latter slowly erased by relentless coastal erosion.[11] More recently, some cities have been given up to others in the demand for fresh water: for example Shi Cheng, the Lion City, which lies in ruins at the bottom of a hydroelectric dam in China, and the city of Igaratá in Brazil, submerged since 1969 after the creation of a reservoir but which recently started to re-emerge after one of the worst droughts in recent history.[12]

The prospect of future drownings due to the effects of climate change – principally rises in sea levels caused by melting ice in the polar regions and Greenland – has been a dominant motif in recent climate change fictions,[13] probably because it resonates with this long history of real and imagined drowned cities as well as providing a way of rendering the effects of climate change in a local context.[14] Within this body of fiction, two types of stories dominate: on the one hand, imagined post-diluvian cityscapes after a catastrophic flood in the

future; on the other, novels that chart the progress of a flood that
gradually transforms an urban environment. In the first category, the
most influential precedent is J. G. Ballard's early novel *The Drowned
World*, published in 1962. Although written long before global warming
was even coined as a term (in 1975), the novel has come to be regarded
as a major influence on more recent climate change fiction and also
prescient of real climate-related disasters, such as the devastation of
New Orleans in the wake of Hurricane Katrina in 2005.[15] Ballard also
self-consciously positioned the novel within an existing English
literary tradition of imagining London's death by water, from Richard
Jefferies's fantasia *After London* (1885) to John Wyndham's *The Kraken
Wakes* (1953).[16] Yet, in explicit contrast to Wyndham's novel, where
the emphasis is on survival and rebuilding, or the more recent reconstruction of post-Katrina New Orleans, where flood defences have
been strengthened, *The Drowned World* posits a transformed urban
world that must be adapted to in order for an authentic human
experience to emerge.[17]

Ballard's novel presents a hallucinatory vision of a future London
that has been sunk beneath vast flood waters created by the melting
of the polar ice sheets, the latter caused by rapid global warming that
resulted from a sudden increase in solar radiation. *The Drowned World*
imagines London as a city that has been literally swamped by exotic
flora and fauna that has reverted back to resemble that of the Palaeozoic
era: an 'impenetrable Matto Grosso sometimes three hundred feet
high' that consumed the city's half-submerged steel-supported tower
blocks; giant iguanas that made their homes in the boardrooms of
former offices; outsized bats that created their eyries in the ruined
buildings; and, in between the last vestiges of the city, a network of
lagoons filled with rotting vegetation and the carcasses of dead animals.[18] Living in the former Ritz Hotel, the novel's isolated protagonist,
Kerans, is part of a group of scientists who are gathering information
about the world's drowned cities before heading to the last remaining
place fit for human habitation – the Arctic – where the remnants of

humanity have gathered. With the air temperature and humidity rising each day, Kerans experiences his own psychic equivalent of regression, eventually embracing the new jungle before him, the novel concluding with this 'second Adam' heading south towards his certain death. Key to Ballard's vision – and the undoubted power of his prose – is the way in which the transformed urban environment functions as a mirror image of the processes going on in Kerans's psyche, whether in his constant confrontation with the submerged city itself (an obvious metaphor for the unconscious mind), the abandoned clock towers he sees, their faces without hands, or a chalk-white colonnade visited by Kerans that reminds him of an Egyptian necropolis.[19]

Although *The Drowned World* presents a powerful vision of a city (and individual psyche) transformed by climate change, it glosses over human responsibility for the catastrophic flooding – it is the Sun that causes London to be drowned, not human activity. Unsurprisingly, this has proved a problematic precedent for fictions that address anthropogenic climate change. Yet vivid images of submerged cities that draw their inspiration from Ballard's novel have been created in a number of recent climate change fictions. Paolo Bacigalupi's *The Drowned Cities* (2012) is similar to *The Drowned World* in both its self-explanatory title and also the fact that the identity of the city it depicts – Washington, DC – is, like Ballard's future London, only revealed towards the end of the novel. Mirroring Ballard's post-diluvian London, the American capital has been overtaken by tropical vegetation, but, unlike Ballard's uninhabited city, this one has become home to rival warlords and scavengers. With Washington's Chinese counterpart, Shanghai Island, remaining a bastion of civilization, Bacigalupi inverts conventional contemporary assumptions about America's enlightened democracy versus China's repressive political regime.

No less savage in its politics, but more satirical, is Will Self's *The Book of Dave* (2008), where London, four hundred years into the future, has been submerged by 100 metres (328 ft) of seawater, turning the city into an archipelago. With its social and political life based on the eponymous 'Book of Dave', the rantings of a London cabbie that are revealed in the segments of the book set in our present-day era, the imagined future world sees Dave's bigoted views and cockney dialect developed into an entire social and linguistic world. The novel's fantastic premise is also grounded in Self's own encyclopaedic knowledge of London, one that closely links this future city to London in the here and now, with all its current dystopian tendencies – increasing social division, the rise in right-wing nationalism, and the globalization of finance and culture – imagined as being played out in the form of a reactionary future *in extremis*. In a completely different vein, Kim Stanley Robinson's *New York 2140*, introduced at the beginning of this chapter, imagines present-day capitalism surviving and even flourishing in a flooded future New York, with the city's island skyscrapers and ruined intertidal districts becoming the target of ruthlessly acquisitive speculators. Although the submerged cities in these novels host social lives profoundly different from our own, they nevertheless draw those lives firmly within the orbit of the familiar, whether through landmarks such as the Washington Monument and the White House in *The Drowned Cities*, the myriad familiar-yet-different street and place names of a future London in *The Book of Dave*, or the still intact buildings and districts of Manhattan in Robinson's novel.

In contrast to these post-diluvian future cities, some recent climate change fictions have used the image of flooded cities to build a different story, namely that of flood-as-duration. These imagine social relations in future cities that are being slowly transformed by rising sea levels, and notable examples include Melbourne in George Turner's *The Sea and Summer* (published in 1987, when awareness of climate change was only just emerging), Bangkok in Bacigalupi's *The Windup Girl* (2009) and London in Maggie Gee's *The Flood* (2004) and Stephen Baxter's *Flood* (2008). In all of these city-based climate change fictions, the relationships between characters in a transforming urban environment take precedence over dramatic descriptions of submerged cities. Yet they do so for varied reasons.

In *The Sea and Summer* the emphasis is on relations between sharply divided classes – as sea levels inexorably rise, Melbourne's tiny urban elite retreat to high ground in secure compounds, while the 90 per cent poor and unemployed eke out subsistence-level living in flood-prone tower blocks. *The Windup Girl* focuses on the relationship between humans and their artificially created cousins (the windup girl of the book's title) in Bangkok, an island-city ringed by enormous defensive walls protecting it temporarily from an outside world in violent turmoil.

Gee's and Baxter's London-based novels centre on near-contemporaneous urbanites dealing with an ongoing crisis – unending rain and rising flood waters – and an impending catastrophe, namely an apocalyptic tsunami in *The Flood* that engulfs the entire city in the final moments of the novel, and an even-greater apocalypse in *Flood* as sea levels continue to rise until they submerge all of the planet's continents. In contrast to *The Drowned World*, the cityscapes in these novels function more as backdrops to social interactions and character development and therefore lack the hallucinatory power of Ballard's post-diluvian London. Yet this focus on social relations forces an acknowledgement that human connections are intimately bound to real places and that in threatening those places, climate change also threatens the characters with whom the reader has identified. In this way, the near-future London depicted in *The Flood* draws us back to the present-day city that we know and experience, rather than forward to a transformation that is only seen as destructive and diminishing.

Taken together, climate change fictions that imagine future drowned cities invite multiple ways of working through possible apocalyptic scenarios. Although most exaggerate the scale and shorten the timescale of future flooding for dramatic effect, they do so in order to galvanize the imagination towards redemptive rather than reactionary ends – whether in the transformation of the individual psyche when confronted with radical change or the evolution of social relations during the progression towards catastrophe. These creative imaginings of future cities are important because they flag up the fact that the ways in which we think and talk about climate change are inevitably both real and fabricated, relying as they do on the work of the imagination as much as scientific enquiry. After all, many non-fictional accounts of climate change also draw on exaggerated apocalyptic imagery for rhetorical effect.[20] Climate change fictions also point to the need for the human imagination to think through *adapting* to the future effects of climate change, something that tends to be sidelined in scientific climate discourse, with its focus on mitigation.

These novels demonstrate a wealth of adaptive strategies taken up by urban inhabitants in the face of catastrophe, from the total acceptance of the solitary contemplative in *The Drowned World* to the communal struggles of *The Flood* and *The Sea and Summer* and the technological and economic ingenuity of *New York 2140*.[21] Finally, even as these fictions project the city forward in time (whether the far future of Ballard's novel or the near-contemporary London of *The Flood*) they nevertheless draw readers back into the world they inhabit in the present, a world already set on a future course that we will – individually, collectively, and all together with the changing climate – play a part in bringing into being.

Postcards from the Future

One of the most striking images of London in ruins is an engraving by Gustave Doré from 1872, which was the final illustration in William Blanchard Jerrold's book *London: A Pilgrimage*. Depicting what was then the world's largest city – and the centre of a global empire – Doré's image was a late expression of the nineteenth-century obsession with the figure of the 'New Zealander', an imagined New World successor to the British who would, in the far distant future, come to gaze upon the ruins of London just as Victorian travellers gazed upon those of ancient Rome.[22] It is also a powerful image of submergence: the city slowly succumbing to ruin from above – its buildings sinking into

the ground – and below, from the waters of the river Thames, long
released from its human-made embankments.

Tapping into late nineteenth-century anxieties about both imperial
decline and London's seemingly intractable social divisions, this image
has persisted as an early precursor to cinema's enduring obsession
with picturing urban destruction. Apocalyptic flood disaster films, from
Deluge (1933) to *The Day after Tomorrow* (2004), use New York's landmarks, such as the Statue of Liberty, in the same way as Doré's image
uses the sunken pillars of Blackfriars Bridge and the ruined dome of
St Paul's Cathedral beyond, to provide memorable visual reference
points for wholly unfamiliar doomsday storylines.[23] The sense of flood
waters restoring untamed nature back to the city resonates with cinematic images of post-apocalyptic cities, perhaps most notably New
York in *I Am Legend* (2007) and London in *The Girl with All the Gifts*
(2016). Indeed, these two aspects of deluge imagery – the apocalyptic
and post-apocalyptic – mirror the two strands already identified above
in relation to fiction, namely the imagination of cities after a catastrophic flood and those that focus on the flooding event or events
themselves. As with fiction, these images tend to emphasize, on the
one hand, the experiences of a solitary survivor (the New Zealander
in Doré's image) and, on the other, the attempts by urban inhabitants
to come to terms with flooding, even if, in the cinematic tradition,
this usually focuses on rebuilding cities rather than adapting to their
submergence.

In relation to more recent predictions about the impact of sea-
level rises on low-lying cities, visual imagery is characterized by
two dominant viewpoints, namely from above and below the flood
waters. Views from above include the predictive flood maps issued
by the UK Environment Agency – conventional map views of cities
like London overlaid with swathes of blue indicating areas at risk
from future flooding – and more creative adaptations of maps seen
in Jeffrey Linn's series of sea-rise maps, in which the artist has shown
how world cities such as London, Los Angeles, Vancouver and Hong

Gustave Doré,
'The New Zealander',
wood-engraved
print from William
Blanchard Jerrold,
London: A Pilgrimage
(1872).

Kong would virtually disappear if sea levels rose by 66 metres (217 ft), the highest level currently predicted by the Intergovernmental Panel on Climate Change.[24] Views from above also include bird's-eye views of cities showing how sea-level rises will alter the sky- and shorelines, as well as the riverscapes, of iconic urban areas – for example, John Upton's digital photomontage of Manhattan skyscrapers used in Al Gore's polemical film *An Inconvenient Truth*, released in 2007.

There is no doubting the powerful effect such imagery can have. It provides a dramatic at-a-glance picture of what cities might look like if flooded by rising sea levels. Yet it also distances viewers from the catastrophic effects of flooding on the ground. What we see in these images are effectively stage sets – cities emptied of their inhabitants and submergence as an inevitable and unstoppable apocalyptic event, even as the process leading to flooding on such a scale would probably take centuries to work itself out.

Views from below are less common than those from above, probably because it is much more difficult to imagine living below the flood waters than above them. These views include digital images of submerged cities, such as François Ronsiaux's Times Square in New York enveloped in submarine blue and Nickolay Lamm's similarly rendered image of Miami under a 7.6-metre (25-ft) rise in sea levels.[25]

Jeffrey Linn's *London Bay*, 2015, a map of London showing how the city might be affected by an 80-m (262-ft) rise in sea levels.

London Bay

Based on 80m sea level rise

Approximate sea level if *all* of the world's ice sheets melted

These images present desolate urban vistas, devoid of any life bar the observer, even as the flood waters are rendered crystal clear. In contrast, in one of a series of five images produced by the UK media production studio Squint/Opera, London's future flood waters support a rich marine ecosystem. Looking up from the bottom of a new shallow sea towards the half-submerged church of St Mary's on London's Strand, this image provides an unfamiliar counter to the otherwise predominantly pessimistic representations of underwater urban futures.[26] Exhibited as part of the London Architecture Festival in 2008, this view from below offers a sense of optimism – in their London of the future, the floods have actually enhanced the urban environment by bringing in abundant wildlife and new opportunities for entrepreneurship.[27] Yet, just how such an improved way of life will come about is far from clear in the image, bar the inclusion of a manned boat that suggests a tranquil human presence. In addition, its depiction of a thriving marine ecosystem in clear, pure waters is entirely at odds with most climate change novels that represent the progress of future urban floods. Thus in *The Flood* the rising waters smell 'of rot, of toilets'; in *The Sea and Summer*, they are filthy, 'full of floating, nameless debris, stinking rubbish' and 'soft slops of slime that touched and clung'; while in *Flood*, they are choked with bodies and wastes, 'murky grey-brown', 'slick with oil' and 'littered with garbage, plastic scraps and bursting bin liners'.[28] Mirroring the experience of many when dealing with the aftermath of real urban floods, when raw sewage often rises up from underground sewers, these fictions undermine the image of any future flood waters as restorative or regenerative.

At first glance, the flood waters in Alexis Rockman's painting *Manifest Destiny* (2003–4) seem to be supporting an equal abundance of life as Squint/Opera's image of a bucolic flooded London.[29] But this is not life as we know it; it is an extraordinary array of organisms made up of a mixture of recognizable flora and fauna (algae, coral, seals, lampreys, carp, an enormous jellyfish, sunfish and lionfish underwater; and gulls, cormorants, egrets and pelicans above) and strange new

Squint/Opera, 'St Mary Woolnath – Rich Pickings', digital image from the series *Flooded London*, 2008.

bioengineered species, including fish sprouting pustules, outsized
deadly viruses (identified by the artist as HIV, West Nile and SARS)
and other bacteria-like creatures and mutant crustaceans.[30] Most of
the non-human life in the painting seems alien, for this is a split-level
panorama of the New York district of Brooklyn in the year 5000, after
global warming has not only submerged the city but transformed its
climate from temperate to tropical. Despite the fact that the landscape
is empty of human beings, the legacy of the latter is evident everywhere. Here, the remains of the built environment – the Brooklyn
Bridge on the right, vestigial skyscrapers in the distance and, perhaps
most strikingly, the city's subterranean infrastructure of tunnels, storage vaults, sewers, and gas and water pipes – not only linger in the

far distant future but have played a key role in the evolution of the organisms that now inhabit them. Scattered throughout the image are also the products of present-day accelerated capitalism that mock the hubris that characterizes our technological age – a floating oil barrel, a sunken oil tanker, stealth bomber and submarine. Finally, Rockman also includes in his painting the remains of projects yet to be built (in 2004), most notably dykes and sea walls meant to protect the city against sea-level rises, but which, in the far distant future, have long been overwhelmed by the inexorable flood waters.

In its extraordinary attention to detail and concern with accuracy – during the process of creating the work Rockman consulted with palaeontologists, biologists, archaeologists and architects – *Manifest*

Alexis Rockman,
Manifest Destiny,
2003–4, oil on board.

Destiny presents not only a dire warning to a pervasive contemporary reluctance to change the destructive course of industrial capitalism but a compelling image of how the human-built world will continue to influence the evolution of the environment long after humans themselves have disappeared. With its mixture of tropical and surreal flora and fauna, the intensity of its sunlight and the absence of humans, Rockman's vision mirrors Ballard's hallucinogenic image of a future London in *The Drowned World*; yet, unlike that novel, it points us back to ourselves in the here-and-now, challenging us to think more seriously and more imaginatively about the long-term effects our collective actions will have on the world to come. As such, *Manifest Destiny* chimes strongly with the emergence of the idea of the Anthropocene in the 2000s as defining a new epoch in geological time in which human activity, and particularly an accelerating urbanism, is as 'geologic' a force as natural ones. Even though the painting transports the viewer to a barely conceivable 3,000 years into the future, it nevertheless spells out clearly the connections between our own time and this long jump forward. The painting breaks down the entrenched humanist distinction between natural and human history – in *Manifest Destiny*, both the future of the city and of nature are thoroughly intertwined. As such, the painting clearly flags up the need to think through those connections today and to recognize that they are already putting us on the road to the future envisaged in the painting. However, as its ironic title suggests, such a future is not inevitable; rather, *Manifest Destiny* invites us to consider how our own small actions are interwoven with the world and how they might be changed to co-create a more sustainable future.

Manifest Destiny also calls into question the current tendency to combat urban inundations with more effective flood defences, as seen in both post-Katrina New Orleans and in many towns in the UK affected by recent flooding. With New York's own future-built flood defences swallowed by the sea, the painting clearly shows the folly of such an approach in its unwillingness to make the deeper changes to both mitigate and adapt to global warming, a point that is perhaps at last being recognized in a shift towards ideas of resilience in the UK government's 2016 National Flood Resilience Review. Such warnings are also characteristic of the climate change fictions discussed previously: the vast sea walls that surround Melbourne in the mid-twenty-first century in *The Sea and Summer* are eventually overwhelmed; the relocation of New York to higher ground in *Flood* proves fruitless; and the seemingly impregnable walls and pumps encircling Bangkok in *The Windup Girl* are finally destroyed by the inhabitants' inability to peacefully resolve their conflicts.

In both literary and visual depictions of submerged urban futures, the intention is clearly to engage our imaginations in thinking through a radically different kind of future urban life. Even though the urban transformations depicted in many fictions and images of the effects of future climate change are extreme or exaggerated, they nonetheless provide intimations of what might be required for genuine human and social transformation to occur. This idea closely reflects the original meaning of the word 'apocalypse' – the Greek *apokalupsis*, meaning revelation or disclosure. In most cases, apocalyptic urban drowning in texts and images is not oriented towards a terminal point in the future but rather produces an ongoing revelation that transforms. These images open up an ambiguous space where a transformed future urban environment can be temporarily *lived in* by readers/viewers in order to establish resonances between their inner and outer worlds.

Just what the outcome of such resonances may be is unknown; yet the insistence in all of these fictions that there can be no clear separation made between outer and inner space chimes with the current emphasis on just such an entwining of the human and non-human environments with their different histories (and future trajectories) – namely, the short spans of individual and collective human history and the 'deep' geological and ecological time of the earth.[31]

Submarine Cities

Although the novels and imagery examined so far describe urban environments radically transformed by rising sea levels, their built environments tend to remain cast in relatively conventional terms: familiar concrete tower blocks and skyscrapers in *The Sea and Summer*, *The Flood* and *Flood* sink beneath the flood waters rather than being adapted in terms of their design; cities are abandoned for giant cruise ships that eventually prove just as vulnerable in *Flood*. Only in *New York 2140* do we witness a city that has adapted its buildings to rising sea levels, whether through the construction of sky-bridges between residential towers, the creation of airborne sky villages or the development of a new aquatic transportation network. By accommodating water in innovative ways, *New York 2140* invites us to imagine how architects might respond to buildings becoming partially or completely submerged.

The exploration and inhabitation of the submarine environment has long held a fascination for many writers and designers, from Jules Verne's *Twenty Thousand Leagues under the Sea* (1870) to the development of scientific and military underwater habitats in the second half of the twentieth century, whether research laboratories like the u.s. Navy-designed SEALAB submersibles in the 1960s, or Jacques Cousteau's experimental Conshelf communities. Stimulated by these technological developments, in the 1960s architects began to imagine the building of entire cities underwater. These included a submarine hotel complex displayed as part of General Motors's 1964 Futurama exhibit at the World's Fair in New York, Warren Chalk's interconnecting spheres in his Underwater City project for Archigram in the same year, and Jacques Rougerie and Édith Vignes' projects in the early 1970s for a submarine village, museum and deep-sea research laboratory.[32]

In recent years, a renewed interest in underwater living has been stimulated by both the threat of rising sea levels and the extreme overcrowding of existing terrestrial cities. In popular media, *National*

Geographic produced *City under the Sea* (2011), a pseudo-documentary charting the construction of an imagined future submarine city built in response to global warming and comprised of communal domes on the seabed linked to rows of living pods for the 'aquanaught' families. In architecture, designers have published their own proposals for underwater cities of the future, most of which adopt semi-submersible structures as their basic units. For example, Phil Pauley's Sub-Biosphere 2 project from 2010 envisions a settlement of eight domes connected to a central spherical support structure,[33] while Alanna Howe and Alexander Hespe's Ocean City, also from 2010, imagines clusters of floating platforms with submerged living quarters that resemble jellyfish in their design.[34] In thrall to a technological optimism in the face of ecological crisis, as well as a libertarian politics that seeks to create new autonomous territories, these projects demonstrate the enduring appeal of the idea of the sea as a hostile environment to be conquered – a frontier for the melding of individual freedom and unfettered technological innovation. Although these projected cities claim to create truly sustainable habitats – self-sufficient communities that recycle all wastes, generate all their energy from renewable sources and grow their own food – they nevertheless fail to articulate any kind of progressive social programme, instead falling back on the elitist libertarian ideals that have characterized utopias of this kind from the early twentieth century onwards. They also fail to engage with the sea as a dynamic environment, one that we know is rapidly changing as it absorbs the carbon dioxide we continue to release into the atmosphere. As the recent wave of mass coral-bleaching events in Australia's Great Barrier Reef testify, the sea is becoming more acidic as it warms, a factor that will irrevocably alter the entire marine ecosystem. To assume that humans can colonize a pristine new environment is a dangerous illusion.

Yet there are currents within the architectural imagination of submerged cities that suggest a richer engagement with the sea as it might become in a warming climate. Back in 1970 – when many were first becoming consumed with fear about the likelihood of grim urban futures of environmental pollution and overpopulation – the architect Wolf Hilbertz and artist Newton Fallis first sketched out a proposal for their Autopia Ampere project, a marine city that would literally grow out of the sea at Seamount Ampere, a site of shallow waters situated about halfway between the Madeira Islands and the tip of Portugal.[35] The city would begin as a series of wire-mesh armatures anchored on top of a sea mountain. Once in place, the wire mesh would be connected to a supply of low-voltage direct current produced by solar panels. Over time, electrochemical reactions would draw minerals from the sea to the armatures, creating walls of calcium carbonate – a natural spiral-shaped dam that would emerge from the sea to create an inhabitable structure that would protect a sizeable population from the otherwise hostile marine environment.

Although Autopia Ampere was never realized, Hilbertz's visionary 'growing' architecture eventually led to his development (in collaboration with the coral scientist Thomas Goreau) of 'Biorock' in 1979 (also known as Seacrete or Seament), a substance formed by the electro-accumulation of materials dissolved in seawater.[36] This material has found a viable use in the restoration of damaged coral reefs, with the Biorock grown to attract corals and other marine life in order to rebuild submarine ecosystems and make them more resilient to changes in the temperature of seawater.[37] In a world where coral has already become one of the first casualties of climate change, Biorock is likely to become an important way of creating new submarine environments out of the ruins of the old. In this sense, Hilbertz's submarine-grown building material is very different from any proposed in more conventional designs for underwater habitats; because it is able to adapt to changes in the constitution of the sea, it is a material that is ideally suited to the age of the Anthropocene. It provides a pertinent model for urban design that seeks to adapt to the waters that will eventually inundate many cities. As many of the future fictions discussed above make clear, such water will not be pristine and

undefiled, but rather filled with a host of human-made substances, whether dissolved carbon dioxide, indestructible plastic or other urban wastes. It may become evident that the only building material that will be able to adapt to submerged cities will be one that is grown in the transformed environment.

    Hilbertz's Biorock is an important precursor to a recent trend in architectural design that seeks to engineer biomorphic materials that mimic nature, thereby questioning conventional interpretations of

Alanna Howe and Alexander Hespe's Ocean City project, 2010.

what sustainable and resilient architecture might be.[38] Such an approach has led to some radical urban design proposals that directly address the prospect of rising sea levels. In her 2009 TED Talk, the synthetic biologist Rachel Armstrong proposed using protocells (chemical agents that behave in lifelike ways) to grow an immense artificial limestone reef structure under Venice to save the city from sinking into the sea.[39] In the same year but in a different vein, CRAB Studio (led by architects Peter Cook and Gavin Robotham) addressed the prospect of a future flooded London with their Soak City project,

Paul Cureton (after Newton Fallis), perspective view of Autopia Ampere, 2013, pencil and ink on paper.

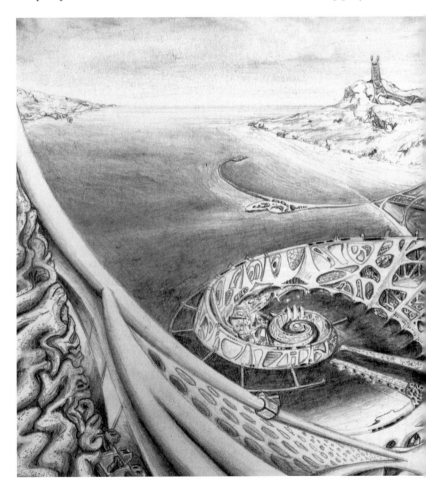

a series of towers sited in East London that would be hand-built from the remains of former buildings and other salvaged materials.[40] The towers themselves were developed from Cook and Robotham's earlier projects for vegetated dwellings, which conceived of buildings taking plants into themselves as part of their ongoing evolution and growth, eventually resulting in hybrid architectures that meld nature and artifice.[41] Enveloped in the dense vegetation that has grown out of the flood waters themselves, the Soak City towers suggest a future semi-submerged urban environment that allows

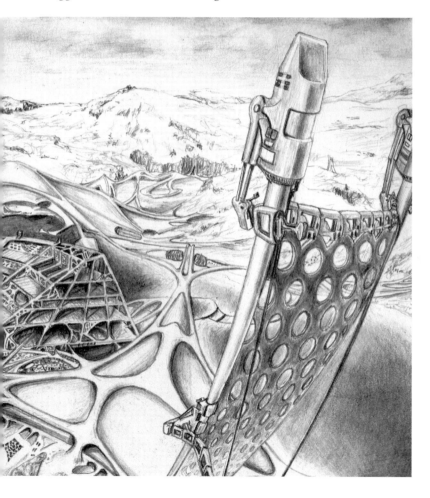

continued inhabitation through a radical form of adaptation. Soak City's vegetated towers mirror the verdant ruins of the Brooklyn Bridge in *Manifest Destiny* and the vine-choked apartment blocks and offices in Ballard's *The Drowned World*, but, in contrast to both, also envisages a thriving human presence that responds to the flooded city with complete acceptance, resulting in a dynamic coexistence with the transformed urban environment.

The kind of architectural conjecture seen in Hilbertz's Autopia Ampere and CRAB Studio's Soak City radically departs from conventional notions of building as deriving from the fabrication of construction materials. Instead, making in these projects is fundamentally a process of growth. As such, it chimes strongly with the arguments put forward by anthropologist Tim Ingold, who has sought a renewal of the notion of design as a process of making that intervenes in 'worldly processes that are already going on, and which give rise to the forms of the living world that we see all around us'. In Ingold's view, architects do not impose their designs on the world as if those two domains were entirely separate; rather they add their 'own impetus to the forces and energies [already] in play'.[42] In relation to climate change and the prospect of future submergence, urban designers must face head-on the challenge of designing *with* these future conditions, rather than falling back on the notions of mitigation and containment that continue to characterize mainstream approaches.

Climate change scientists may attempt to predict likely outcomes of rising sea levels on cities using empirical evidence, but those predictions are usually stated in bald statistical terms, avoiding engagement with the emotional consequences of presenting such alarming news. Climate change fictions, whether they take the form of texts, images or architectural conjecture, fill the gap here, making room for other kinds of forecasts, not of a predictive nature, but centred on the creation of future narratives – stories that we can latch onto in terms of imagining what it would be like to *live* in these possible future urban worlds. They also anchor those possible futures in human experience

in the here and now, but each in different ways. Climate change novels focus on the subjective and social responses to submerged cities, and ask us to work through our own feelings in relation to a disturbing future; images of future urban flooding show us transformed cities that are nevertheless grounded in familiar landmarks or views that we already know; architectural speculation shows us how the urban spaces we live and move in today might be reworked to allow us to continue to inhabit them.

CRAB Studio, Soak City, 2009, perspective view.

These fictions are not suggesting mere resignation in the face of the threat of rising flood waters, or that political, economic and social life should remain as it is; rather, they demonstrate that change – the kind of transformational change that is and will be undoubtedly required of us in the face of a new global climatic order – can only come about by showing how to *live* that change, rather than merely accept that it is necessary. So, post-diluvian novels show us how the radical transformation of the built environment might change both individual psyches and social relations, while flood-as-duration novels present that change on a more incremental level. Images of future submerged cities emphasize how the everyday aesthetics of the urban environment will be transformed, leading us to change how we see and experience our cities in the here and now. Finally, speculative architecture asks us to think through how we might change how we live in cities by opening up new possibilities for inhabitation and for the making and unmaking of our buildings. If we agree that our cities really are made and unmade in the imagination as much as in their material spaces – a meld of matter and mind – then imaginative texts, images and designs must mutually inform each other to encourage holistic ways of approaching how we think about the future prospect of urban submergence. This is how we incubate radical responses to it.

2
Floating: Water and Urban Utopias

Stephen Baxter's 2008 apocalyptic novel *Flood* begins with a familiar scenario in climate change fictions. In the near future (2016 in the novel), global warming has resulted in a sea-level rise of around 5 metres (16 ft), which, combined with a storm surge, overwhelms London's Thames Barrier, causing catastrophic flooding across the city. However, this opening plot device is a ruse – for the rise in sea levels continues relentlessly, not as a result of melting ice but rather of vast subterranean waters being released into the existing seas. Just 35 years later the tip of Mount Everest disappears to leave a world without land. Throughout the novel, the billionaire business tycoon Nathan Lammockson oversees the creation of a panoply of floating structures to give him, and those he chooses to be with him, an advantage over the rising flood waters. Yet each of these structures is shown to be vulnerable: the group of luxurious floating buildings at the beginning of the novel are overwhelmed by a tidal storm surge; while the colossal cruise liner – *Ark Three* – that is launched as the seas begin to overwhelm the Andes mountains is eventually attacked and destroyed by other more desperate survivors.

The novel concludes with Lammockson and the remnants of his entourage floating on a raft made from bioengineered seaweed, literally grown out of the new marine environment, and only possible because of Lammockson's foresight, grounded throughout the novel in his unwavering faith in technology. Hyperbolic as its flood narrative may be, Baxter's novel provides an insight into the many ways in which floating structures might be used to adapt to a world in which sea levels are inexorably rising. It also calls attention to the folly of hubris in relation to technologically based solutions to rising sea levels, as well as to the necessity of foresight – of some belief in that technology's ability to ensure human adaptation to, and survival in, the transformed environment.

History is littered with rich imaginaries of floating cities: artificial urban environments on water conceived by entrepreneurs, architects, novelists and artists as utopian. These range from reactionary 'island' cities – elitist floating communities that have territorial and social autonomy – to countercultural social experiments, where new kinds of collective urban life have been imagined. More so than drowned cities, the imagination of floating cities has had a measurable impact on architectural practice, with many structures now being designed and built to foster a new kind of aquatic urbanism.

Floating cities are places for potential social relations to be both imagined and lived, ranging from a regressive isolationism on the one hand to radical forms of connectivity on the other. They draw not only on cutting-edge technologies for their architectural forms but on a long tradition of utopian politics that envisage radical social change through imagined urban environments that are conceived as entirely isolated from the existent world. By engaging with the imagination of floating cities, we can tap into a wide range of utopian impulses that desire the built environment and social relations to be *other* than they are. Floating cities offer stories about possible futures – some more pragmatic than others, some more socially progressive than others, but all collectively setting down their respective anchors in order to speak to and challenge what we regard as possible.

Island Utopias

There is a long history in Western society of viewing the ocean as a barrier that, when surrounding an island, creates a distinct and inviolate territory, subject to its own laws and social codes and free from the corrupting influence of the world beyond. Thomas More's 1516 text *Utopia* took up Plato's conception of islands as perfectly bounded, whole and separate spaces, but grounded it in a biting critique of his own urban world, namely Tudor London.[1] The emphasis on inviolate and tightly controlled cities in More's text had its own mirror in the contemporaneous city-states of Italy, perhaps most notably Venice, an island city that reached its apogee of power in the fifteenth century but which had already begun to decline when *Utopia* was published. Yet the example of medieval Venice lives on today in island-cities such as Singapore, with its combination of a deregulated finance sector to concentrate wealth and a socially conservative political regime. Imagining islands as utopias also finds expression in the creation of artificial urban islands inhabited by those wealthy enough to afford a socially exclusive environment, perhaps most notably in Dubai's colossal Palm Island resort and the thus-far incomplete World Islands development – an artificial archipelago of small sand islands off the coast of Dubai to be constructed in the shape of a world map.[2]

Even as island-cities have long been imagined and built, the idea of a self-contained urban environment that floats on the ocean did not take root until technological developments made that idea feasible. As the oil industry grew in the early twentieth century, so did the need to extract oil from under the sea and, by the 1940s, drilling platforms had been constructed many kilometres offshore of the United States.[3] Together with seaforts and large pontoons developed and built by the British military during the Second World War, these fixed and floating sea-based structures inspired many post-war architects to propose the appropriation of this industrial and military technology to create entire floating cities. Initially these proposals

Kenzō Tange, Tokyo Bay project, 1960.

were driven by a modernist faith in the power of technology and the mass production of building components to create an entirely new type of urban environment that was free from the traditional restraints of land-based cities. Thus both Kenzō Tange's and Paul Maymont's Tokyo Bay projects, both dating from 1960,[4] envisaged an enormous expansion of what was still a bomb-damaged Tokyo by means of colonization of the city's shallow seas on interconnected floating platforms not unlike the ones actually built by Stalin in the 1950s to extract oil off the coast of Baku (in what is now Azerbaijan).[5] Later, the American architect and inventor Buckminster Fuller would develop several proposals for floating cities, including Triton City (1968), also for Tokyo Bay and financed by the U.S. Department of Housing and Urban Development, and, with the architect Shoji Sadao, the gargantuan Tetrahedron City

(c. 1968), a megastructure with immense honeycombed concrete walls rising to a 2,500-metre (8,200-ft) peak and intended as an earthquake-proof structure for any vulnerable urban environment, such as Tokyo or San Francisco.[6]

These early proposals for vast floating urban agglomerations were principally envisaged as extensions of terrestrial urban environments. Yet in their full embrace of the stark utilitarianism of architectural modernism and industrialized modular construction, and their abolition of hierarchical architectural – and, by implication, social – typologies, they could not have been more different from conventional cities. By the early 1970s, as the technological optimism of the 1960s waned and was replaced by growing fears about the environmental costs of industrialization and the vulnerability of a global economy dependent on oil, proposals for floating cities with an emphasis on organic forms that were in tune with nature softened the hard-edged technological modernism of their 1960s forebears. Significantly, they also increasingly conceived of marine cities entirely separated from their terrestrial counterparts, reflecting the earlier utopian tradition of island-based other-worlds.

Jacques Rougerie and Edith Vignes' designs for floating and submarine structures were inspired by both the sense of wonder brought to light by the marine explorer Jacques Cousteau in the 1970s and also contemporaneous anxieties about the decimation of inhabitable land by overpopulation and pollution.[7] Their proposals ranged from Thallasopolis 1 (1971), a city of 45,000 inhabiting an aggregation of floating villages built from locally sourced materials for indigenous peoples in Indonesia,[8] to a recent self-sustaining floating research centre shaped like an outsized manta ray and intended to study the effects of changes in the marine environment due to climate change and pollution.[9] The 1970s also saw the first structures being built for these anticipated marine cities, including Rougerie and Vignes' Galathée (1977) and Aquabulle (1978) structures and Kiyonori Kikutake's Aquapolis, a floating pavilion modelled on oil-drilling platforms and

created for the 1975 Expo in Okinawa, Japan.[10] Although Aquapolis
was visited by thousands and demonstrated not only the technical
viability of marine construction but also its symbolic potency in suggesting that humans could live harmoniously on the sea, Kikutake's
pavilion was the high point in this period of experimentation with
floating habitats; thereafter – at least until the present day – the idea
fell out of favour. A viable market for these structures never materialized; the costs of building marine cities would have been prohibitive
to would-be investors, particularly in comparison to their terrestrial
counterparts.[11]

Much of the enthusiasm for marine cities in the 1960s and '70s
was driven by a belief that they would relieve problems in existing
cities, such as overpopulation and congestion, and contribute
towards a progressive social vision, even though this was rarely
spelled out explicitly by architects. A recent renewal of interest in
floating cities has largely drawn on the older model of island cities
as havens from the outside world, utopias for the exclusive few rather
than the many. Nowhere is this more evident than in the work of
the Seasteading Institute, founded in 2008 by software engineer and
political theorist Patri Friedman and billionaire technology entrepreneur Peter Thiel, co-creator of the online payments system PayPal.[12]
The aim of the Institute is to build a floating city that will be politically
and economically autonomous, where the kind of entrepreneurial
culture found in California's Silicon Valley can be nurtured, but free
from any political, social and economic constraints.

Drawing on the Objectivist philosophies of Ayn Rand and Robert
Heinlein, the Seasteading Institute greatly expands the remit of existing libertarian attempts to colonize the sea.[13] These include the
establishing of several marine micro-nations in the 1960s and '70s,
such as Sealand (1967), an abandoned seafort off the Essex Coast in
Britain declared to be a sovereign nation by British pirate-radio
broadcaster Roy Bates and his family.[14] More recent examples of
speculative floating structures specifically intended as tax havens

include the *Freedom Ship* (2003–), a giant cruise liner proposed to house a population of 40,000 super-wealthy full-time residents that will slowly circle the globe,[15] and the Principality of New Utopia (1996–), a settlement to be constructed on a seamount in the Caribbean Sea's Cayman Deep, which, being 160 kilometres (100 mi.) from any other territory, would be eligible to declare itself a sovereign state. Established by U.S. citizen Lazarus Long when he discovered an unclaimed section of the Caribbean Sea and filed a territorial claim to the United Nations, New Utopia is now run by Long's daughter, Elizabeth Henderson, and has apparently already attracted over $500 million from worldwide investors. The floating city is currently scheduled for completion in 2021, but building has yet to commence, the evolving designs seemingly fixated on creating an exotic medley of forms drawn from the retail and leisure architecture of Las Vegas.[16]

Jacques Rougerie, SeaOrbiter project, a proposed floating oceanic research laboratory, 2013.

The Seasteading Institute has brought a sense of professionalism to their own proposals that is notably absent from the New Utopia project, as well as a great deal more investment from supporters such as Thiel. It has also scaled up the ambition of projects like the *Freedom Ship* in proposing the construction of an entire marine city. In 2015 the Institute launched an architectural competition for a future floating city. As stated on their website, the Institute invited participants to submit designs for a small marine city made up of at least ten inter-connected platforms that would support a mixture of commercial office buildings and retail and leisure units, as well as housing and green spaces. The brief asked for modular designs – reflecting the earlier proposals by Tange and Maymont for Tokyo Bay – that would give the city flexibility (modules could be repositioned as required), as well as sustainable and self-sufficient energy sources such as solar, wind and wave power.[17]

The winning entry – Roark 3D's Artisanopolis – proposed a branching arrangement of interconnected pentagonal platforms supporting a variety of geometric housing and office and retail units interspersed with tropical vegetation. The hexagonal modular housing shown in the foreground of the 3D image submitted by the architects was based on Kisho Kurokawa's iconic Capsule Tower (1972) in Tokyo. Yet, in its updated marine setting, the original intention of the Capsule Tower – to provide low-cost mass-produced housing in cities where space was at a premium – has been replaced by a sense of exclusivity and luxury, confirmed by the presence of enormous cruise liners seen in some of the images. Indeed, despite the inclusion of 'green' structures like biodomes to grow food and an emphasis on efficiency and sustainability, the architectural forms of Artisanopolis remain rooted in a culture of contemporary architecture that has been dictated by the neoliberal transformation of cities, namely one that is intent on attracting the wealthy and driving out the poor.

Artisanopolis explicitly marketed itself as 'an alternative model that allows new communities to form beyond the limiting jurisdictions

of existing nation states in order to promote freedom and competition in the marketplace'.[18] Just who would form these communities is unclear, but, given the enormous cost of building a floating city, it would most likely be the super-wealthy who desire political auton-omy in order to protect their riches. For all the rhetoric of liberation, the aims of the Seasteading Institute are narrowly selfish; even as Artisanopolis proclaims itself as a refuge for creatives, it elides any reference to other kinds of work, particularly the work of those who would need to maintain the city in service of the liberated elite. As such, the freedom offered in this floating city is only one that can be bought; in short, a commodity like any other.[19] For the moment, it seems, the eye-watering price tag of such freedom has put off most investors, with even Thiel admitting in 2015 that the cost of building a floating city would be prohibitive. The Institute seems to have con-ceded its dream of a new sovereign nation in favour of seeking 'cost-reducing solutions within the territorial waters of a host nation'.[20]

Gabriel Scheare, Luke and Lourdes Crowley, and Patrick White (Roark 3D), Artisanopolis, the winning entry in the Seasteading Institute's 2015 floating city design competition.

Ship Cities

Even though floating cities such as those envisaged by the Seasteading Institute and others before them have yet to become a reality, communities of people have inhabited the oceans since humans first learned to build waterborne vessels. When ships group together, such as the 130-strong Spanish Armada that sailed from Flanders in 1588 to unsuccessfully invade England, they effectively become mobile cities, namely large groups of people kept together by architecture, networks of communication, local laws and social codes, and a common, usually military, purpose. In another vein, histories of piracy at sea have brought to light the formation of many different kinds of countercultural maritime shipboard societies.[21] The closest equivalents today have traded warfare and counterculture for leisure and pleasure: of the supersize cruise ships that circle the globe, the largest currently is *Harmony of the Seas*, which was launched in Southampton in 2016, its sixteen-deck-high superstructure housing 6,780 passengers and 2,100 crew members.[22]

At the other end of the scale are houseboats, a ubiquitous presence in cities with relatively calm waterways, particularly canals. In Amsterdam alone, lining the city's waterways are an estimated 3,000 houseboats, comprising traditional narrowboats, commercial vessels converted into accommodation and multi-storey floating homes, some of the more recent examples demonstrating high levels of architectural literacy and often luxurious facilities.[23] Despite crowding almost every available space at the edges of Amsterdam's numerous canals and rivers, houseboats still offer an attractive self-sufficient alternative and largely cheaper way of living in a city where space is at a premium. What conglomerations of houseboats produce is an architectural bricolage: an unplanned and mostly unregulated mix of fixed structures (for example, jetties and mooring posts) and mobile elements – the houseboats themselves and their accruements, such as ropes and chains, solar panels, wind turbines, bicycles, smaller boats and makeshift gardens.

Houseboats are a common presence in many urban environments, yet they are also separate from those environments, often literally so with their off-grid energy sources bypassing the networked infrastructure that most land-based urbanites take for granted. Nevertheless, they are usually dependent on the terrestrial city for their continued survival – the city provides secure and safe mooring points as well as all the services that urban houseboat owners clearly require. It is much more difficult to imagine such agglomerations of inhabited boats existing on the open seas, entirely cut off from existing cities.

It is only in the realm of fiction that such cities have been realized. Two novels – Lloyd Kropp's *The Drift* (1969) and China Miéville's *The Scar* (2002) – imagine floating cities of a very different kind from those proposed by both modernist architects and contemporary seasteaders. *The Drift* was published at the very end of the 1960s and is suffused with an elegiac tone and melancholy mood reflecting the loss of countercultural optimism in this period. The narrative centres on a disaffected middle-aged American, Peter Sutherland, who, having left his family for a solo boat trip, is rescued after losing consciousness during a storm, only to find himself marooned on The Drift – a ship-city that has accumulated over centuries at the still centre of the Sargasso Sea. Inhabited by a hundred or so people who, like Peter, have also been marooned there, the city is an extraordinary assemblage of marine architecture – hundreds of ships of all sizes and ages that have ended up being gathered together:

> Some of the ships listed at steep angles; others lay on their sides, apparently suspended by thick growths of Sargasso Weeds. Some were nailed together, and some had walkways that connected them with others. Some rested across or on top of other ships that had been almost completely submerged in thick growths of strange sea flowers and exotic green plants that Peter had never seen before. In some places there were pools of decaying wood where ships had rotted away. Again,

the weeds had apparently not allowed them to sink. In other places, parts of ships had decayed and fallen together with parts of other ships to form a weird progeny of shapes in which it was impossible to tell where one ended and another began.[24]

What is notable about the architecture of The Drift is the almost complete lack of human agency involved in its creation. The ships themselves have been, and intermittently continue to be, brought to the site by the centrifugal currents of the Sargasso Sea; their location and materiality being determined solely by the Sargasso Weeds that also collect in this part of the sea. The 'weird progeny of shapes' that results could hardly be more different from the geometric order of the planned floating cities discussed earlier.

Yet, despite its unplanned nature, The Drift nevertheless has a profound affect on the social lives of those who come to inhabit it. Initially fiercely resistant to what he regards as his imprisonment on the ship city, Peter gradually learns to accept his fate, mainly through his encounters with other people who have ended up there. Divided into different clans who inhabit distinct zones of The Drift, the agglomeration of ships has produced a society in which the imagination has taken precedence over rational thought – where, according to Tabor, one of the long-standing inhabitants, 'life is [viewed as] a series of metaphors . . . a series of correspondences. The better you are at metaphors, the more you can bring into your circle of feeling and understanding.'[25] As one of the eldest residents, Rose, says to Peter, stillness is central to nurturing these metaphorical correspondences; and The Drift reverses the conventional associations of ships as moving structures by gathering them to a still point. When Peter eventually leaves The Drift after talking with one of its disillusioned residents, the enigmatic Hatchmaker (feared by all the others), he returns to his conventional life in the United States. He has nevertheless been transformed by his experience, which had 'taught him the desire to give in, to drift, to follow the course of experience for its own sake and to open his mind to sensation, to the color and texture and shape of things, and not merely to their uses'.[26] In short, Kropp's novel fuses floating architecture and a countercultural social vision, creating a powerful allegory of the late 1960s sense of deflation and despair about the crushing effects of stifling the human imagination and the seeming failure of the fervent countercultural dreams of the 1960s to have any long-lasting effects on society.

China Miéville borrowed Kropp's imagining of a city made out of ships in his 2002 fantasy novel *The Scar*.[27] In inventing the floating pirate city of Armada – Miéville's own version of The Drift – he brought to bear a different kind of politics to the floating city, one that would later inform his own stinging criticism of the Seasteading vision.[28] In contrast to the contemplative stillness of The Drift, Miéville's Armada is a super-dense, bustling, floating and mobile metropolis of hundreds of thousands of inhabitants, with most of its innumerable ships tethered together with chains and bridges, and long since built over with 'tall brickwork, steeples, masts and chimneys and ancient rigging'.[29] The underside of the city is no less vibrant – 'wire-mesh cages tucked into hollows and dangling from chains, crowded with fair cod and tunny' are harvested by the Cray, a hybrid human/crayfish race who live underwater in coral-like dwellings attached to the ships' hulls.[30] Below water, 'a moving ecology and politics were tethered to the city's calcified base', while above, the buildings were all 'licked by constant damp, contoured with salt – steeped in the sounds of waves and the fresh-rot smell of the sea'.[31]

Taken by force while sailing into exile from Miéville's other invented city of New Crobuzon, the central protagonist, academic Bellis Coldwine, becomes part of an alternative society made possible by piracy, whether stealing ships to add to the city's fabric or people to augment its population.[32] And, unlike The Drift, Armada moves – initially very slowly, pulled across the endless oceans by dozens of tug boats, but later much faster under the steam of a gargantuan deep-sea creature (the avanc) that the city authorities successfully tether. The architecture of Armada is imagined as chaotically hybrid. On the one hand, this is evident in its 'countless naval architectures': 'Stripped longships; scorpion-galleys; luggers and brigantines; massive steamers hundreds of feet long down to canoes no larger than a man' have been reclaimed 'from the inside out', with 'structures, styles and materials shoved together from a hundred histories and aesthetics into a compound architecture'.[33] On the other, such hybridity also extends to the social life of the city. Although 'ruled by cruel mercantilism, existing in the pores of the world [and] snatching new citizens from their ships', Armada's social codes are also fiercely egalitarian – the former Remade slaves now freed and equal to any other citizens – and democratic.[34] Like The Drift, Armada is divided up into discrete kingdoms, each controlled by a powerful leader but with its own distinct social customs. Although one of these kingdoms – Garwater – gains control of the fate of the entire city, this power is never safe from democratic challenge, as demonstrated in the mutiny that occurs in the latter stages of the novel.

What Miéville's imagined floating city does so well is to provide a vivid and sustained sense of the material, mental and social life of such a city. A fantastical creation it may be, but in fleshing it out over the course of nearly seven hundred pages, Miéville provides a far more convincing picture of what it might mean to *live* in such a city than any of the 3D renderings produced by architects in response to the Seasteading Institute's design competition. Perhaps more significantly, Miéville's Armada also reimagines the possibilities of social life in such a city as much as its urban fabric; by doing so, he stretches our imaginations to think much more broadly and openly than the Seasteading vision.

Yet there are more positive comparisons to be made between architects' visualizations and Miéville's fiction in projects that envisage the kind of architectural hybridity suggested in *The Scar*. In Hans Hollein's photo-collage *Aircraft Carrier City in Landscape* (1964) from his *Transformations* series (1963–8) and James Wignall's *Inverted Infrastructure* (2010) from his Port of London Authority project, vast aircraft-carrying ships are repurposed for new, non-military ends: respectively, as a surreal addition to an otherwise agricultural landscape and as safe havens for iconic British buildings to rest on in the event of London being overwhelmed by rising sea levels.[35] Anthony Lau took Hollein's idea a stage further in his 2008 student project Flooded London 2030, in which a variety of marine structures – oil rigs, cruise liners and other large ships – are linked together alongside the banks of the river Thames by aerial walkways, mobile infrastructure and aquatic transport, creating an entire floating city.[36] In a similar manner to the ships in Armada, Lau's floating structures are foundations for informal architectures, in this case shipping containers repurposed as housing. With cranes hoisting the containers into place, Lau proposes an organic urban fabric that grows over time rather than being planned in advance. In all of these projects, familiar floating structures become estranged, whether in their incongruous settings or in the unexpected uses to which they are put. This sense of estrangement links these projects with Miéville's pirate city; for

Anthony Lau,
Flooded London
2030 project, 2008.

in each case, it is the hybrid nature of the floating structures that produces their quality of strangeness. This, in turn, makes us question the norms we have accepted for otherwise bizarre structures. What these seemingly fantastical imaginings draw attention to is the fact that floating cities already exist. Perhaps all that is required is for us to inhabit them.

What at first seem much more improbable future floating habitats than the slick 3D visualizations produced by architects in response to the Seasteading Institute are in fact more believable, because they give voice to a utopian vision of floating cities that grows out of present conditions rather than reacting against them. The architectures of both *The Drift* and *The Scar* have been created organically from familiar structures and materials, ostensibly without human intervention in the case of The Drift, and through a radical countercultural pirate politics in the case of Armada. These bricolage architectures contrast sharply with the sterile built environments endorsed by the Seasteading Institute, their shiny surfaces and ordered geometries having only a superficial appeal that seems to exclude the messiness that characterizes genuinely diverse social life in cities. Indeed, in filling the informal architectures of Armada and The Drift with vibrant human and non-human presences, these fictional floating cities communicate far more than the Seasteading Institute about what kinds of social life might result from a radically altered urban environment.

As they stand, design proposals such as Artisanopolis provide very little sense of what it might be like to inhabit these floating cities – the favoured bird's-eye 3D views only serving to distance viewers. We may find the residents of Miéville's Armada to be excessively fantastical, merging as they do the human and non-human, flesh and machines; but, in this excess, Miéville demonstrates the rich possibilities that can be sketched out through an imaginative reading of floating cities. This is clearly at odds with the Seasteading vision, which, for all its rhetoric of radical freedom, seems to fall back on existing certainties – the sterile alienating architecture of neoliberalism

– in order to convince potential investors of the viability of their vision. Such an approach cannot but close down possibilities because it sacrifices the freedom of the imagination to the dictates of the real. What might be a more fruitful way of maintaining openness is an approach, like Kropp's and Miéville's, that aims to create a series of metaphors, or correspondences, that are not primarily concerned with an end product (the actual construction of a floating city), but rather with enlarging a sense of what might be possible, in challenging us to see familiar places and architectures in a new way so that, if necessary, we might create our own floating cities.

Lived Utopias

The Seasteading vision has its roots in architectural technologies that have already been tried and tested, particularly in the Netherlands, where floating houses have been constructed in the last decade that anticipate the effects that climate change will have on a country in which 26 per cent of the land is below current sea levels. On a bitterly cold but dazzling morning in January 2016, I visited the largest collection of floating houses to date: a group of nearly one hundred homes that has developed since 2013 on one of Amsterdam's numerous reclaimed islands on the eastern fringes of the city.[37] Straddling the IJmeer lake are the two sections of the IJburg project: on the west side, 55 gleaming white modular two- and three-storey floating houses crowded together around purpose-built jetties and designed by Marlies Rhomer Architects and Planners; on the east, a more colourful collection of bespoke homes, currently numbering 38 but still being added to, each box-shaped but featuring an array of unique elements such as colourful cladding, roof terraces and individual moorings for boats. Each of the houses is supported by a concrete tub submerged in the water to a depth of half a storey; a lightweight steel structure sits on top, infilled with cladding panels and glazing. With as many residents per hectare as the most densely populated parts of

Marlies Rhomer
Architects and
Planners, modular
floating houses in the
IJmeer lake, IJburg,
Amsterdam, 2013.

Amsterdam's old city, this aquatic community realizes a floating city in miniature.

While this agglomeration of floating houses demonstrates a more flexible approach to urbanism than is usually seen in terrestrial-based construction, the planned nature of the IJburg development, as well as the high-tech construction materials and methods used, could not be more different from the anarchic bricolage of Miéville's Armada. This is no countercultural community like that which inhabited the pirate city and as one might still find in Amsterdam's houseboat culture; rather, it is an exclusive development clearly favouring the wealthy, with some of the bespoke houses worth around €1 million (as of mid-2016). Despite this, its vision of marine urbanism is very much at odds with that put forward by the Seasteading Institute, even as the construction materials and modular approach to design are similar.

Rather than responding to a dream of autonomy – the desire for an isolated and autonomous floating community – the building of the IJburg homes necessitated close engagement with the elements that connect water and land. During construction, some of the modular houses began to list alarmingly and a new solution had to be found to give them extra buoyancy. The numerous jetties that link the land and water have become hybrid streets, with elements from the houses spilling out, most noticeably the many bicycles chained to them. In addition, essential utilities (drinking water and electricity) are brought to the floating houses from the land via plastic tubes that are suspended in mid-air – these connect directly into the houses in structures rather like outsized vacuum cleaner tubes. In contrast to the idealized visions of the Seasteading Institute, these houses demonstrate a delicate and vulnerable relationship to the environment in which they are situated. The sea may offer the dream of an architecture that can escape future crisis, whether ecological, economic or political; yet actual floating houses draw attention to the city's interconnectedness – the points of vulnerability that require working with rather than against. In this light, the IJburg development offers a model of how an aquatic urbanism might be grafted onto conventional terrestrial cities that are already vulnerable to the future effects of climate change; it demonstrates how those cities might maintain social and geographic connectedness to their existing contexts even as they also adapt to what is to come.

Vulnerability and connectedness also inform the work of contemporary art practice that engages with floating structures. For five months in 2009, the American artists Mary Mattingly and Alison Ward lived on their self-designed Waterpod project in New York City, assisted by numerous volunteers.[38] The artists rented a barge and installed two metal-framed geodesic domes on it that were 6 metres (20 ft) high, creating a multifunctional and entirely self-sufficient habitat which they sailed to each of New York's five boroughs, mooring every day to enable visitors to experience the artwork. As Mattingly has made clear, the Waterpod grew out of a desire to 'encourage innovation as we visualize the future fifty to one hundred years from now', when New York will likely be threatened by rising sea levels caused by climate change.[39] Drawing on the example of Robert Smithson's 1970 *Floating Island* – a commercial shipping barge filled with earth and transplanted trees which was towed by a tug-boat around New York – the Waterpod project was designed to challenge conventional mitigation-focused responses to the threat of rising sea levels. Constructed entirely from recycled and donated materials, using a hydroponics system to grow food and collect, purify and recycle water, and employing an off-grid network of solar panels and other renewable energy sources, Waterpod clearly responded to a bleak vision of the future when it is assumed that rising sea levels would force communities to adapt in radical ways. In this vein, Waterpod anticipates themes seen in Mattingly's more recent work, such as her Flock House project (2012–14), in which the artist designed a mobile, self-sufficient geodesic structure that could easily be moved in the event of an apocalyptic disaster, and which could also float on an improvised raft.[40] Her WetLand project, launched in 2014, was more ambitious in terms of its scale: a floating 'mobile, sculptural habitat and public space constructed to explore resource interdependency and climate change in urban centers'.[41] In developing partnerships with educational institutions and community-based groups, WetLand articulated a more thoroughgoing vision of participation and education than Waterpod, demonstrating how to build structures and living environments that were completely self-sufficient and which, Mattingly has argued, would create 'thriving local environmental economies'.[42]

The geodesic domes that form the main components of both the Flock House and Waterpod works are clearly indebted to the work of Buckminster Fuller, particularly in the sense of them being self-contained living environments. Like Fuller's pioneering domes of the

1960s and more high-profile contemporary geodesic structures such as the Eden Project in the UK, Mattingly's floating structures have been criticized for being too generalized and disconnected from existing urban conditions.[43] In creating sealed-off worlds, geodesic structures limit our ability to imagine how such radically separate environments can have any meaningful links to the ones we actually generally inhabit in cities.[44] Countering this criticism, Mattingly has argued strongly that her projects are grounded in existing social practices – whether the relationships forged in learning to live along-side others self-sufficiently for extended periods on the Waterpod; educational programmes in both the Waterpod and WetLand projects that centre on outreach to a wide range of community groups; or collaborations with environmentalists and sustainability experts in designing and building the floating structures.[45] Yet her projects will undoubtedly seem extreme to those who are used to living in more conventional urban environments. Despite their hands-on and

Mary Mattingly and Alison Ward, The Waterpod Project, South Street Seaport, New York City, 2009.

bottom-up approaches to design, projects like the Waterpod fall into the same trap as some of the many countercultural communities set up in the 1960s in that they adopt the perilous position of supposing themselves to be avant-garde – lone pioneers showing others how to live differently rather than working with those others to engender incremental change. Unsurprisingly, many of Mattingly's collaborators and Waterpod volunteers were those who were already attracted to alternative living – fellow artists and other people accepting and embracing the countercultural basis of the project. What the Waterpod project lacks is precisely the compromised and messy connections that characterize the much more conventional IJburg floating community.

In this light, the work of British artist Stephen Turner might seem like an even more extreme retreat into isolated and self-contained floating structures. In both his *Seafort* (2005) and *Exbury Egg* (2013–14) projects, the artist spent an extended period of solitude on marine structures. The first was on a dilapidated Second World War seafort in England's Thames estuary.[46] The second was a twelve-month residency on board a wooden, egg-shaped floating living pod, designed and constructed by Turner, Space Place & Urban Design and the architects PAD Studio and moored on the river Beaulieu in Hampshire, England.[47] Even as both projects contained educational elements – a school in Whitstable, Kent, corresponded with Turner during his residency on the seafort, and engineering workshops, talks and other public events took place during his time living on the Exbury Egg – the driving force behind each was Turner's interest in the experience of extreme solitude and the creativity that might come out of such an experience.

In both projects, Turner's creative output took the form of an online diary, published throughout the course of each residency and made up of a mixture of personal observations about the natural world, the experience of solitude and how the latter might contribute to an enhanced ecological awareness.[48] Where the Exbury Egg was

constructed as a utopian, womb-like structure for creative meditation
on the relationship between the human and non-human, Seafort was
an altogether more unsettling work. In this project, Turner spent 36
days alone on one of the group of Maunsell forts (named after their
designer, the engineer Guy Maunsell) located at Shivering Sands off
Herne Bay, at the mouth of the Thames. The length of Turner's residency corresponded to that of a typical tour of duty in the days when
the forts were occupied by hundreds of British military personnel
during the Second World War and were used as gunneries to target
German bombing aircraft.[49] Throughout his residency, Turner
restricted his world to that of the interior of the fort – an inward
exploration that revealed traces of its former occupants. His plan for
the 36-day project was simple: he would document each of the fort's
interior rooms in minute detail before moving on to the next. Thus
narrowed down and explored very slowly, Turner's world went against
the grain of the emphasis on speed and continuous connectivity in
today's globalized world. His self-imposed isolation was a deliberate
attempt to find ways in which intense solitude can nurture contemplation of the past and present in order to resist such a world.[50]

   Turner's observations while living alone on the seafort resonated
with me when I visited an identical group of structures in May 2016,
built at Redsands, a few kilometres west from the fort that Turner
lived on. For the visitor approaching by boat from the Medway estuary,
the forts first appear as a group of vague smudges on the horizon
which very gradually grow larger and larger until, all of a sudden,
one is upon them. Even in their current dilapidated condition – the
walkways long collapsed, the gun placements broken off, and the
steel boxes stained red with rust – they are still striking structures.
They are both alien in their improbable location, and in their uncanny
similarity to the merciless tripods in H. G. Wells's *The War of the Worlds*
(1898), and familiar in their anthropomorphic appearance and simple
formal arrangement: four precast concrete legs sunk into the seabed
which support a steel, box-like superstructure that used to contain

overleaf:
Redsands Maunsell
sea forts, Thames
Estuary, 2016.

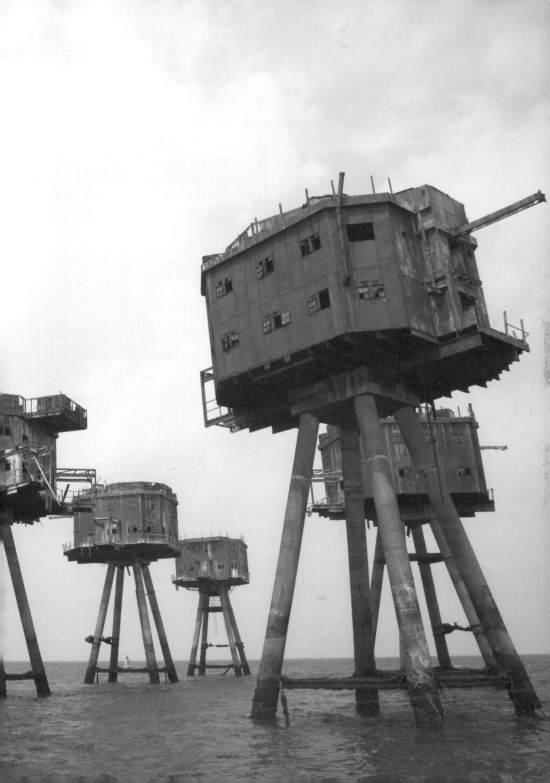

all the accommodation and defence equipment. For a while, the boat
I was on circled and passed between the seven forts in a slow dance,
while the dozen or so passengers took photographs. It was a moment
of shared wonder at the audacity and strangeness of these marine
human habitats, long abandoned but still possessing a charismatic
hold on the imagination. They summoned up not only the dream of
living autonomously, free from the enmeshing webs of conventional
life, but the nightmare of what must have been a prison-like existence
for the hundreds of men who were once forced to live on them.
Turner's reliving of that experience was a form of vigil to those lost
memories – a way of connecting with the past through a sustained
period of enforced solitude within the ruins of the environment which
those men used to inhabit. Such connections are very different from
those envisaged by and enacted in Mattingly's work, but they are no
less important in contributing to future visions that seek to integrate
rather than ignore or reject history. Even in intense solitude, there
are still connections to be forged, ones that can and should inform
how we think about the future.

Turner's act of reinhabiting one of the Maunsell seaforts was very
different in its intention from that currently being proposed for the
similar structures at Redsands. Although the seven forts have recently
been acquired by the charity Project Redsand, which has partially
restored one and is trying to raise funds to secure the future of all
seven, it seems unlikely that a new public use will be found for structures that are 9.7 kilometres (6 mi.) from the nearest shoreline.[51]
However, a recent proposal has been put forward by Aros Architects
to turn the derelict forts into a luxury resort, complete with executive
apartments, a museum complex, a sea spa and a helipad for guests.[52]
This proposal draws us back to the isolationist dreams of the social
elite embodied in the vision of the Seasteading Institute. As Turner's
Seafort project has demonstrated, it is not that the desire for a room
of one's own is inherently regressive, but rather that we must always
understand that perfect security is only ever to be found in the

imagination; even some way out to sea, the world will still be connected to us, no matter how wealthy or privileged we may be. The Seasteading Institute may desire to build a scaled-up version of micro-nations like Roy Bates's Sealand – inviolate territories that have severed connections to the larger world. Yet, as every healthy person knows, it is precisely our lack of a hard protective shell – our vulnerability – that in the end draws us into a larger world that encourages us to share and allows us to grow.

3
Airborne: Architecture
and the Dream of Flight

I n August 2016, the longest aircraft ever built – the 92-metre (302-ft) *Airlander 10* helium-filled airship – was launched at Cardington Airfield in Bedfordshire, England.[1] First developed for the U.S. government as a surveillance aircraft, *Airlander 10* was to be the first of a new fleet of enormous airships, reviving memories of the golden age of this form of transport in the 1920s and 1930s. But when *Airlander 10* crash-landed on only its second test flight, damaging not only the craft but the entire programme of the company, it revived a much darker memory: the fatal crash of the *Hindenburg* passenger airship, which was destroyed by a catastrophic fire in 1937, effectively bringing the era of the airship to an abrupt end.[2]

The double-edged sense of nostalgia – both of an age-old dream of conquering the air and the nightmare of air's intractable resistance to such conquering – afforded by the *Airlander 10* encapsulates our relationship to the air. Even as many millions of us have quite literally taken to the air in mass-transit air travel, we still do not engage with the air as a truly habitable space. If jet aircraft allow us to be in the air, they equally rigorously exclude that air from their interiors, though for good reason. Can air ever be a space in which we can truly live? Or will it remain a hostile terrain, a medium in which the innate heaviness of ourselves and the buildings we inhabit have no place?

Although airborne living may seem like an impossible dream, there are many ways in which air has come to occupy our minds. At the most basic level, we are irrevocably entwined with air – breathing

Urban Future Organization, CR-Design in collaboration with Karin Hedlund, Lukas Nordström, Pedram Seddighzadeh at Chalmers Technical University, and Expedite Technology Co., Cloud Citizen scheme, Shenzhen, 2014.

is an action that demonstrates that we are not separated from the outside world but rather the reverse: the air outside continually enters our bodies and vice versa.[3] At the same time, in the modern era air became the subject of rational inquiry: initially, isolated by scientists in vessels and chambers as an object of study; later, analysed by climatologists and supercomputers in their ongoing attempt to understand the impacts of climate change.[4] In order to even think about air, we must be able to imagine it, to put some boundaries on its infinitude. Perhaps even as we constrain air by trying to imagine it, we nevertheless open ourselves up to it by recognizing the limits of our ability to grasp it.

It is possibly in our dreams that air becomes most open to inhabitation. Explored in depth by the phenomenologist Gaston Bachelard, dreams of air come from a primal place: 'the great timeless memory of an aerial state, one in which everything is weightless, in which our very own matter is innately light'.[5] Variously cast as our spirit, soul or inner being, this imagination of lightness sometimes manifests itself as recurrent dreams of flight – an image of the human body lifting off the ground by volition alone, without the wings that we see are necessary for powered flight in other creatures and most flying machines. For Bachelard, in the poetical and philosophical imagination, air stands for lightness, freedom and inspiration, the upward movement of the spirit that he regards as 'one of the most profound instincts in life'.[6] Here, the imagination of air is not so much of a material element but rather of 'a future with a vector for breaking into flight'.[7]

Developing Bachelard's focus on aerial images in poetry, philosopher Luce Irigaray has argued that twentieth-century Western philosophy, under the influence of Martin Heidegger's work, has 'forgotten' air, founded as Western thought is on ideas of density and of privileging rootedness to the earth. Mirroring Bachelard, Irigaray argues for a rehabilitation of air in philosophical discourse, with dwelling being recast as being 'at peace within the free sphere [of air] that safeguards each thing in its nature'.[8] Here, dwelling isn't a hunkering down in the earth and erecting a protective shield against all that is outside, but rather an opening up to the vast abundance of what is outside – the infinity of air itself.

Irigaray's criticism of the overly earthbound phenomenology of Heidegger can also be read as an indirect attack on architecture itself, with its almost unquestioned reliance on the solid, the dense and the heavy for its forms throughout history.[9] Although all architecture, by definition a mixture of solid surfaces and spaces in between, contains air, it does so in almost complete ignorance of the latter's existence, let alone responding to its material qualities. For architects, the space of inhabitation should possess a uniform atmosphere, excluding, as far as possible, the unstable air outside with its unpredictable draughts, vortices, swirls and fluctuating temperatures. Yet hidden away in and under our houses are the circulatory networks that bring us essential services: invisible flows of air, gas, electricity and information.[10] Such flows have sometimes been made a virtue of by architects by exposing the normally concealed tubes and pipes and displaying them instead as aesthetic features, as in Richard Rogers's Lloyds Building (1978–86) or Renzo Piano and Rogers's Pompidou Centre (1971–7). More recently, 'green' architecture has increasingly deployed a whole panoply of high-tech devices and materials to make buildings 'breathe' – whether this refers to architecture's inhalations (temperature control and energy intake) or its exhalations (waste removal and recycling).[11] However, such conceptions are invariably ones that emphasize the control of air – even as buildings are now said to breathe air, they are still distanced from it because their architects only ever cast air as a substance to be manipulated, pressed into the service of buildings and their (human) occupants.[12] The architectural control of air reaches its apotheosis in desert-based cities like Dubai, where the enormous expansion of the built environment is a direct result of the ruthless subjugation of air in architecture's omnipresent energy-guzzling air-conditioning units.[13]

The air around buildings – and particularly agglomerations of buildings in cities – has come under increasing scrutiny since the nineteenth century, as industrialization and rapid urbanization saw both the deterioration in the quality of city air – at first, imagined as a dangerous miasma – and a decreasing tolerance among the urban populace of noxious odours.[14] Early attempts at climate control in architecture, such as that engineered in the Crystal Palace in London in 1851, were indicative of a desire for a hermetically sealed interior space that would be a haven from the increasingly hostile air of the industrial city;[15] while the advent of the automobile witnessed the emergence of a new kind of air pollution, one that particularly affected urban-design debates in high-rise cities like New York in the second half of the twentieth century.[16] Built into the very foundation of main-stream architectural modernism, and particularly post-war urbanism, the reaction against industrial miasma and urban overcrowding saw cities transformed by high-rise buildings that reached for the pure air and unbounded light of the skies, with architects like Le Corbusier drawing on aerial views to envision the wholesale transformation of cities such as Paris.[17] Some of these high-rises even introduced 'streets in the sky' – an explicit engagement with the idea of aerial living. Estates like Park Hill (1958–61) in Sheffield and the Barbican (1965–76) in London included multi-level pedestrian walkways that sought to remove residents from the congestion and dirt of the urban street into the purer air above.[18]

As industrialization has now moved to the Global South, so have architectural responses to the air pollution that has become an environmental hazard in many of the new industrial cities in China.[19] Streets in the sky now link many of Hong Kong's skyscrapers, a means by which people can escape the increasingly polluted streets.[20] At the same time, some Asian skyscrapers have taken up the idea of aerial living more directly, as seen most dramatically in Singapore's Marina Bay Sands resort, completed in 2010, in which a SkyPark, 340 metres (1,115 ft) long, complete with a 150-metre (492-ft) swimming pool straddles the rooftops of three skyscrapers. Even more ambitious is CR-Design's prize-winning Cloud Citizen scheme for Shenzhen, a hypermodern business district recently approved for construction and comprised of a single cluster of very tall skyscrapers joined in the air by several connecting buildings.[21] In both of these projects, the aerial city is not defined by a responsive relationship between architecture and air but rather by a continuation of the modernist dream of both escaping the insalubrious air of the city's lower levels and subjugating the air above for the urban elite.

Castles in the Sky

To build a castle in the sky means to have an unrealistic and unattainable dream. Where the phrase originates is unclear, but it reflects a long-standing association of air with what might be termed 'airiness', signifying a lack of intelligence in a person (an 'air-head') or a lack of substance in a concept (an idea being 'hot air').[22] In this understanding, lightness is equated with the superficiality of appearance, heaviness with the true essence of things.

Jonathan Swift's fantastic image of the flying island of Laputa in *Gulliver's Travels* (1726) seems to reverse this conventional order of things. In Swift's story, Gulliver becomes stranded on a rocky island after being forced off his ship by pirates while on a voyage to the East Indies. Pondering his fate on the island, he becomes aware of 'a vast opaque body between me and the sun . . . it seemed to be about two miles high . . . the bottom flat, smooth and shining very bright from the reflection of the sea below . . . the sides encompassed with several gradations of galleries and stairs', which led upwards to the royal palace that crowned the island.[23] Taken up to the flying island via a system of pulleys, Gulliver meets a strange race of people who are permanently lost in 'intense speculations' centred on geometry and astrology. Their minds are so bound to the dictates of pure geometry that their houses are completely impractical, the structures being without any right angles because of the Laputans' contempt for 'practical geometry'.[24] Their politics are intolerant of any dissent, the floating island raining down rocks onto or simply flattening any opposition. With his fantastical flying island, Swift satirized a tendency in Enlightenment thinking that sought essences in the disembodied world of pure geometry, and he probably had figures such as Isaac Newton very much in his sights.[25] The Laputans may have gained victory over the forces of gravity but, by doing so, they lost touch with the reality of the material world, most notably their own bodies.

Swift's Laputa has inspired several more recent reimaginings of flying-island states, including space-travelling cities in James Blish's *Cities in Flight* (1955–62) series of novels, the anime film *Laputa: Castle in the Sky* (1986) and the video game *BioShock Infinite* (2013). Although the flying cities depicted in these media are very different, they share, with Swift's Laputa, an allegorical intent. If the future spacecraft *Manhattan* in the first book of the *Cities in Flight* quartet, which cleaves itself from the rest of New York City by means of super-powerful antigravity devices called spindizzys, seems almost absurdly fantastical, it can be read as an allegory of the rapid suburbanization in many U.S. cities from the 1950s onwards.[26] The disappearance of the centre of New York in Blish's fantasy provides a powerful image of the literal emptying out of the city's urban core that would leave parts of it in ruins by the early 1980s.

In a completely different vein, the flying citadel-island in Hayao Miyazaki's *Laputa: Castle in the Sky* seems at first to be a remnant of an ancient paradise: a series of tranquil gardens and stone ramparts crowned by a citadel, all built around colossal tree roots and a core of crystalline power. Yet this flying city contains a dark secret: an immensely powerful weapon controlled by a supercomputer and capable of unimaginable destruction, which is eventually neutralized by the actions of the two children at the centre of the film's narrative. Miyazaki's flying city is an allegory of the unresolved conflict between human technology and the natural environment that so dominates urban life today.[27]

The equally improbable flying city of Columbia in *BioShock Infinite* gives free rein to the fantasy of an alternate American state in the clouds: a city characterized by extreme architectural pastiche – a veritable cornucopia of late nineteenth-century buildings – and a deliberately nostalgic visual feel, with its almost overexposed brightness and old-fashioned aerial transport (airships and balloons) and cultural activities.[28] Yet this apparently bucolic city-state is as brutal as Swift's Laputa: governed by the religious fanatic, fascist and xenophobic figure of Comstock, the city is shown in one sequence of the game to attack and destroy New York City. As *BioShock*'s creative director, Ken Levine, has stated, Columbia is 'the memory of America that people think existed but never quite did' and, as such, is a metaphor of the xenophobic nationalism that is increasingly marking the political landscape in the u.s. and elsewhere today.[29]

If the allegorical meaning of Swift's Laputa has inspired others to take up the flying city as a fantasy motif, then its ideal of a gravity-defying architecture anticipated a dominant concern of architectural modernism, namely for a new sense of lightness, transparency and,

The flying city of Columbia in *BioShock Infinite* (2013).

to some extent, flexibility in construction. In early Soviet projects, dreams of a mobile architecture fed into the almost unbridled technological optimism that characterized this period. Georgy Krutikov's City of the Future, submitted for his architecture diploma in Moscow in 1928, presented, in a series of technical drawings, a vision of a levitating future city powered by yet-to-be-discovered atomic energy. In exquisitely precise drawings, Krutikov showed all the main elements of his new urban world, including three types of residential apartments suspended in the air and connected to industrial zones on the ground, which would all be traversed in universal travel capsules that could move through the air, along the ground and through – even under – water.[30] By presenting a host of other materials detailing the evolution of aerial structures and transportation, Krutikov gave weight to the idea of his proposal as a natural evolutionary step from the hot-air balloon through to powered flight in airships and aeroplanes. His future city also linked aerial living with social progression, namely the disappearance of the state and the realization of a socialist utopia with no territorial boundaries.

A residue of Krutikov's optimistic technological and social vision can be found in American architect Lebbeus Woods's speculative project for an aerial city to be located 2 kilometres (1¼ mi.) above Paris, developed in a series of drawings in the early 1990s. In asserting that he had declared himself 'against gravity', Woods's self-declared 'Anarchitecture' challenged the static, museum-like city of Paris beneath it as being unfit for purpose in a society where everything else was in ceaseless motion and flux.[31] Anticipating the global sea of flows in which we are now immersed in the digital age, Woods's flying city imagines an architecture that is entirely provisional and responsive to the flux around it and to the individual desires and needs of its inhabitants, resisting any tendency towards hierarchical organization. There is clearly an honesty to Woods's speculations; however, it is very difficult to imagine the inhabitants of such structures, ones who would be willing to radically forgo architecture's traditional role as a fixed shelter – a place of stasis in an otherwise turbulent world. If we were to become Laputans, we might forge a victory over an oppressive establishment, whether social, political or – in the case of architecture – physical; but we would also undoubtedly lose touch with our humanity in our newfound godlike freedom.[32]

Contemporary visions of aerial cities tend to underplay the radical politics seen in these earlier proposals in favour of an emphasis on ecology. John Wardle Architects' Multiplicity project, exhibited as

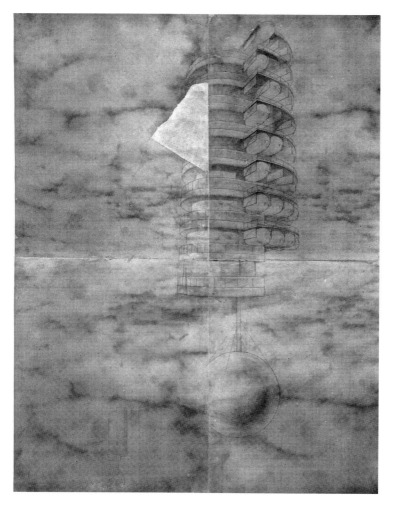

Georgy Krutikov, levitating apartment buildings, City of the Future, 1928.

part of the Australian *Now + When* entry at the 2010 Venice Biennale, imagines Melbourne in 2110, when a floating architectural island hovers over the traditional urban fabric below.[33] This new aerial structure would harvest the rain, generate energy and produce food, freeing up land on the ground while providing a model of high-tech sustainability as well as a protective shield for the city below. In a different vein, Clive Wilkinson's Endless Workplace project (2015) envisages a giant shared-office structure that hovers above London. A solution to what the LA-based architect sees as the crippling congestion of London as well as its reliance on traditional cubicle-style offices, Endless Workplace attempts to bring Californian tech-based innovation in workspace design to the British capital, providing an almost infinite office that would make work more creative and cooperative by eliminating what Wilkinson describes as 'the numbing isolation of working at home'.[34] Yet what is notably absent in both of these contemporary proposals for aerial cities, and what makes them so different from

John Wardle Architects, Multiplicity, 2010.

Lebbeus Woods, project for an aerial city above Paris, 1990s.

earlier modernist utopian visions, is any sense of progressive social life or politics. Indeed, Endless Workplace seems predicated on the future intensification of what many regard as current dystopian tendencies in our cities, whether a 24/7 work culture that leads not to personal freedom but rather to endless toil, or the hyper-stratification of cities, which precipitates the decay and ruin of the street level. The Multiplicity proposal may project an image of optimism with regard to the future of cities in an age of overpopulation and resource scarcity, yet it is so sketchily defined that one is left wondering how such a proposal could ever be realized. We are, once again it seems, back to building castles in the sky.

Air-filled Architectures

We might quite justifiably regard visions of flying cities as solely belonging to the realm of fantasy; yet many of them grew out of concrete technological developments from the late eighteenth century onwards. When the Montgolfier Brothers launched the first manned hot-air balloon in November 1783 in Paris, witnessed by a crowd of hundreds of thousands, they ushered in an era of intense fascination and experimentation with lighter-than-air structures.[35] While balloon flights are now largely understood in terms of leisure and pleasure, they were, during this time, objects of wonder and excitement, offering, as they did, a radically new way of experiencing the world. Even today, riding in a hot-air balloon corresponds much more closely to our dreams of flight than do journeys in jet aircraft. In balloons, as in reverie, we ascend effortlessly, without the need of the wings that we see in all other animals that can fly.

Fantasies of flying cities emerged alongside the first hot-air balloon flights, the most outlandish being the Belgian physicist Étienne-Gaspard Robert's Minerva balloon (1820) – a permanent habitation in the sky for global trips of scientific discovery.[36] The 46-metre-diameter (150-ft) balloon was to be connected to a large ship, which

Étienne-Gaspard
Robert, Minerva
balloon, 1820.

would in turn be linked with a host of other structures, including a
recreation room, kitchen, theatre, study and living spaces for the
'air-marines'.[37] Although lampooned on its publication, the Minerva
balloon nevertheless perfectly captured the vaunting ambition of the
early ballooning era and what it might conceivably produce in the future,
eventually feeding into the proto-science fiction of French illustrator
and novelist Albert Robida in the late nineteenth century.

Robida's trilogy of illustrated futurist novels – particularly the
first, *Le Vingtième Siècle* (The Twentieth Century), published in 1883
– drew directly on the emerging technology of powered flight that
would result in the first airships.[38] Henri Giffard was the first to

successfully demonstrate a dirigible balloon in 1852, but it wasn't until 1903 that the first fully controlled flight took place, with an airship designed by the Lebaudy brothers.[39] In Robida's anticipatory future world – Paris in the 1950s – a multitude of airships provide the principal form of passenger transportation in the city. Unusually for a futurist writer, Robida also illustrated his novels; *Le Vingtième Siècle* contained hundreds of engravings that did not merely embellish the accompanying text, but rather provided a 'stereoscopic' view of the future.[40] Just one example – Robida's view from above the towers of Notre-Dame cathedral – suffices to demonstrate this. With its hovering viewpoint, presumably from one of the many dirigibles arriving and departing from the restaurant perched atop the cathedral on a suitably Gothic-looking cast-iron structure, this image brings the viewer *into* the future world being described. We experience this image not as onlookers, but rather as participants: we become one of the multitude of passengers experiencing this congested aerial urban future. In Robida's illustrations and text, the daily life of the future civilization described becomes the main character, the anodyne plots of the novels mere pretexts 'around which a guided tour of the novelist's potential world unfolds, layer by layer'.[41]

The general tone of *Le Vingtième Siècle* is optimistic. Although future Parisians live at a hectic pace, technological developments made possible by the mastery of electricity lead to the development of an instantaneous communications network (a harbinger of the Internet) and safe and efficient mass transit by a whole fleet of exotic *aerocars*, *aerocabs* and *aeronefs-omnibus*. However, the second book in the trilogy – *La Guerre au Vingtième Siècle* (War in the Twentieth Century), published in 1887 – chimed with darker portents about the possible future of an aerial urban life. As early as the 1780s, when the first hot-air balloons were developed, their use in military conflicts was already being tested. In *La Guerre au Vingtième Siècle*, with its aerial convoys of military vehicles, Robida anticipated the eventual use of Zeppelin fleets during the First World War to terrorize urban populaces

Alfred Robida, view of Notre-Dame cathedral from *Le Vingtième Siècle* (1883).

from the air – a development that would culminate in the levelling of entire cities by bombs from aeroplanes at the end of the Second World War.[42] Aerial terror would also come from other sources – namely in the catastrophic failure of technology: balloons crash-landing, hydrogen-powered airships disintegrating in spectacular conflagrations or, more recently, aeroplanes disappearing, being blown up or used as weapons to destroy buildings. Such terror from the air continues to provide a disturbing counter to the general sense of optimism towards aerial technologies, particularly hot-air balloons, which remain to date a popular, if expensive, form of leisure activity. Today, the dark undersides of aerial technologies are revealed in remote-controlled drone strikes on unsuspecting combatants or civilians, or 'swarm intelligence models' – namely, self-organizing flying robotic blimps that are currently being developed and which suggest a nightmarish future mutation of warfare.[43]

The 2016 launch of the *Airlander 10* airship demonstrates that, although the era of passenger travel by airship came to an abrupt end after the *Hindenburg* disaster of 1937, this form of transportation still has a viable future, especially as fossil-fuel-powered aircraft become both more expensive and, perhaps, less culturally acceptable. At the same time, in the literary and visual genre known as Steampunk, airships have come to signify nostalgia for a 'lost' form of technology as well as ways in which to imagine alternative futures – ones in which airships win out over powered flight (or, simply ones in which aeroplanes had not been invented). The prevalence of all manner of airships and other dirigibles in Steampunk novels – from Bruce Sterling and William Gibson's *The Difference Engine* (1991) to China Miéville's *Perdido Street Station* (2000) – demonstrates how the revival of seemingly redundant technologies infuses them with a sense of magic that, in turn, revives how these structures were originally perceived.[44]

In Steampunk, the aerial urban worlds imagined by Robida in the late nineteenth century are cast both as speculative futures and alternative pasts, ones that imaginatively rework the relationship between past, present and future. For example, in Miéville's *Perdido Street Station*, the imagined city of New Crobuzon, with its extraordinary array of hybrid architectures and its population of human/non-human splices, extends into the air in a rich profusion of airborne life, including aerostats that 'oozed from cloud to cloud . . . like slugs on cabbages', militia-pods that 'streaked through the heart of the city to its outlands' and a cornucopia of flying creatures that centre on the monstrous slake-moths that are inadvertently released.[45] The air in Miéville's imagined city is infused with both magic and menace, the airships in particular cast as objects of wonder and also military tools of repression, reflecting the double-edged historical meaning of these structures. In other speculative fictions, particularly ones that think through urban futures without fossil fuels, airships supersede jet aircraft – the dirigibles that come and go in the future Bangkok imagined in Paolo Bacigalupi's *The Windup Girl* (2009) providing the only means of international transport in a world where coastal cities have been decimated by rising sea levels.

These speculative visions of lighter-than-air structures in alternative urban worlds – whether past, present or future – are important because they open up a range of possibilities that enrich and expand conceptions of aerial life in cities beyond the conventional world of jet aircraft, which are almost always far removed from the urban skies, unless you are unfortunate enough to live next to an airport. If some stress the environmental qualities of airships over their oil-guzzling, jet-powered cousins, then others emphasize air-filled structures as more expressive of human ideals of liberty and equality than aeroplanes.[46]

In the experimental fervour of the 1960s, many architects turned to air-filled structures because they were seen to embody that decade's spirit of optimism and reaction against the perceived social conformity in Europe and the United States in the 1950s. In addition, for architectural collectives like Ant Farm, Archigram and Utopie, pneumatic structures were diametrically opposed to the heavy concrete masses of the then fashionable Brutalist style.⁴⁷ Although only ever realized at a small scale, air-filled structures in the 1960s nevertheless came with high levels of ambition. For some, they were an expression of unfettered personal freedom and mobility; for others, they created a new kind of sensory environment that would transform human consciousness. For radical groups like Utopie, inflatables represented the overturning of bourgeois everyday life, with its emphasis on solidity

Anish Kapoor and Arata Isozaki, Ark Nova concert hall being erected in Lucerne, 2013.

and permanence, and Utopie demonstrated the potential of this in their 'Structures Gonflables' (Inflatable Structures) exhibition in Paris in March 1968, which featured designs not only for inflatable houses but for all manner of air-filled objects, from machines and tools to furniture and vehicles.[48]

Such subversive and utopian ideals for pneumatic structures proved short-lived. Even as the 1970 Osaka Expo was dominated by ambitious inflatable buildings – the largest, at 30 metres (98 ft) high, being the Fuji Pavilion by Yutaka Murata – they had already lost much of their subversive charge and, from the 1970s onwards,[49] would increasingly become limited to the worlds of entertainment and leisure, particularly as stage props at popular music concerts.[50] Although, in more recent inflatable works, like Anish Kapoor and Arata Isozaki's Ark Nova concert hall, the original promise of pneumatic structures to be flexible to new forms of urban living has been revived for different ends.[51] With its doughnut-shaped outer walls made from a flexible plastic membrane, the inflatable concert hall provided a demountable venue for music, theatre, dance and art that toured those regions of Japan devastated by the 2011 Tōhoku earthquake and tsunami. Here, the highly expressive and colourful pneumatic structure embodied the hope of adaptation and flexibility in the face of disaster.

Even though air-filled architectures have yet to transform urban life in the ways in which 1960s visionary architects and artists wanted them to, their utopian potential is still being mined in some recent speculative projects. In 2010 the architect Vincent Callebaut published his Hydrogenase plan for a new kind of city made up of a fleet of enormous airship structures that would produce their own fuel (hydrogen gas) by farming specialized breeds of seaweed, which would soak up sunlight and carbon dioxide to generate hydrogen.[52] By casting airships as the building blocks of future cities – each of his structures would also be a permanently inhabited urban neighbourhood – Callebaut's proposal argues for a radical overhaul of urban

Tiago Barros, Passing
Cloud, 2011.

design. With breathtaking ambition, he claims his future airship-city
will embody the highest ecological and humanitarian principles (with
his mobile cities providing disaster relief around the world) and would
supersede what Callebaut regards as the dying industry of carbon-
fuelled aviation. More utopian still is Tiago Barros's Passing Cloud
project from 2011 – an airborne assemblage of Zeppelin-like spheres
held together with tensile nylon fabric over a featherweight skeletal
steel structure.[53] Propelled only by the wind, Passing Cloud would
transport passengers in a manner almost diametrically opposed to
current air travel, namely slowly, erratically and with full exposure
to the aerial environment. With its goal being to transform airborne
travel from a stressful experience to one 'with an open schedule and

unknown final destination' that gives travellers the opportunity to experience 'a full floating sensation', Passing Cloud clearly draws on Bachelard's understanding of flight in human dreams, namely of rising into the air without the aid of wings.[54] Although both Hydrogenase and Passing Cloud draw on technologies that have already been developed, particularly in relation to lightweight materials and cleaner energy production, they are nevertheless firmly grounded in the fantasies of air-filled structures that stretch right back to the first hot-air balloons at the end of the eighteenth century. Technologies may evolve or become redundant, but the dream of flight will always be there.

Cloud Cities

In the context of aerial architectures, and particularly proposals for aerial cities, the work of the Argentine artist and architect Tomás Saraceno deserves to be considered at length because it represents perhaps the most thoroughgoing engagement with the subject to date. In a practice that continues to evolve in his Berlin-based studio, Saraceno has fused the speculative futurism seen in so many proposals for flying cities with a hard-edged practicality that is rooted in scientific research and collaboration. By doing so, he has created some of the most convincing representations of what a city in the sky might look like, and, in his numerous exhibitions and installations, how one might actually build and live in it. Many of his projects are ongoing series of works that collectively contribute to the artist's stated purpose to realize the world's first aerial city, or rather in his words to 'explore new, sustainable ways of inhabiting and sensing the environment towards an aerosolar becoming'.[55]

Like many of the works already discussed in this chapter, this aim may sound impossibly utopian, but in his projects, such as the ongoing series *Air-Port-City/Cloud City* (2001–), Saraceno has painstakingly built up a body of work that demonstrates the constructive principles that might eventually inform the building of such cities. The last decade has seen him installing accessible spheres and geodesic domes seemingly suspended in mid-air in his Düsseldorf installation *In Orbit* (2011).[56] He also built a cluster of habitable polygonal modules on the roof of the Metropolitan Museum of Art in New York in his 2012 'Cloud City' exhibition.[57] In a different vein, in 2007 he inaugurated the world-travelling solar balloon/museum space *Museo Aero Solar*. Made up entirely of recycled plastic bags and assembled by participants at each successive launch site, the balloon continues to travel the globe to date.[58] In addition, in his *Becoming Aerosolar* project, Saraceno has created an open, collaborative work that solicits responses to air in order to foster a new kind of collective awareness of it.[59] Such an evolving body of work ranges from research at the micro scale – Saraceno's long-standing interest in the structural mechanics of foam and bubbles, the design of optimal modular packaging, and the tensile strength of spiders' webs – to the macro scale of agglomerations of habitable structures in the air in his speculative drawings for the *Cloud City* series.[60]

In 2008 I was able to experience Saraceno's work at first hand in his *Observatory/Air-Port-City* installation on the roof of the Hayward Gallery in London, part of the exhibition 'Psycho Buildings: Artists Take On Architecture'. This installation was an early example of Saraceno's aerial structures – effectively a prototype module for a flying habitat – and consisted of an accessible geodesic dome where visitors could sit or lie down on inflatable pillows and observe and interact with the environment while seeming, to observers below (such as the friend who photographed me inside the installation), to float in the air. This sense of floating was an optical illusion – the structure did not actually levitate but rather, through the manipulation of transparent and reflective surfaces, merely appeared to do so. In a similar vein, in Saraceno's *In Orbit* of 2011, the multi-level spheres that seemed to be suspended in the air below the glass dome of the Kunstsammlung Nordrhein-Westfalen in Düsseldorf were actually

held in place by a huge net and countless ropes attached to the floor of the exhibition space.

Saraceno's installations allow participants to experience a power-ful sense of being suspended in the air that foregoes the obvious dangers associated with the reality of any genuine airborne experience, such as the record-breaking manned solar balloon flight undertaken in November 2015 by Saraceno himself in the desert of New Mexico.[61] They are not primarily concerned with the realization of a genuine flying city but rather affecting the human experience of air to thereby change attitudes towards it. Thus my recollection of experiencing the *Observatory/Air-Port-City* installation in 2008 was of being trans-ported back to childhood – of recovering and experiencing a renewed sense of wonder in relation to the air. The nets that suspended the spheres in *In Orbit* were also a means by which human responses to the work might be measured – according to Saraceno, with every installation he creates, each action participants take influences the

Tomás Saraceno,
*Observatory/
Air-Port-City*
installation,
Hayward Gallery,
London, 2008.

acts of others and elicits a response. This has the effect of changing 'the responsibility and the social behavior in a space . . . in this case a new flying space'.[62]

This emphasis on participation in Saraceno's installations links his work with that of Ant Farm and Archigram in the 1960s and early 1970s, both groups publishing 'do-it-yourself' guides to encourage people to make their own pneumatic structures.[63] However, Saraceno has taken the notion of participation much further than any of his predecessors, making it a fundamental element in his practice. Indeed, he has argued that his future aerial cities will come into being by a process of emergent organization and organic agglomeration rather than through the genius of visionary individuals. Some commentators on Saraceno's work have argued that this participatory method has a

Tomás Saraceno,
In Orbit installation,
Kunstsammlung
Nordrhein-Westfalen,
Düsseldorf, 2011.

specific ethical-political meaning, namely in striving to produce an inhabitable social space that is 'defined by multiplicities, that hold together without containing, accommodating different risings, fallings, directions, velocities, agencies, materials'.[64] Like those before him who have proposed the human inhabitation of the air, Saraceno has an explicit agenda that argues for airborne cities that transcend existing territorial boundaries, in effect creating social spaces that will generate entirely new – and, by implication, utopian – ways of inhabiting the world and being with each other.

The sociologist Bruno Latour has gone further, broadening Saraceno's emphasis on participation to include his engagement with the non-human world.[65] With reference to the work *Galaxies Forming along Filaments, Like Droplets along the Strands of a Spider's Web*, exhibited at the 2009 Venice Biennale,[66] Latour has argued that, in experiencing Saraceno's work, we realize – both visually and experientially – 'that no identity exists without relations with the rest of the world'. Thus, in engaging with a work like *Observatory/Air-Port-City*, participants become simultaneously aware of their spatial relationship with each other through the flexing of materials – whether inflated plastics, fabric meshes or steel ropes – and what is outside of the transparent spheres: other people, the city, the air. Latour contends that it is this double awareness that offers 'a powerful lesson for ecology as well as for politics: the search for identity "inside" is directly linked to the quality of the "outside" connection.' For Latour, this is an ecology that grows out of the broader cultural moment of the Anthropocene, namely the realization that human activity has been shaping and will continue to shape the earth as a force that is commensurate in scale with geological upheavals. Latour regards Saraceno's work as offering up a model of what transformed human relationships to each other and to the non-human might look like in this new epoch: a non-hierarchical social and ecological structure that connects human subjects with 'the rest of their support systems', including the air that they breathe and live in.[67]

With endorsement from such a prominent theorist as Latour, it is not surprising that Saraceno's work has come to be invested with a level of seriousness not seen in any previous proposals for aerial cities. His sense of commitment to the idea of aerial cities is unprecedented, demonstrated in the experimental rigour of his practice. However, it is also important to flag up some of the difficulties in his work – problems that I would argue have yet to be addressed by the artist and which temper the high level of optimism that is invested in his work by critics such as Latour. First, although Saraceno's projects are committed to sustainable ideals – particularly apparent in his demand that all future flying structures be powered by solar energy alone – the materials he uses for many of his inflatable works cannot be regarded as sustainable. Transparent plastic polymers (PVC and polyethylene) may produce aerial structures that use far fewer materials than their conventional cousins on the ground, but those plastics are nevertheless petroleum-based and therefore a non-renewable product of a carbon-releasing production process. Second, Saraceno's emphasis on radical mobility in his projects – a form of nomadic living that echoes the work of Ant Farm and Archigram – leaves unquestioned the ethics of such deterritorialized movement. In relation to 1960s projects for moving cities, such as Archigram's airborne Instant City (1968–70), unfettered movement is often presented as being liberating without fleshing out the politics of such freedom.[68]

There is also a clear sense that the aerial mobilities proposed by Saraceno would be restricted to the fit and able – namely, those willing to climb, roll, tumble and crawl in his structures. What place for the less able, whether those with physical disabilities or mental ones such as vertigo? Even as the rhetoric of aerial mobility promises freedom for all, flying cities would undoubtedly favour those who are already the most mobile. And what of those who simply desire to stay still, to remain where they are, but who have been forced by necessity to become nomads – the world's refugees, asylum seekers and economic migrants? Unfettered movement might represent freedom for some and frightening upheaval for others.

Saraceno's conception of the relationship between architecture and air can also be read as overly simplistic. While it is laudable for his aerial cities to aim to transcend the earthbound territories and politics of nation-states, particularly in an age of rising nationalism, there is nevertheless a danger in viewing the air as a frontier – an empty, non-territorial space that is ripe for colonization. Such air is imagined as benign, offering itself up to habitation by humans if only we would have the courage to do so. In the Anthropocene, we already know that climate change is producing increasing turbulence and extremity in our atmosphere – that the air itself is being changed by us and that our engagement with it to date is in fact making the air increasingly resistant to human habitation.[69] Will Saraceno's featherweight flying cities engage with *this* air – the unpredictable atmosphere of ever-more wild extremes? Or will they, like Archigram and Ant Farm's inflatable pods, actually end up protecting us from those extremes, merely offering up another architectural engagement with air that is also a retreat from it?

All of these questions lead us back to the complexities of air itself and our relationship to it. Even as our very survival, moment by moment, is bound up with our intermingling with air, we are not creatures of this element. Earthbound in design, we take to the air only with great difficulty, often with great trepidation and always with extreme vulnerability. Jet aircraft may shield us from the hostile air that they rush through, but many travellers never lose the terror of boarding those lumbering machines. A ride in a hot-air balloon may expose us to a less hostile part of the air above us, but as a form of transportation, balloons are extremely susceptible to air's vagaries and are almost diametrically opposed to the efficiency and speed we have come to take for granted in air travel. If we are ever to take to the air as Saraceno imagines we might, we would be required to transform almost everything we expect of the world we currently inhabit. With air – the atmospheric sea above our heads – being the key driver of climate change, such a transformation may be desirable but it must be able to accept and work through our limitations and vulnerabilities as earthbound creatures.

It is easy to mock the desire to take to the air as indicative of a Laputan imagination, whether manifest as a tendency to abstract speculation, arrogant assertion or fanciful imagining. Yet our relationship with air is founded on the gap between what we actually know and experience of it and what we dream about it. Perhaps this is a gap that can never be bridged; however much technology leads us into the air in the future, we will always remain separated from it. Yet, in a world where the air is being irrevocably changed by our collective actions, there is a pressing need to think through the consequence of air becoming more unstable. Far from a place of repose and harmony imagined in Saraceno's projects, the air will become more and more convulsive, turbulent and hostile. It is *this* air – the air we are currently creating – that requires our attention. This should not be an attention that seeks to dominate or control air, but rather one that respects and accepts our dependence on it.

II
VERTICAL CITIES

4
Skyscraper: From Icons to Experience

I n late June 2009, what would eventually become the tallest building in Western Europe – Renzo Piano's £1.5 billion Shard – was still little more than a deep pit in the ground, the gathered pile-driving cranes probing the earth and installing the skyscraper's foundations. Surrounding the site were hoardings that promised the building of a 'vertical city', words that could not but be redolent of futuristic visions of high-rise, multi-level urban landscapes that have dominated architectural speculation ever since the birth of the sky-scraper in Chicago in the 1880s.[1] Yet, once completed in 2012, the Shard fell far short of its original promise. For despite being a multi-use skyscraper, those uses hardly match the richness of what we would expect in a city, consisting as they do of a luxury hotel and apartments, high-rent offices and an expensive tourist attraction with restaurants and retail facilities.[2] The much vaunted 'public' spaces of the Shard's viewing galleries, for which you must pay around £25 to enter and undergo airport-style security checks, mock conventional definitions of what constitutes public space.[3] Like the vast majority of skyscrapers, the Shard's relationship to the wider city is one of visual dominance on the one hand, particularly at night, and hermetic isolation on the other. However, isn't this isolation an inevitable consequence of building high? Of building an environment that is profoundly at odds with the human experience?

Unlike the imagined urban visions so far discussed in this book – sunken, floating or flying cities – the skyscraper city is one that has entered fully into urban life as a built reality for well over a century. Indeed, in recent years, skyscraper construction has accelerated – rapid urbanization in the Middle East and East Asia has propelled the skyscraper to ever greater heights as the premier symbol of cities entering the world stage, joining and vying with the old-world dominance of American skyscraper cities, most notably New York.[4] According to the Council on Tall Buildings and Urban Habitat – the world's leading organization dedicated to skyscraper research – in 2015 more skyscrapers were built than in any other year in history, namely 106 buildings more than 200 metres (656 ft) tall. In the super-tall (above 300 m/984 ft) and mega-tall (above 600 m/1,969 ft) categories, numbers have risen sharply: before 2001 there were only 23 completed skyscrapers taller than 300 metres and none taller than 600 metres; from 2001 to 2016, 74 super-tall skyscrapers were built and, for the first time in history, three mega-tall buildings were completed, with several more currently under construction.[5]

Such a proliferation in skyscraper construction means we must engage more fully with the city's vertical axis, both above and below ground level.[6] So many of the world's new skyscrapers serve the interests of a tiny super-wealthy elite, functioning as containers of globalized flows of capital; they nevertheless have an almost overwhelming visual presence in cities that affects all urban citizens.[7] As literary historian Paul Haacke has argued, a progressive idea of the imagination 'requires a higher vantage point from which to perceive the multiple horizons of the future, as well as the multiplicity of historical pasts, while at the same time acting in the time of the now'.[8] Even though the heights of the skyscraper speak of the power of a global elite, they nevertheless provide us all with a tool for developing such a progressive imagination. Placing these all-too-real material artefacts against a host of imaginative visions of skyscrapers allows the very notion of the vertical city to be brought down to earth, back into the realm of the collective, of us all.

Icons

Today, skyscrapers of all kinds are often described as 'icons', meaning objects regarded as representative symbols of a dominating power. This reflects a much longer-term veneration of skyscrapers that dates back to the origins of this building type. The sense of awe that greeted the first buildings that were recognized as skyscrapers in Chicago and New York in the 1880s and 1890s came from a well-established tradition of viewing tall buildings in cities as iconic landmarks. In London guidebooks throughout the nineteenth century, the rapidly growing city was often represented, to the foreign visitor, as a series of landmark buildings seen from a high vantage point that could anchor experience of a complex and confusing city within the context of tall buildings.[9] In addition, what are now familiar height-comparison charts of skyscrapers originated in the Victorian information explosion, which saw a proliferation of printed material that included similar charts for the pre-skyscraper age, where the vertical dimension of urban space was dominated by church spires and domes. Thus, even before commercial skyscrapers emerged and overtopped these existing religious buildings at the end of the nineteenth century, there was already a well-established culture of viewing tall buildings – both religious and secular alike – as iconic structures.

Yet the emergence of the skyscraper in America was nevertheless regarded as inaugurating a new architectural epoch, one based on both distinct structural principles (a multi-storey steel frame supporting

Skyscraper
height-comparison
chart, 2016.

a curtain wall) and a strictly commercial use. Structural frames of iron and steel had already been used for industrial buildings in Europe from the late eighteenth century onwards, but their application to city-centre commercial buildings came later and, until the building of William Le Baron Jenney's 42-metre-tall (138-ft) Home Insurance Building in Chicago in 1885, were not recognized as possessing the necessary character of skyscrapers.[10] As these tall buildings grew in stature, so their prominent visual presence in American cities began to draw comparisons with much older buildings – a means of investing their unprecedented visual effect with some familiarity, some continuity with history. Thus visitors to New York in the 1890s and 1900s regularly compared the new vertical landscape of tall buildings with ancient Babylon, the impression of the latter deriving from imaginations steeped in biblical texts and well-known paintings of the Tower of Babel by artists such as Pieter Bruegel the Elder.[11] As the Dutch architect Hendrik Petrus Berlage said of the city's sky-scrapers in 1906: 'they seem a consummation of that dream of Babel's towers, these buildings that arise and towering seem almost to touch

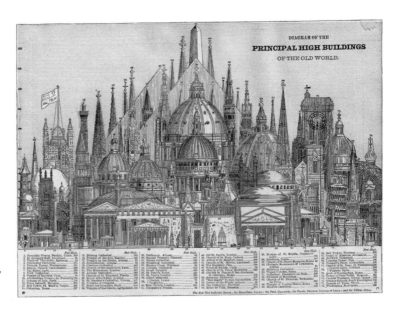

Height comparison chart for the tallest buildings in the world, printed in London, 1870s.

the skies.'[12] Some likened the emerging New York skyline of towers to those of medieval city states: in Karl Lamprecht's book *Americana* (1906), a contemporaneous image of New York's skyline is directly compared with a photograph of the towers of San Gimignano in Italy.[13] Others saw visual parallels with the temples of ancient Egypt or the ziggurats of Mesopotamia. Here, the imaginative overlaying of such architectural iconography onto skyscrapers demonstrated that entirely new forms can only be assimilated by relating them to existing ones.[14]

The first period of skyscraper construction culminated with the first super-tall buildings of the 1920s and '30s, the highest being the 381-metre (1,250-ft) Empire State Building (1930–31). Designed to accommodate strict zoning laws introduced in New York in 1916, these buildings deliberately introduced 'step-back' forms into their vertical construction, producing, in some cases, a startling resemblance to ancient ziggurats. The artist and architect Hugh Ferriss invested these step-back forms with extraordinary visual power in his 1929 publication *The Metropolis of Tomorrow*, where dark charcoal drawings of both real and imagined skyscrapers placed an almost overwhelming emphasis on the geometric forms of tall buildings and their visual effect from afar, as if half-obscured by mist or semi-darkness. If Ferriss's iconic buildings overwhelm in their archaic Babylonian forms, they do so with a strong sense of ambivalence as to whether this indicated either a 'headlong ascent' into a future characterized by extraordinary wealth and culture, or a descent into catastrophic destruction, mirroring the tragic end of the Tower of Babel in the biblical story.[15]

The host of symbolic references and overt historicism of these early skyscrapers were challenged by modernist architects from the 1920s onwards, resulting in the familiar overly functionalist geometric box-shaped towers that were commonly built in urban centres across the world in the three decades after the end of the Second World War. Yet the recent proliferation of skyscrapers in both old- and new-world cities has seen a powerful, if discomfiting, reinvesting of the tall building with powerful symbolic meaning. Skyscrapers such as César Pelli's Petronas Towers (1998) in Kuala Lumpur, which marked, for the first time, a shift to Asia from the u.s. in its claiming of the title of the world's tallest building (until it was surpassed by Taipei 101 in 2004), were conceived as both markers of global status

Hugh Ferriss's imagined future skyscraper city, a drawing included in *The Metropolis of Tomorrow* (1929).

Dubai's Burj Khalifa (2004–10) and its probable historical model: Frank Lloyd Wright's 1957 proposal for the mile-high Illinois Tower (opposite).

and signifiers of local identity – the pinnacles of the Petronas twin towers being overt visual references to Islamic minarets.[16] The tallest of the new generation of skyscrapers also establish their historical meaning by seeming to execute previously speculative proposals: in the case of the Petronas Towers, Arne Hosek's 1928 proposal for a City of the Future, showing twinned towers joined by a sky bridge;[17] and in the 829.8-metre (2,722-ft) Burj Khalifa in Dubai (2004–10; currently the world's tallest building but soon to be overtaken by the Jeddah Tower in Saudi Arabia, at 1 km/over ½ mi. high), Frank Lloyd's Wright's 1957 proposal for the mile-high Illinois Tower.[18] These visual references do more than invest new skyscrapers with architectural literacy; they also provide them with a sense of historical continuity that paints these projects as realizations of former dream images that Western powers were unable or unwilling to realize. The iconic nature of skyscrapers like the Petronas Towers and the Burj Khalifa resides in a sense of their declared *inevitability* – they are cast as products of the evolution of the skyscraper as already foretold in the past.

If some of the skyscrapers of the future are drawing from the past in order to be seen to both fulfil and overcome it, then how might we read the iconic nicknames penned for some of London's newest tall buildings: whether the Shard, Gherkin (30 St Mary Axe, opened in 2004), Cheesegrater (122 Leadenhall Street, finished in 2004) or Walkie Talkie (20 Fenchurch Street, completed in 2014)? Or, indeed, those that are already being built: the Spire (due to be completed in 2019), the Scalpel (2018) or the Can of Ham (2019)? The icons referenced here are decidedly ordinary, everyday objects – ways of summing up the dominating visual profile of these buildings in a memorable, if banal, image. These nicknames are not necessarily the products

of public acceptance – signs that the new buildings have entered comfortably into everyday urban life – but were in fact incorporated into the design and marketing strategies right from their conception. Indeed, it was the architect Renzo Piano himself who coined the name of the Shard during the design stage when he described his building as a 'shard of glass'.[19] The nicknames function as free-floating signifiers of distinction in an increasingly crowded and competitive skyline; they help developers and planning authorities sell the buildings to the wider public.[20] However, in contrast to the first generation of u.s. skyscrapers, whose iconic status lay in their projection of civic values grounded in a benevolent vision of corporations, today's iconic tall buildings merely project a 'branded' image; they appropriate the language of public space to cover up the fact that they are really creating highly securitized spaces for a tiny global elite.[21] As anyone who visits the Shard will discover, the 'public' status of its viewing galleries belies that fact that the overwhelming majority of the building's interior is carefully sealed off from the public gaze. Asserting an air of privilege to visitors only adds to the separation of the wider public from those who normally use these buildings, namely those who conduct business or who can afford to live in extreme luxury.

According to geographer Maria Kaika, these luxury skyscrapers are an 'autistic architecture' in that they exhibit a pathological self-absorption that severs them from the outside world.[22] For the citizen who does not work or live in one of these skyscrapers, they appear as highly mediated objects in the urban landscape. Usually apprehended favourably only from a distance, skyscrapers are increasingly becoming enlivened by special effects, particularly sophisticated lighting at night or images projected onto their surfaces, either to advertise products or mark the occasion of a special event.[23] In addition, the mediated nature of contemporary skyscrapers feeds into imaginative visions of vertical urban landscapes in cinema: for example, the illustration that introduced this book – a photograph of a projected image on a smog-enshrouded high-rise building that seemed to reference *Blade*

Runner. Although such blurring of the boundaries between the fictional and the real can be understood as revealing the interconnectedness of urban experience at the material and mental levels, it also exacerbates the tendency to focus almost exclusively on the visual effect of tall buildings, leading to a fixation on their exterior surfaces and thereby occluding their interiors.

Icons may be objects of veneration, but they also have a tendency to become targets, particularly when iconoclasm underlies an ideology – in the case of 9/11, a highly iconoclastic form of Islam. Iconoclasts fixate on the icon as an object to be destroyed, the acknowledged power of the icon fuelling the will to overcome it. A related, but 'benevolent', iconoclasm has fuelled a long-standing cultural fascination with the destruction of New York's tall buildings: from the obliteration of the city's emerging skyscraper skyline by German airships in H. G. Wells's novel *The War in the Air* (1908), to pre- and post-9/11 cinema that seemed to anticipate/replay those events, such as *Independence Day* (1996) and *Cloverfield* (2008).[24]

Within the long tradition of disaster fiction and film, there are examples of specific works that focus directly on the dissolving of the rigid distinction between the interior and exterior of skyscrapers. These fictions directly challenge the hubris of those – the privileged insiders – who imagine the skyscraper interior as an inviolate space. A key narrative motif here is the invasion of the skyscraper from outside: for example, from terrorists intent on destroying an enormous fortress skyscraper city in Los Angeles in Larry Niven and Jerry Pournelle's novel *Oath of Fealty* (1981); or from marauding zombies finding a way into a corporate skyscraper in George A. Romero's film *Land of the Dead* (2005). Yet invasion can also come from within, when the social and material structure of the interior of the skyscraper is imagined to disintegrate, perhaps most famously in J. G. Ballard's 1975 novel *High-Rise*, but also seen in David Cronenberg's debut film *Shivers*, also released in 1975, in which an elite high-rise condominium becomes infected by parasites that turn its residents into sex-crazed zombies. Both *High-Rise* and *Shivers* end with social disintegration spreading outwards from the skyscraper's interior: to other high-rise buildings in Ballard's novel, and to the rest of the city in Cronenberg's film, as the deranged residents leave the building in their cars ready to infect the outside world.

The early to mid-1970s was a particularly fruitful period for dystopian novels depicting the degeneration of skyscraper communities. In addition to *High-Rise*, Mack Reynolds's *The Towers of Utopia* (1975) saw high-rise buildings fall victim to planned obsolescence. In this novel, a 119-storey skyscraper owned by a giant corporation is being deliberately run down in order to create the need for a new one – economic growth being almost entirely dependent on the construction industry. In a different vein, Thomas M. Disch's *334* (1972) charts life in run-down New York tower blocks in a bleak authoritarian future where social stratification is rigidly maintained. More fantastical is Robert Silverberg's *The World Inside* (1971), set in a distant future where innumerable 3-kilometre-high (1.9-mi.) towers house almost the entire global population of 75 billion.[25] The proliferation of dystopian urban visions in the early 1970s reflected a growing awareness of the environmental costs of urbanism; but they often centred on the high-rise because of the perceived failure of what were then predominately buildings for social housing. This was seen in the structural failure of the Ronan Point tower block in London in 1968, caused by shoddy construction methods, and also the perceived social failure of the Pruitt-Igoe housing projects in St Louis, demolished in 1972, and the Hulme Crescents in Manchester, which began to deteriorate almost immediately after their completion in 1972.[26]

The resurgence of the tall residential tower in recent years has been predicated on an almost complete discrediting of the tower block as a viable form of social housing. The current tendency to 'luxify' city skies through the building of privately funded elite skyscrapers is underpinned by a focus on the few problematic examples of tower-block social housing that ignores the many success stories, in order to justify neoliberal policies that have systematically disassembled public housing in order to transfer it into private hands.[27] In this sense, the dystopian fiction of the early 1970s, rather than offering insights into the neglect of social housing by irresponsible construction firms and municipal authorities, might have actually contributed to the more recent ideological – and literal – running-down of high-rise social housing. Yet, that fictional mode of critique might also be revived again to undermine the current ideology that is based on the assumption that wealthy high-rise dwellers are not subject to the same social pressures as those who are disempowered. Here, Ballard's *High-Rise* still provides a potent challenge to this hubris, as the social breakdown he depicts in his tower block is tellingly middle class, radically undermining the overly classist bias of much of the current discourse on skyscraper construction.[28] Perhaps new invasion narratives might be directed at those who believe themselves to be inviolate – cocooned in their luxury apartments high above the city? New fictions might use the dissolution of the skyscraper interior/exterior to issue a warning against hubris and also to call for reconnection, that is, for the elite to both acknowledge and embrace their vulnerability.

Alastair Reynolds's novel *Terminal World* (2011) has done precisely this, but in the context of the imagined vertical city Spearpoint, seemingly located on another planet and occupied by a mixture of humans, sentient machines and cloud-dwelling angels, which are in fact humans that have evolved to live at otherwise impossible heights. Although Spearpoint is a fantastic creation – a city of 30 million inhabitants that occupies the surface of a vast human-built pinnacle rising to an immeasurable height – it nevertheless cleverly inverts conventional assumptions about vertical buildings and draws attention to the ways in which skyscrapers always seem to fall short of their self-proclaimed promise to become vertical cities. Seen from a distance, the vast, vertiginous city of Spearpoint appears iconic in the same way as today's mediated skyscrapers: 'the city-districts appeared to be little more than a coating of light, a phosphorescent daub on the rising, screw-like structure.'[29] However, the lights of Spearpoint are not mere surface expressions projecting outwards; rather they are visual reminders of inhabitation, of the vertical city's vibrant life itself. Although Spearpoint is structured vertically, the buildings that cling to its substructure are mainly low-rise, grouped around a railway that winds its way up and down the distinct urban districts in a steep spiral, calling to mind the spiral minaret of the ninth-century mosque in Samarra, Iraq. In addition, the built fabric of those districts is determined by seismic variations that emanate from the core of Spearpoint to create distinct zones within the vertical city, the transition points requiring anti-zonal drugs to temper the effects of moving between zones on its citizens.

Throughout the novel, as the central protagonist Quillon – a fallen angel – leaves Spearpoint to escape almost certain assassination, the vulnerability of Spearpoint is emphasized: first, in its connections with the world beyond, symbolized by a welter of ropeways and pulleys that carry raw materials into the city; and, second, by a catastrophic zonal shift early in the novel that almost destroys Spearpoint, resulting in its once sister city Swarm – a massive conglomeration of interconnected airships – returning to rescue the stricken pinnacle. The city may appear at first reading to be the epitome of urban self-sufficiency, gathering as it does an enormous population into an immensely old vertical structure; but even this fortress city proves vulnerable to forces it cannot control. In short, Spearpoint's iconic status is always undermined by its need to connect with what is outside of its vertical ramparts. As Ricasso, leader of Swarm, argues, in isolation, Spearpoint is 'an evolutionary dead end: a form that can't adapt'. In his view, in order to continue to thrive Spearpoint must reconnect with the 'perilously delicate thing' that is Swarm, a counter-city in which 'the whole was no stronger than any of its constituents'.[30] As an allegory of the need for the strong to reconnect with the weak, *Terminal World* speaks powerfully to the contemporary skyscraper icons that increasingly make a virtue of isolation.

Experience

Ever since observation decks were incorporated into the Eiffel Tower in 1889, the ascent of tall buildings to see the city from an elevated position has become an essential ritual for urban tourists. In December 2016 I added myself to the millions who have already ascended London's Shard since its observation platforms on floors 69 and 72 were opened in 2013. The commodity that is 'The View from the Shard' draws on a long fascination with seeing London from above that dates back to at least the early nineteenth century, when a mania for panoramas (enormous painted views of the city housed in specially designed rotundas) and hot-air balloon rides gripped the British capital (and others across Europe).[31] The popularity of these views from above came at precisely the same time as London was undergoing swift transformation and exponential growth in the wake of the Industrial Revolution. Today, an arguably even greater transformation is underway in light of an escalating property market that is seeing many hundreds of new residential and mixed-use towers being erected across the city.[32]

The desire for the sense of serene mastery experienced when contemplating the complex city from a great height is intensified when cities are undergoing rapid change. From the Shard's 244-metre-/800-ft-tall observation platforms, London is simultaneously a readable network of orderly flows, with road and railway tracks fanning outwards towards the horizon; a sublime spectacle in the hours of darkness when it becomes a fairytale multicolour tapestry of twinkling grandeur; and a city that seems to hold you, the individual viewer, at its centre. Of course, such a sense of mastery is a product of being so distanced from the chaotic sensory bombardment experienced on the ground.[33] Indeed, the overwhelming emphasis on the visual at the expense of the other senses replicates in reverse the iconic view that separates the exterior and interior spaces of the contemporary sky-scraper. On floor 72 of the Shard, the rest of the building doesn't seem

overleaf:
View from the observation platform on floor 72 of London's Shard, December 2016.

to exist – and visitors are not permitted to experience it anyhow – while London itself becomes an icon seen from afar, just as the skyscraper at night becomes when seen from a distance.

Viewing platforms in tall buildings also serve to illustrate how skyscrapers tend to restrict how the body can move around verticalized space. As an illustration of this, one might imagine the Shard being moved from the vertical to the horizontal axis – in other words, a ground-scraper, namely a very long and narrowing low-rise building. What would result is a city of multitudinous interior cul-de-sacs with a small number of entrance/exit points clustered on only one end of the building. It might be argued that a horizontal building would never be this spatially limited in reality, but the illustration serves to reveal just how different the vertical built environment is from the rest of the city. Skyscrapers cannot help but reduce the range of choices that are open to urban citizens in terms of how they negotiate the city's spaces. On the ground, cities offer 'a fine interconnection of streets, where an almost infinite number of lateral interconnections are possible'; in the vertical city, those interconnections are always much more limited and usually heavily proscribed.[34]

Building vertically will inevitably mean a reduction in urban interconnectedness, but contemporary skyscraper architects do not seem too willing to engage with a long history of designers and planners challenging the overwhelming dominance of the vertical axis in tall buildings. At the dawn of the skyscraper age many speculated that future high-rise cities would incorporate multiple horizontal levels connecting tall buildings that effectively multiplied what counted as the urban ground. Thus, in the early twentieth century, numerous speculative visions of vertical cities articulated a radical vision of an enhanced sense of horizontality. This is seen most strongly in perspective views of imagined future versions of existing cities, such as New York in Richard Rummell's frontispiece to the book *King's Views of New York* (1911) and Harvey Wiley Corbett's engraving of the 'City of the Future' (1913).[35] In both Rummell's and Corbett's future

Richard Rummell, illustration for Moses King, *King's Views of New York* (1911).

New Yorks, the building of skyscrapers of ever-increasing height necessitates the construction of an elevated transportation network that connects the skyscrapers on multiple levels. In a similar vein, early cinematic visions of future cities, such as *Metropolis* (1927) and *Just Imagine* (1930), envisaged a similar interconnectedness of the vertical and the horizontal axes.[36] The burgeoning skyscrapers of New York also inspired H. G. Wells's 1910 novel *The Sleeper Awakes*, in which a far-future London is transformed into a city of impossibly tall buildings connected by vertigo-inducing walkways. Many of these visions were predicated on the rigorous separation of different forms of urban transport, ostensibly to relieve traffic congestion at ground level; but they also envisaged an enriched horizontal experience for inhabitants in the future city that encompassed multiple grounds.

Despite some successful attempts by urban planners to implement elevated transportation networks – for example, Chicago's 'L' railway and Bangkok's Sky Train, and pedestrian skywalks linking many tall buildings in Minneapolis and Hong Kong – the radical visionary tradition of multi-level cities has mostly been sidelined in favour of the dominating paradigm of vertical stacking in tall buildings.[37] Even recent attempts to reintroduce the horizontal dimension into skyscrapers have usually failed to embrace the social dimension of these earlier visions. Although both the China Central TV Headquarters (2012–14) in Beijing and the Marina Bay Sands Hotel (2010) in Singapore feature striking horizontal elements that offset their vertical towers, neither use the former to connect those towers with the city beyond. Indeed, as already stated in Chapter Three, the luxury swimming pool that straddles the rooftop space of the Marina Bay Sands Hotel is but another instance of the skyscraper's appeal to the privileged elite by offering a place of sanctuary from the city below. Even the most ambitious proposals being put forward at present, such as Shimizu Corporation's Mega-City Pyramid, a vast vertical city proposed by architects Dante Bini and David Dimitric,[38] or CR-Design's Cloud Citizen scheme for Shenzhen, conceive of their high-rise built environments as only self-referentially interconnected – that is, they are all enclosed vertical cities entirely separated from the existing urban environment. Although high-rise living of this kind might not produce the social breakdown predicted by novelists like Ballard, the tendency towards vertical isolation inherent in the stacking model has been shown to be a contributing factor in the dissatisfaction experienced by residents of tall buildings.[39]

SKYSCRAPER: FROM ICONS TO EXPERIENCE

It is not surprising therefore that it is skyscraper fictions, rather than real buildings, that have articulated most clearly the recovery of the horizontal experience in vertical built environments. In a negative vein, this has taken the form of narratives of tall buildings turning on their residents – for example, the apocalyptic fire that engulfs the skyscraper in *The Towering Inferno* (1974) or the tit-for-tat confrontation between terrorists and Bruce Willis that witnesses the skyscraper becoming a sentient being in *Die Hard* (1988).[40] In these films, the stacked vertical environment turns from a place of safety to one of extreme danger, horrifically entering real life in the televised coverage of 9/11, when lack of escape routes in the burning World Trade Center towers led many to leap to their deaths. That said, the danger of horizontal movement at great height has also been exploited by film-makers to heighten drama and tension in their narratives. The climax of *Blade Runner*, for example, sees Harrison Ford dangling by his fingertips into the yawning void below a skyscraper rooftop in a future Los Angeles, before being rescued by the replicant he is trying to kill. In the more recent film *Cloud Atlas* (2012), a high-tech, but flimsy, pop-up skybridge is deployed by a hunted couple to escape between tall buildings in a fantastically vertiginous future Seoul. Exposure to the horizontal in a vertical built environment might also take on more realist forms, as witnessed in a scene in Andrea Arnold's film *Red Road* (2006), where impoverished residents of the 24th floor of one of Glasgow's soon-to-be-demolished Red Road tower blocks open the windows to experience the power of the wind on their faces and bodies. In all of these fictions, the vertigo induced by moving 90 degrees to the vertical axis can be understood as both terrifying and exhilarating.

Vertigo and skyscrapers dovetailed perhaps most powerfully in Philippe Petit's high-wire walk between the Twin Towers on 7 August 1974, dramatized twice in cinema as *Man on Wire* (2008) and *The Walk* (2015), even though the actual event was never filmed. As well as offering uncanny images of the construction of the Twin Towers, cementing their post-9/11 significance as icons aiding memory, the films also dramatize a breathtaking horizontal experience that temporarily bridged the vertical void between the Twin Towers. Petit's walk has readily been cast as a heroic act, with Petit himself a 'superhero', referencing a long history of fantasy figures such as Spiderman who were able to climb the exterior walls of skyscrapers effortlessly.[41]

Scaling skyscrapers for enjoyment and enhanced kudos is a key part of the variety of activities known as urban exploration. In what has become an increasingly extreme form of urban sport, explorers vie with each other to become the first to reach the tops of skyscrapers nearing completion, the final stages of these expeditions usually involving scaling cranes or gantries in dangerously exposed positions.[42] As urban explorer Bradley Garrett has argued, the motivation for such illicit climbs ranges from a desire to test the limits of one's fears, to an urge to experience an extraordinary sense of freedom or to feel like a superhero in the mould of Petit or even Spiderman.[43] Much of the imagery produced by explorers climbing tall buildings emphasizes above all the spectacular nature of the vertiginous view from above, and the sense of the explorer as hero. A corollary to this has been the increasing commercialization of the images that explorers produce and their appropriation by advertisers to imbue their products with a sense of subversive edginess.[44]

Many urban explorers climb skyscrapers because they want to experience cities freely in whatever way they see fit. They question why they should be forced to pay to access viewing platforms in tall buildings; why their experiences should be constrained by the rules of others. Yet, in putting the desire for individual freedom above everything else, are urban explorers not expressing the same desire that attracts tourists to the heights? For both practices are about gaining freedom *from* the city precisely by escaping it. In the same ways as visitors to the View from the Shard gain pleasure from feeling a sense of mastery over the city, of being placed at the city's centre, so urban explorers do so by getting to the top in their own way. Whichever way up, the viewpoint is still the same – a lofty vantage point that ends up simplifying the messy connectedness of the city, of the things that cannot be controlled or wrenched free from in everyday life. These views from above don't help to bring the skyscraper back into a fruitful relationship with the city that lies beyond it.

The vertigo-inducing climbs of urban explorers do, nevertheless, provide tantalizing glimpses into what are perhaps the most hostile spaces of skyscrapers, namely their exterior surfaces. In many super- and mega-tall buildings, windows are permanently secured shut to prevent accidents, as the exterior walls at these heights are often buffeted by fierce and unpredictable winds. Perhaps understandably, the outside walls of skyscrapers rarely galvanize the imagination in the same way as their interiors or visual effect from a distance. However, one novel – K. W. Jeter's *Farewell Horizontal* (1989) – is based on the fantastic premise that a colossal skyscraper, the Cylinder, supports an entire human ecosystem on its sheer exterior walls. Probably inspired by the architect Friedrich St Florian's 1966 Vertical City proposal – a cluster of 300-storey cylindrical towers – Jeter's Cylinder is so large and so high that no one knows its true extent. All life on the exterior of the building occurs above the cloud barrier, beneath which is an uncharted region that might continue downwards for ever.[45]

The novel's leading protagonist, Ny Axxter, is a graphic designer who decides to leave his staid life inside the building to 'go vertical', with a plan to sell his graphic logos to one of the warring tribes who vie for supremacy on the building's exterior. Axxter uses a lichen-eating motorbike to traverse the skyscraper's walls, while eking out a living filming and then selling-on unusual sights, such as copulating angels. Both Axxter and his machine are attached to the skyscraper wall via a complex tangle of steel cables, clips, specially adapted boots, and a canvas bivouac sling for shelter. When Axxter reaches a 2,000-strong camp of the Havoc Mass – one of the leading tribes that inhabit the exterior of the Cylinder – he enters an entire built environment adapted to the vertical walls, comprising:

gaudy tents, crested with fluttering pennants ... set in random
profusion, creating a chaos of intertwining pathways, dangling
catwalks, rope ladders, and nets. The division had been sta-
tioned in this one spot long enough for a second and third
layer of tents and platforms to have grown out from the first,
like overlapping limpets protruding from the building's wall.[46]

Drawing on many of the themes that characterized cyberpunk fictions
of the 1980s and '90s – the blurring of the boundaries between the
real and the virtual, the melding of high and low technologies, and
the glamorizing of a 'cool' counterculture – Jeter's novel plunges the
reader into a fantastical world. That world's central premise – that
human life might evolve on the outside of a skyscraper – is explored
with admirable conviction.[47]

The heady vertigo that is palpable in *Farewell Horizontal* contrasts
with more literal attempts to represent human experience of the
exterior walls of skyscrapers, perhaps most notably the film *Mission
Impossible: Ghost Protocol* (2011), which used the exterior walls of
Dubai's Burj Khalifa as a site for one its action set-pieces. In this
sequence, Tom Cruise dons specially designed sucker-pads to ascend
eleven storeys on the outside of the Burj Khalifa (starting from floor
119), the tension enhanced by camerawork that focuses on both the
extreme drop below and its mirroring in the reflective glass of the
building. While employing all the tricks in the book to escalate viewers'
experience of vertigo, this sequence nevertheless fails to go beyond
the conventional view of the skyscraper exterior as an exceptional
space. The real strength of Jeter's novel is to convince us otherwise:
it concludes with Axxter returning to live permanently on the exterior
of the Cylinder, 'the old fear and nausea gone', ready to explore the
full extent of the 'curved empty territory of the vertical world'.[48]

Nature

When the second tallest building in the world, the Shanghai Tower, was completed in the summer of 2016, it was also declared to be the first 'green' mega-tall building, being awarded the top Platinum rating by LEED, the most widely used third-party verification for green buildings in the U.S.[49] As well as employing a panoply of devices for both sustainably sourcing and bringing down its energy use – for example, two hundred wind turbines at the top of the tower, tanks for collecting rainwater and reusing wastewater, and a double-skin of glass for natural cooling and ventilation – the spiral form of the Shanghai Tower also referenced similar ones found in the natural world. Yet while it is clearly important for tall buildings to reduce their carbon footprints, such greening rarely extends to the sourcing and prefabrication of the vast quantities of raw materials required to construct mega-tall buildings.

In fact, the building of the first generation of mega-talls has been accompanied by environmental destruction on an unprecedented scale – the result of the quarrying, mining and fabrication of industrial quantities of building materials required for such colossal structures.[50] It might be argued that any urbanization at this scale – whether vertical or horizontal – is inevitably predicated on such destruction; but when many of the world's new tall buildings contain so much unoccupied or, in some cases, unoccupiable, 'vanity' space,[51] it is more likely that the touted environmental credentials of these skyscrapers are just another form of 'greenwashing' – a smokescreen that camouflages the powerful symbolism of extreme vertical architecture as an agent of increasingly environmentally destructive capitalism.[52]

Despite the questionable environmental qualities of skyscrapers, investing them with 'nature' can also be read as an attempt to soften the edges of these implacable human-created objects. In the early twentieth century, Manhattan's skyscrapers, both real and imagined, were regularly cast as natural objects. Tall buildings were likened to

Shanghai Tower, completed in 2016.

giant trees competing for sunlight; famous mountains were equated with the city's iconic skyscrapers; and frozen fountains symbolized the idea of arrested motion in the Chrysler (1928–30), Empire State (1930–31) and RCA buildings (1931–4).[53] In Ferriss's 1929 book *The Metropolis of Tomorrow*, skyscrapers morphed into outsized crystals, drawing on European Expressionism's obsession with such mineral accretions, while skyscraper height-comparison charts articulated a supposed 'natural' genealogy of tall buildings. Similar charts continue to dominate contemporary representations of super- and mega-tall buildings, thus reinforcing the long-standing rhetoric of natural evolutionary growth, despite the increasingly destructive nature of building ever taller. In these images, the sense of skyscrapers as a force of nature is a powerful way to account for their increasing visual dominance, even as it obscures the all-too-human forces that produce them.

This evolutionary model also accounts for the dominant tendency in futuristic urban fictions to depict cities as more verticalized than those of the present-day, from the colossal Art Deco skyscrapers of *Metropolis* to the future-tech towers of Neo-Seoul in *Cloud Atlas*, Kansas City in *Looper* (2012) or Washington, DC, in *Minority Report* (2002). In this largely dystopian mode, the intensification of the city's vertical axis may be cast as organic in its evolution; but, like the tropical jungle, it suffocates in its overwhelming dominance, leading to ever increasing social inequality and the threat of urban collapse. Modernist promoters of tall buildings introduced a different, and much more positive, mode of apprehending the relationship between skyscrapers and nature that focused on bringing what was perceived as natural *into* the building, principally by creating more permeable exterior surfaces. That nature was just as symbolic as in the expressionist mode it ostensibly reacted against, forgoing any engagement with how the making and use of a skyscraper might relate to nature in favour of a conception that pitted the solid building against the immaterial nature of light and air.[54]

In recent years, as awareness of the destructive environmental impact of the construction industry has grown, some architects have formulated new approaches to building tall that meld the programmatic and the symbolic in skyscrapers' engagement with nature. The practice of the Malaysian architect Ken Yeang, in partnership with T. R. Hamzah, has been key in developing the notion of green skyscrapers. In a host of built and speculative projects, as well as many publications, Yeang was one of the first to think through how the design of skyscrapers might evolve as the tallest examples moved from the temperate U.S. to the tropical regions of Asia.[55] Yeang's resulting 'bioclimatic' buildings, such as the Roof-Roof House (1984) in Kuala Lumpur, incorporated many features designed to make use of natural ventilation and shade from the sun to mitigate the effects of the hot and humid local climate.[56] His later works, such as Menara Mesiniaga (1992), a small office-tower also in Kuala Lumpur, incorporated more advanced features, including a tilting landscaped base, a radial glass curtain wall at mid-height wrapped with spiral sunshades, and sky courts and shaded terraces at the top of the building.[57] Yeang's unbuilt competition proposals, such as the Chongqing Tower in China, the Elephant and Castle EcoTowers in London, and the EDITT Tower in Singapore, are more ambitious in scale and each combine the architect's well-developed design features with an emphasis on the literal greening of towers, namely by bringing vegetation directly into the building itself via ramps and terraces.

To date, the most startling realization of such greening has been in the work of the Italian architect Stefano Boeri, most notably his Bosco Verticale (Vertical Forest) in Milan (2014) – two tall residential towers that host nine hundred trees and over 2,000 plants – and a similar project currently under construction in Nanjing, China.[58] With plans to build entire cities in this way, Boeri argues that green buildings create natural 'islands' in cities with their own distinct ecologies; plants absorb CO_2 from the urban atmosphere and produce oxygen that enhances it; they also provide natural shade and an acoustic barrier for residents, mitigate horizontal urban sprawl, and act as a magnet for birds and other animal life.[59] Although Boeri's vertical forests are startling in their appearance, the tall buildings that the vegetation partially obscures are constructed from conventional materials (mostly reinforced concrete) to an equally conventional design (multiple stacked floors). In addition, there is very little information about the environmental costs of extracting soil from the ground to cultivate these green skyscrapers, let alone the future costs of maintaining them. It may be a step too far to suggest that the vegetation in Boeri's skyscrapers amounts to yet another form of 'greenwashing', one

Ken Yeang, EDITT Tower proposal, Singapore, 2008.

Stefano Boeri, Bosco
Verticale (Vertical
Forest), Milan, 2014.

that covers over the true environmental costs of skyscrapers; but it
certainly does not represent a radical departure from existing models
of building tall.

    In this respect, skyscraper-design speculation is far ahead of built
reality, most notably evidenced in the thousands of projects already
submitted to the ongoing skyscraper competition hosted by the design
and architecture magazine *eVolo*.[60] Begun in 2006, this annual event

has become an important testing ground for speculative designs that engage with questions of vertical density; in 2009 alone, *eVolo* received 489 entries from 36 countries, with only a select few of the projects published in the magazine.[61] With such an enormous number of speculative proposals, it is a difficult task to find overarching themes that link them together, let alone any unified formal language; yet, from 2006 to date, a large number of the skyscraper proposals have been grounded in ecological concerns that often extrapolate wildly on what might be possible in the near future. In the 2009 group of entries, some of the imagined skyscrapers morph into vertical farms, thus bringing high-density agriculture and permaculture back into cities, freeing up land outside of them.[62] Other proposals demonstrate how cutting-edge technologies might turn skyscraper facades into giant environmental filters, where assemblages of cleaning cells embedded into a double skin purify both air and rainwater;[63] or, following Yeang, provide light, thermal insulation and natural ventilation.[64] At the same time, these overtly ecological programmes occur within often startlingly biomorphic forms, whether the giant helical structure of the Urban Nebulizer project,[65] the outsized petal-like towers of Sky-Terra,[66] or the insides of the human lung in Trabeculae.[67]

When one of the 2009 *eVolo* projects – Kwonwoong Lim's Space High-Rise – proposed building a skyscraper in space by means of a tower 1,000 kilometres (621 mi.) high,[68] it is hard not to sympathize with those critics who regard many speculative skyscraper designs as exhibiting a 'fetish for mere form', paying no attention to how such structures might be realistically built or inhabited.[69] Yet even the most fantastic proposals in these competitions are grounded in technologies that are actually viable and, in some cases, already beginning to be implemented. For example, Stefan Shaw and John Dent's Bio-City proposal features two biomorphic skyscrapers, 1.2 kilometres (¾ mi.) high, sited above the English motorway intersection at Birmingham that is known as Spaghetti Junction.[70] The facades of these towers would contain thousands of photo-bioreactors that would cultivate vast quantities of algae, its nutrients sourced from sunlight and the otherwise polluting exhaust fumes churned out from the vehicles passing beneath the towers. The algae would then be turned into biodiesel and liquid hydrogen to provide energy for the buildings and the city's transportation system. The fact that the proposed facade of photo-bioreactors was subsequently incorporated into a real building, namely Splitterwerk Architects and Arup's BIQ House (2014) in Hamburg, only serves to demonstrate that even the most fantastical proposals cannot easily be dismissed as irrelevant to practice.[71] Surely the great strength of speculative design is to stretch the limits of what we regard as possible at any given time; to forgo all of the constraints of the practising architect in order to sketch out multiple possibilities that do not predict but rather incubate many possible futures? Proposals like Bio-City also radically reconceive the 'skin' of the skyscraper as something living, a hybrid of human-created and non-human technologies that prevent any facile distinction between the inside and outside of the buildings. In a similar vein to CRAB Studio's Soak City proposal discussed in Chapter One, nature enters the towers of Bio-City not to soften their artificiality, but rather to meld with it, producing a new kind of nature that is set within rather than against the building.

The ongoing *eVolo* skyscraper competitions prove that the tall building continues to be a building type that exerts a powerful hold on the imagination worldwide, where tallness is still equated with prosperity, as if a building's height were itself a talisman for economic growth. Skyscrapers have been and still are a constant presence in the imagination of future cities, even as, in cities like Dubai, those futures are increasingly becoming wedded to the present. It is therefore an urgent task to think through the imagination of vertical cities with a whole range of creative practices that are all affecting the realm of the possible in terms of the actual construction of tall buildings.

How might a more socially progressive conception of the skyscraper emerge more fully in contemporary architectural practice? First, the forms of tall buildings need to be more heavily invested with

Stefan Shaw and John Dent, Bio-City project, 2009.

historical meaning – a meaning that goes beyond mere branding and which can challenge us to think anew about what skyscrapers might yet become. It remains to be seen if a truly vertical city can be constructed – one that holds within it the rich currents of urban life on the ground; yet examples like Spearpoint in *Terminal World* at least show how they might be imagined, thus expanding what may be possible in the future. Second, skyscrapers need to be experienced more fully. It might be that tall buildings by their very nature cannot but help to reduce what is possible in terms of how we inhabit buildings, but the standard model of vertical stacking that tends to isolate inhabitants can at least be questioned. By focusing on a number of fictions that dramatize the human experience of skyscrapers – for example, Jeter's *Farewell Horizontal* – I suggest that the range of possibilities for such experience have not been as fully embraced by architects and urban planners as they might have been. Perhaps new kinds of horizontality might be introduced into tall buildings that reconnect them with what is outside, and which provide residents with more freedom to make those connections. Finally, designers of skyscrapers must acknowledge the destructive capacity of tall buildings and seek to work against that rather than covering over it with green rhetoric. Instead of being destructive of and divorced from nature, skyscrapers like Shaw and Dent's Bio-City might lead the way in promoting design that bridges the gap between the artificial and the organic, creating a meld of both.

At the moment such transformations seem unlikely, at least when skyscrapers are so wedded to neoliberal capitalism, where differentiating form and function is key to their acceptance by urban populations, and where they sit among us as seemingly inviolate citadels of the elite. That shocking realization of the vulnerability of tall buildings that so many experienced on 9/11 has not yet led to an embracing of the *weakness* of the skyscraper – which will be key to these citadels being reconnected with what's currently kept firmly outside of them. On the contrary, the last decade has seen in skyscrapers a renewed and intensified arrogance in the face of mounting threats. One can only wonder what it might take for such a perverse attitude to be reversed. It need not mean the kind of destruction practised by hate-filled iconoclasts on 9/11; rather, merely the skyscraper coming down to meet the earth or the earth being raised up. In the meantime, we can inhabit tall buildings in this way in our imaginations.

5

Underground: Security and Revolution

I n the Victorian novel *The Coming Race* (1871), a hyper-evolved race of humans – the Vril-ya – are discovered by the curious narrator living in underground cities beneath a mine. In describing the entrance to this subterranean urban world as 'a broad level road . . . illumined as far as the eye could reach by what seemed artificial gas-lamps placed at regular intervals',[1] the author, Edward Bulwer-Lytton, drew directly on descriptions of the world's first underwater tunnel – the Thames Tunnel in London, built from 1825 to 1843.[2] Widely regarded as a modern wonder of the world, the Tunnel was visited by many in search of a new kind of urban experience. When artist Edmund Marks went there in 1835 he described an 'indescribable feeling of subterranean vastness': 'the amazement and delight I experienced, quite overcame me, and I was obliged to turn from the friend exploring with me, to cry and ponder in silence.'[3] But as its novelty wore off, so did these strong feelings, and the Tunnel was incorporated into the emerging underground train network in 1869, relegating it from wondrous to workaday space.

Today, plans are being put forward to find new uses for abandoned underground infrastructure in cities across the world. In London and Paris, long-abandoned Tube and Metro stations are being turned into swimming pools, skating parks or galleries, offering novel experiences again to urban citizens.[4] In New York, a disused tunnel in Manhattan's Lower East Side is being touted as the 'Lowline', a subterranean equivalent of the city's famous High Line, an abandoned elevated railway that has recently been transformed into an urban park.[5] Meanwhile, in Beijing, a million people now live underground in shelters built in the 1950s to protect the city's population in the event of a nuclear attack; these inhabitants have been forced into these spaces because of a shortage of land in this rapidly growing megalopolis.[6] If fiction and reality were bound up together in *The Coming Race*, how might today's subterranean incursions inform how we imagine these spaces? If inhabited, will utilitarian infrastructure open up imaginative gateways to alternative worlds, as they did over a century ago for Victorian writers like Bulwer-Lytton; or will their novelty value simply cause them to be abandoned again?

As *The Coming Race* demonstrates, even as cities are increasingly dominated by underground spaces that are overwhelmingly utilitarian in their function, whether sewers, subways, railway tunnels or other forms of infrastructure, these spaces nevertheless exert a powerful hold on the imagination.[7] We are aware of the necessity of underground spaces in cities, and we use some of these – particularly subways and underground railways – on a regular basis. But usable underground spaces are almost always places of transit – to be moved through quickly rather than dwelled in for any length of time. They are still replete with our fears and anxieties about venturing below the surface, accentuated today by the threat of terrorist attacks such as those carried out on the London Underground on 7 July 2005.

The imagination of the underground conveys very different meanings from the city above. If skyscrapers have risen to a position of visual dominance in the city, underground spaces are still full of dark and invisible recesses. Our ability to move around underground spaces in cities may be as limited as that in skyscrapers, but it is limited in a very different way. The depths may be constricted spaces, but unlike their skyward capsular equivalents, they also harbour the potential for revolutionary subversion. The very invisibility of underground spaces – their disconnectedness from the world above – lends them an air of impregnability and security. Yet, as the recent phenomenon of basement construction by the uber-wealthy in London demonstrates, or increasingly sophisticated 3D military surveillance shows,[8] that revolutionary potential may easily become yet another domain of the elite. How might the imagination of underground spaces generate an urbanism that digs in order to enrich, not impoverish, the social life of the city? The rich layering of many different histories in underground spaces may yet inform the ways in which we build and inhabit these spaces.

Domes

Hermetically sealed human environments have a long history, perhaps dating back to the origins of the human species itself, when we made our homes in caves. Yet the desire to enclose entire cities under artificial protective canopies only emerged with any force in the nineteenth century, when the new engineering technologies of iron and glass suggested that this might actually be possible. Thus the self-contained utopian communities imagined by the French socialist thinker Charles Fourier in the 1820s, or the vast covered arcade encircling London proposed by Joseph Paxton in the 1850s, were both essentially scaled-up versions of already existing structures, such as the iron-and-glass arcades built in Paris and London from the early nineteenth century onwards.[9] At the same time, increasingly large-scale iron-and-glass structures were being constructed as greenhouses for the display of exotic nature or buildings to house the international exhibitions that began with Paxton's Crystal Palace in London in 1851.[10] Using iron and glass allowed architects and engineers to develop covered spaces of both unprecedented scale and transparency: the first visitors to the Crystal Palace expressed a sense of awestruck wonder at the sense of lightness experienced in this enormous enclosed space created by these two materials.[11] For an unnamed contributor to Charles Dickens's journal *Household Words*, the interior of the Crystal Palace was 'a wondrous fabric, sublime in its magnitude, beautiful in its simplicity';[12] while for the German visitor Lothar Bucher, it seemed to transcend ordinary architectural experience: 'Instead of moving from the wall at one end to that at the other, the eye sweeps along an unending perspective which fades into the horizon. We cannot tell if this structure towers a hundred or a thousand feet above us.'[13]

The development of these iron-and-glass buildings went hand-in-hand with the exploitation of materials below ground, particularly in the coal mines that provided the raw materials for the production of iron. Thus the excavation and inhabitation of mines in the nineteenth century was equally important as iron-and-glass buildings in promoting the idea of a wholly man-made hermetic environment.[14] If these two sealed worlds – iron-and-glass above ground, the mine below – could not have been more different in their spatial qualities, they were nevertheless linked: both envisaged a new kind of ground level within the inhabited space, namely an enclosing envelope or barrier above that effectively made both spaces subterranean.

Despite the ambition and scale of iron-and-glass buildings in the nineteenth century, these visions of covered cities failed to materialize, mostly on account of the expense that would be incurred in their construction. It would only be in the 1960s that the imagination of artificial urban environments would resurface again with any force. That decade saw an emerging environmental consciousness of Earth as a globe. When one of the first photographs of Earth from space was broadcast from the U.S. *Apollo 8* mission in 1968, people saw just how vulnerable our planet was – its fragile life-sustaining atmosphere surrounded on all sides by the hostile vacuum of outer space.[15] Coupled with a growing awareness of threats to our planet's ecosystem, such as pesticides, human population growth or an exploitative capitalism, this heightened awareness of the Earth's vulnerability led to an obsession with enclosure.[16] As architectural critic Douglas Murphy has argued, throughout the 1960s and '70s, again and again the notion of the spherical environment, the dome or bubble, came to represent the new-found sense of the earth as a small, vulnerable globe . . . and the quest, for some, was to expand that protective interior to encompass ever-greater aspects of life.[17]

An enormous range of projects from this period envisaged new urban communities under protective canopies of one kind or another. These included the geodesic bio-domes developed by Buckminster Fuller and realized most dramatically in his 76-metre-diameter (249-ft) Bio-sphere built for the 1967 International and Universal Exposition in Montreal. Fully enveloping a seven-storey exhibition building, the dome's innumerable interconnecting equilateral triangles, made from lightweight steel tubes, created an extraordinary visual display of delicate enclosure.[18] At the same exposition was architect Frei Otto's German pavilion, made up of a vast translucent, polyester canopy anchored to the ground with steel cables. The sweeping parabolic curves of the canopy produced dramatic spatial effects and came to be regarded as a blueprint for a new kind of humanitarian architecture that could respond quickly and flexibly to human needs.[19]

Geodesic domes
at Drop City,
Colorado, c. 1970.

The late 1960s environmental movement in the United States also saw the establishment of new countercultural settlements, such as Drop City, founded in 1966. This community realized the technology seen in Fuller's geodesic domes on an everyday scale – the improvised domed structures of Drop City were made possible by a do-it-yourself culture promoted in such works as Stewart Brand's *Whole Earth Catalog* (1968) and Steve Baer's *Dome Cookbook* series from 1970.[20] The Drop City domes were grounded in the new technologies of super-light structures that sought to reduce their ecological footprint on the Earth: they were also powerful symbols of cosmic interconnectivity.[21] With geodesic structures based on the complex interactions of innumerable structural members, the technology of these domes dovetailed with a desire for a countercultural way of life based on the idea of 'roundness'. The imaginative connotations of roundness and domes to 1960s counterculturists were clear: in a round house, everything seems to be in repose – the earth connects with the sky, human beings with the cosmos.[22] Yet, very soon, Drop City began to disintegrate, its initial social cohesion compromised by an increasingly itinerant population of drug-addled dropouts and a chronic shortage of funds. By the early 1970s, most of Drop City's domes lay abandoned or in disrepair.[23]

The failure of alternative communities like Drop City in the 1970s fed into the widespread sense of disillusion and pessimism that characterized that decade. In imaginative visions of enclosed cities in this period, the dome stood not for cosmic connectivity or ecological awareness, but rather human imprisonment and social stagnancy. In Michael Anderson's 1976 film *Logan's Run*, set in the year 2274 and based on the 1967 novel by William Nolan and George Clayton Johnson, a vast domed city has been created to house the population that formerly lived in Washington, DC, now in ruins.[24] This ostensible urban utopia gives its residents a life of unbridled hedonism but with a savage catch – all citizens are ritualistically killed at the age of thirty in order to control population levels. Mixing contemporaneous fears of overpopulation with a satirical swipe at 1960s countercultural values, the domed city in *Logan's Run* creates an ultimately sterile urban environment that cannot countenance any subversion. When one of its policemen (the Logan of the film's title) rebels against his own prescribed death, he flees the city with his girlfriend, escaping outside to the ruined, but fecund, former capital city in order to be free.

This clearly dystopian vision of an enclosed city has its roots in an earlier tradition of science fiction writing that was grounded in a mistrust of technology, particularly industrial technology that threatened human freedoms. As early as 1909 in E. M. Forster's short story 'The Machine Stops', a hermetically sealed future urban environment, in this case underground rather than under a dome, results in the complete disconnection of its citizens not only from the world above but from each other and their own bodies.[25] In Forster's enclosed city, human bodies wilt into mere 'lumps of flesh', with most of its citizens never leaving their rooms, communicating only via handheld devices rather like prototype electronic tablets or mobile phones. The eventual failure of the machine that maintains the city results in its total annihilation, the only survivor a rebel who has already found a way out to a verdant world above. Less apocalyptic but no less negative is Arthur C. Clarke's imagined city of Diaspar in *The City and the Stars* (1956) – a megalopolis of 10 million inhabitants that has survived unchanged for millions of years into the future as the rest of the planet around it has succumbed to the forces of entropy, being mostly ground down into a vast desert.[26] Protected by an all-powerful computer – the Memory Banks located in the city's underground – and an environmental filter that surrounds the city, Diaspar is eventually revealed to be the product of cowardice – of a human race that had rejected the outside world in favour of a perfect form of shelter. In the end, the unchanging order of this city breaks down in the face of the rebel Alvin, who finds a way outside and leads a quiet revolution to once again embrace the riches of the outside world.

Even in the pessimistic post-war period, domed environments remain ambivalent in their meanings. In Isaac Asimov's 1953 novel *The Caves of Steel*, each of the Earth's eight hundred cities has been relocated underground as a 'semi-autonomous unit, economically all but self-sufficient. [Each city] could root itself in, gird itself about, burrow itself under . . . a steel cave, a tremendous, self-contained cave of steel and concrete'.[27] Here, a future underground New York City is contrasted with an adjacent domed settlement inhabited by so-called Spacers – interplanetary colonists who are trying to convince the urban troglodytes to join them in space exploration.[28] Here, domes once again stand for cosmic connectivity, for living lightly on the Earth, and for technology as a positive evolutionary tool.

Viewed alongside *The Caves of Steel*, Buckminster Fuller and Shoji Sadao's 1960 proposal to build a domed structure of 3 kilometres (1¾ mi.) diameter over the midtown area of Manhattan can be read as both a call to resist the desire to burrow to safety, and also an act of environmental domination that creates freedom inside by severing connections to the city outside.[29] Although Fuller justified the project on economic and environmental grounds – his dome would reduce the amount of energy needed to heat and cool the city's skyscrapers and provide 'uninterrupted contact with the exterior world' without the 'unpleasant effects of climate, heat, dust, bugs, and glare' – there is a strong sense of technological determinism in his vision that subjugates the complexity of the human/non-human ecosystem in favour of a reductive model of environmental control.[30] When the novelist Frederik Pohl imagined a similar doming project being carried out in a future New York in his *The Years of the City* (1984), twin domes – or 'blisters' – are raised as the city becomes increasingly socially divided and mired in violence, reflecting fears about the escalating crime rates that plagued New York in the early 1980s.[31] In Pohl's vision, the domes do not create a Garden of Eden as such; rather the structures co-exist within a chaotic city riven by opposing political and economic interests which the domes seek, unsuccessfully, to sidestep.

Richard Buckminster Fuller and Shoji Sadao, proposal for a 3-km-diameter dome over midtown Manhattan, 1960.

Pohl's vision was brought to realization on a much smaller scale in the Biosphere 2 project from 1991. The brainchild of countercultural figure John Allen, an American ecologist and engineer, Biosphere 2 was built by Allen's company, Space Biospheres Ventures. Intended to demonstrate how humans could establish a more sophisticated and less domineering relationship with nature, Biosphere 2 was a series of domes covering 1.2 hectares (3 acres) – the largest fully sealed habitat ever created. The eight individuals who spent two years inside Biosphere 2 were living out an experiment to see if humans could thrive in an entirely closed system – there would be no transfer of food, waste, air or water between the Biosphere and the outside world for the entire period of isolation.[32] Plagued by serious difficulties from the start – a gradual loss of oxygen inside and barely enough food grown to support the human occupants – the project ultimately failed due to a lack of cooperation among the participants, revealing that perhaps the biggest obstacle in the way of the successful realization of a domed city will be the city's inhabitant themselves. When a second crew entered Biosphere 2 in 1994, the project lasted less than six months, sabotaged by two of the crew, who opened the airlock.[33]

The obvious failings of the Biosphere 2 project has not stopped an ongoing preoccupation with creating enclosed built environments. Structures such as London's Millennium Dome (1999), the Eden Project (2000–2001) in Cornwall and the 2016 designs for Google's new headquarters in Seattle have all drawn on the idea of the dome as an image of connectivity, fertility and creativity – in effect, continuing the optimistic current seen in the 1960s.[34] Yet the revival of the domed environment in recent years has seen the potent social meanings inherent in earlier projects like Drop City sidelined in favour of a superficial reading that views domes as exclusive habitats for either leisure, consumption or corporate business.[35] Perhaps most dramatically demonstrated in Dubai's proposed Sunny Mountain Ski Dome (put on hold after the 2008 financial crisis) and the more recent proposal for a pedestrian mall, 7 kilometres (4.4 mi.) long, covered with a retractable domed roof, these recent proposals tend to focus on the creation of exclusive climate-controlled enclaves in a world now threatened by the ravages of global warming.[36] In the future, desert cities like Dubai are likely to become uninhabitable outside of their proposed domed enclaves. Simply put, domes over cities signal exclusion – a tendency that cannot be evaded no matter how progressive the design rhetoric may be.[37] A recent rash of popular visions of domed environments – the eponymous location of *The Hunger Games* (2012), the reality-TV-like domed world seen in *The Truman Show* (1998) or the nightmare alien interference of the U.S. television series *Under the Dome* (2013–15) – take up the dystopian tradition, portraying the deterioration of social relations in enclosed environments and rebellion against them.

However, the idea of domes, bubbles and spheres has also come to represent, for some, the fragile interconnectedness of life today, where human life and the built environment are seen as interconnected spheres, both physical and conceptual.[38] As explored in relation to the work of the artist-architect Tomás Saraceno in Chapter Three, enclosed environments – principally transparent spheres and geodesic domes in Saraceno's case – serve to connect the inhabitants of those environments with what is outside. In this sense, the transparent dome, in its very artificiality, can make us aware of the limited nature of what we usually take to be the infinite space of the atmosphere above our heads. As cultural historian Rosalind Williams has argued, in actual fact, 'we have always lived below the surface, beneath the atmospheric ocean, in a closed, sealed, finite environment.'[39] In a very real sense, domes do in fact symbolize the reality of our existence as earthbound creatures, rather than our disconnection from that reality. A more hopeful expression of the dome as vulnerable shelter can be seen in Matsys Design's Sietch Nevada project from 2009.[40] As explained by the architects, the project was inspired by

The CBS television series *Under the Dome* (2013–15).

the imagined subterranean dwellings on the desert planet in Frank Herbert's novel *Dune* (1965). Sietch Nevada envisages a future world with depleting supplies of fresh water, responding with a design proposal that mediates above and below with a honeycomb formation of verdant underground cities topped with retractable domes. Designed to make the storage, use and collection of water essential to the functioning of future cities, it recognizes and responds to the vulnerability of human life in the face of the future effects of climate change.

Matsys Design, Sietch Nevada project, 2009.

Resolutely opposing the exclusive luxury domed environments being proposed for Dubai, Sietch Nevada promotes a dense, underground community that nevertheless continues to be intimately tied to the world above.

Bunkers

Domed cities mediate above and below ground. When urban environments move entirely below ground, they become another type of city altogether, a bunker city. Bunkers embody individual or collective desire for a physical retreat into a place of confinement entirely sealed off from the outside world, with the underground offering an ideal environment for such structures.[41] Although bunkers emerged as a building type only in the twentieth century, the creation of secure living spaces below ground dates far back in history, with some of the most notable examples being the underground cities and Christian churches of Cappadocia, located in modern-day Turkey but excavated from the Roman period onwards when Christians were a persecuted minority.[42] What was different about the twentieth-century bunker was its basis in technological advances in warfare, most notably the advent of widespread aerial bombing of cities during the Second World War and the threat of nuclear conflict in the Cold War period. Entire landscapes of bunkers were constructed during the Second World War, including the vast Atlantic Wall built by the Nazis and comprising around 15,000 individual and groups of concrete bunkers and other structures scattered over the entire Western European coastline from the south of France to the northernmost tip of Norway.[43] Responding to anxieties about a nuclear war in the 1950s and '60s, military and civilian deep-level bunkers were constructed under major cities across the world, many of which remain today as relics from that period, even as some have become tourist attractions and others housing for the urban poor, as is the case in Beijing.[44] Most of these shelters were designed and constructed by military engineers, with occasional architectural examples such as Oscar Newman's 1969 unexecuted design for a spherical replica of Manhattan to be created deep beneath the city's bedrock, the cavernous underground space ironically to be cleared out by controlled nuclear blasts.[45] If the Second World War saw bunkers inhabited mostly by small groups of soldiers and other military personnel, in the Cold War era the bunker was envisaged as an idealized 'survival machine' for many thousands of inhabitants – usually a military or social elite deemed necessary to rebuild society decades or even centuries after a nuclear war.[46]

Given that the world has, thus far, evaded a widespread nuclear conflict, stories of how these deep-level bunkers might be populated have remained thankfully in the realm of fiction. Yet fiction enables reflection on what it might mean to live in a nuclear bunker. In Cold War era bunker-based fictions, such as Mordecai Roshwald's *Level 7* (1959) and the television film *Threads* (1984), bunker complexes are shown to be wholly inadequate to the task of keeping a human population alive in the aftermath of a nuclear war. In the case of *Level 7*, a global nuclear conflict results in millions of Americans being housed in vast underground shelters, ranging from shallow civilian bunkers right down to the Level 7 of the book's title – an elite military shelter 1,341 metres (4,400 ft) below the surface. Narrated by one of the button-pushers who initiated the nuclear conflagration – known only as x-127 – the novel charts his experience in this sealed-off world. At the beginning, he feels secure in his detachment from the rest of humanity: 'like an omniscient being, severed from contact with other human beings, but knowing all about what is going to happen to them'.[47] But as each successive level above is gradually contaminated by radiation, he begins to sense his own vulnerability. The novel ends bleakly with x-127's own death from radiation sickness, apparently the last surviving human anywhere on or under the earth.

Cold War bunker fictions tend to end on such a note of extreme pessimism because they were polemical texts that directly challenged the hubris of those who believed that nuclear conflict could be contained and survived. In more recent examples of fictional bunkers, the threat of nuclear conflict tends to fade into the background, as befits the cultural and political shift in the wake of the collapse of the Soviet Union in 1991. At the same time, social relations in such underground structures take centre stage. Thus in Hugh Howey's 'Silo' trilogy of novels – *Wool* (2011–12), *Shift* (2013) and *Dust* (2014) – the entire population of the world appears to live in innumerable silos, each structure extending 144 levels beneath the ground. Although the second novel, *Shift*, reveals that this subterranean existence resulted from a catastrophic nuclear conflict, the focus of the trilogy and particularly the first book, *Wool*, is on the organization of social life below the ground. Howey cleverly inverts conventional notions of social stratification in cities by stressing that the most important people in this underground society – the engineers and maintenance workers who mine the materials required for the silo to function – live at the very bottom of the silo. As *Wool's* heroine, the depth-dwelling engineer Juliette, observes:

> the forbidden dreams of the outside world, she saw, were sad and empty. They were dead dreams. The people of the up top who worshipped this view had it all backwards – the future was *below*. That's where the oil came from that provided their power, the minerals that became anything useful, the nitrogen that renewed the soil in the farms.[48]

The sustaining of the silo comes at a heavy price, though: any desire to leave it is forbidden – subversives are sent outside the silo to their deaths, but not before they are forced to ritually clean the sensors that project an image of the devastated and toxic world above to the residents below.

In common with other recent underground fictions, such as the young-adult novel *City of Ember* (2003) and its film adaptation in 2008,[49] *Wool* takes place in the distant future – around 2345 – nearly

View of the multi-level underground city in George Lucas's *THX 1138* (1971).

three hundred years after the building of the silos. This has the effect of eliding any clear sense of cause and effect in the production of the underground city; but this does not result in the distancing of the story from contemporary concerns – rather, the reverse, reflecting as it does the more generalized anxieties we now have about incarceration and control by whatever powers that seek to exert this. In *Wool*, the longevity of the prison-like city is the result of ruthless domination by a tiny elite, perhaps a reflection of the current tendency of global capitalism to increasingly concentrate wealth in the hands of the few.

In cinema, imaginative visions of bunker cities tend to focus on the experience of a lone individual or a small group trying to escape the carceral urban world, with or without the motif of nuclear Armageddon. George Lucas's remarkable debut film *THX 1138* (1971) follows the efforts of the film's hero, only ever known by his number, THX 1138, to leave the underground city in which he lives. This shaven-headed drone-like figure works in servitude to a twenty-fifth-century world dominated by consumer capitalism and overseen by omnipresent computerized surveillance and a sinister robot police force. As in Fritz Lang's *Metropolis*, these workers are portrayed as dehumanized and rigidly controlled, their emotions constantly sedated by a cocktail of drugs. The film is noteworthy for the production design of its sleek, modernist underground city, characterized by brightly lit white spaces and a hyper-efficient transportation network – and the film focuses throughout on the movement of the human body through this mall-like multilayered network of spaces. Eventually THX 1138 manages to escape the city by stealing a car and driving through its kilometres of tunnels before climbing a shaft, the film ending with his body silhouetted against the setting sun.

Just as prison-like are the underground cities in the films *A Boy and His Dog* (1975), *La Jetée* (1962) and its loose remake *12 Monkeys* (1995), and *City of Ember*. In the case of *A Boy and His Dog*, adapted from a 1969 short story and novella by Harlan Ellison, after a nuclear war underground life has been chosen by the conservative element of America's population ('downunders') in favour of the scavenging world of libertarian inhabitants above, mostly violent young men called 'roverpaks'; both novel and film centre on the life of one rover-pak, Vic, and his telepathic dog Blood.[50] When Vic is lured into the underground city of Topeka by a nubile female sent up from below in order to improve the city's limited gene pool, he reacts as any countercultural 1960s teenager might to the 'square' life below – with ridicule and disgust at the rows of 'neat little houses, and curvy streets, and trimmed lawns', all expressing a nostalgia for suburban life in 1950s America.[51] *A Boy and His Dog* shows that, even in the most apocalyptic circumstances, prisons might be chosen rather than coerced, and a prison for one person might be a paradise for another.

Bunker cities tend to symbolize societal dead ends through their prison-like spaces; more user-friendly examples of designed sub-terranean habitats can be seen in so-called 'depthscrapers' – a term first coined in 1931, when the magazine *Everyday Science and Mechanics* provided an illustration of an inverted skyscraper proposed for Japan and designed to be resistant to earthquakes.[52] In more recent exam-ples, inverted skyscrapers have been proposed to save valuable land in rapidly growing cities, such as a variety of proposals by the Malay-sian architect Ken Yeang,[53] and BNKR Arquitectura's 2011 plans for an underground skyscraper under the Zócalo, the oldest part of Mexico City.[54] Ten storeys deep and containing homes, shops and offices, the inverted pyramid design aims to provide high-density

Proposed 'depth-scraper' for Tokyo, illustrated in *Everyday Science and Mechanics*, November 1931.

• "Depthscrapers" Defy Earthquakes' •

MIRROR ON CIRCULAR TRACK FOLLOWS SUN

SUN LIGHT REFLECTOR

ELEVATORS

CIRCULAR HALL

VENTI-LATORS

WINDOW PRISM LIGHT REFLEC-TORS

LIGHT RAYS

REENFOR-CED CONCRETE WALL

IRIS ROOF SHUTTER

THE "Land of the Rising Sun" (Japan) is subject to earthquakes of distressing violence at times; and the concentration into small areas of increasing .city populations invites great destruction, such as that of the Tokio earthquake of 1923, unprecedented in magnitude of property loss, as well as life.

It was natural, then, that the best engineering brains of Japan should be devoted to the solution of the problem of building earthquake-proof structures; and a clue was given them by the interesting fact that tunnels and subterranean structures suffer less in seismic tremors than edifices on the surface of the ground, where the vibration is unchecked.

The result of research, into the phenomenon explained above, has been the design of the enormous structure illustrated, in cross-section, at the left—the proposed "Depthscraper," whose frame resembles that of a 35-story skyscraper of the type familiar in American large cities; but which is built in a mammoth excavation beneath the ground. Only a single story protrudes above the surface; furnishing access to the numerous elevators; housing the ventilating shafts, etc.; and carrying the lighting arrangements which will be explained later.

The Depthscraper is cylindrical; its massive wall of armored concrete being strongest in this shape, as well as most economical of material. The whole structure, therefore, in case of an earthquake, will vibrate together, resisting any crushing strain. As in standard skyscraper practice, the frame is of steel, supporting the floors and inner walls.

Fresh air, pumped from the surface and properly conditioned, will maintain a regular circulation throughout the building, in which each suite will have its own ventilators. The building will be lighted, during daylight hours, from its great central shaft, or well, which is to be 75 feet in diameter. Prismatic glass in the windows, opening on the shaft, will distribute the light evenly throughout each suite, regardless of the hour.

Making the Most of Sunlight

In order to intensify the degree of daylight received, a large reflecting mirror will be mounted above the open court, and direct the sun-
(Continued on page 708)

LIQUEFACTOWER
The Sinking City

Eric Nakajima,
Liquefactower
project, 2014.

housing on a historically sensitive site without disturbing it at ground level. Covered by a huge glass floor to bring in natural light, the surface would also enhance the public square on which it is built by providing a novel view of the subterranean habitat. In the same year, architect Matthew Fromboluti proposed to refashion abandoned mines in Bisbee, Arizona, into a 'mantlescraper' – an entirely self-sufficient subterranean city that included areas for crops to grow by means of skylights.[55]

There is a sense that these designs are intent on negating the characteristic darkness of the underground through natural lighting descending from above, thus 'erod-[ing] the differences between above and below which banishes anything more interesting', namely a more nuanced approach to urban layers that engages with their distinct material conditions and meanings.[56] More unusual in this respect is Eric Nakajima's Liquefactower project, which received an honourable mention in the 2014 *eVolo* skyscraper competition.[57] Designed to accommodate unstable soil conditions in earthquake-prone Christchurch in New Zealand, the inverted tower would be formed as the soil liquefied, gradually sinking into the earth, the urban habitat expanding in the process and drawing its energy from geothermal sources as the city sinks. With a design that engages with the distinct material qualities of its underground landscape, the Liquefactower proposal demonstrates how bunker cities might not necessarily be sterile spaces and social cul-de-sacs.

Revolution

If imagined future domed and bunker cities centre on the provision of security against external threats, whether real or imagined, then subterranean space can also be read as a place of revolution. Thus, even as the late-Roman underground cities of Cappadocia were undoubtedly constructed to escape persecution, Christians fled to the underground because they themselves were viewed as a threat – a group of people with a dangerous idea that overturned the stable order of Roman society. Once ensconced in the safety of the underground, those revolutionary ideas can continue to ferment, undisturbed by above-world conventions.

Perhaps the most well-known underground spaces associated with revolution are the quarries, or *carrières*, that lie beneath Paris.[58] Comprising more than 285 kilometres (177 mi.) of disused quarries, parts of which were turned into a municipal ossuary – or catacombs – at the end of the eighteenth century, the *carrières* were used by insurgents as hideouts during the 1832 and 1848 revolutions and the 1870 uprising that saw the establishment of the Paris Commune.[59] Such real-life events fed into imaginative renderings of the quarries as places of subversive activity, as seen in Élie Berthet's *Les Catacombes de Paris* (1854), Alexandre Dumas' *Les Mohicans de Paris* (1854–9) and, most famously, Victor Hugo's *Les Misérables* (1862).[60] In the latter, the relationship between underground space and revolution is made explicit. With reference to the forces that stoked the 1832 revolution, Hugo wrote that beneath the surface of human society are various symbolic mines:

There is the religious mine, the philosophical mine, the political mine, the economic mine, the revolutionary mine [where] one person digs with an idea, another digs with numbers, yet another digs with rage.

In the safety of the deep, subversive ideas continually ferment 'in an immense teeming infestation' until, at last, they are ready to burst out to the surface with disruptive force.[61] Drawing on many metaphorical images – volcanoes, disease, mining, even a proto-unconscious – and not without a sense of ambivalence, Hugo invokes the underground as a powerful site in which new and threatening ideas can develop, ready to challenge stable conventions of all kinds.

Unsurprisingly, for a city characterized by a long history of political and social upheaval, Paris's underground has often featured in fictional depictions of the city below as a space of subversion. In the twentieth century, these came to a head in the wake of the May 1968 *événements*, the first period of sustained revolutionary fervour in Paris since 1870. With their rallying cry of 'the beach beneath the street', the group of radical artists and writers known as the Situationist International drew on Hugo's suggestive imagery of Paris's underground spaces to meld revolutionary ideology with the material spaces of city.[62] On a lighter note, the satirical film *Les Gaspards* (The Holes, 1974) imagined the *carrières* as 'a countercultural playground of misfits, eccentrics, and romantics, safe and nurturing' except when they were forced to confront the world above them. In the film, this confrontation centres on the contemporaneous redevelopment of the city's central market – Les Halles – into an underground shopping mall and railway station.[63]

Similar associations between the underground and subversion also characterize some future visions of cities, including the subterranean workers' city in Fritz Lang's *Metropolis* (1927) which eventually explodes into full-scale revolution as its servile population rebels to overthrow its oppressors, who rule from the skyscraper heights above ground. *Metropolis* borrowed heavily from H. G. Wells's earlier fictions of future cities characterized by extreme social division. For example, *The Time Machine* (1895) projects into the far future the widening gap between rich and poor that Wells witnessed in late Victorian London. In this far-flung future, the time traveller finds a world starkly divided into above-ground-dwelling Eloi – childlike and carefree – and the underground Morlocks, the monstrous workers who now prey on their distant human cousins. In a similar vein, the subterranean work-ers' spaces of a nearer-future London in Wells's *The Sleeper Awakes* (1910) are discovered by the narrator to be the squalid and brutal underlying foundation of what seems like a spectacular utopia above ground. In all of these fictions, the urban underground is used as a tool of critique, borrowing from Victor Hugo the sense of the sub-terranean as a site of truth.[64] Here, the act of reconnecting above and below is critical in exposing truth; yet gaining awareness of that truth often comes at the expense of the entire social system, suggesting instead its overthrow and destruction.

More conciliatory, but no less subversive, is the underground world created by Neil Gaiman in *Neverwhere*, first written as a BBC television series broadcast in 1996 and published as a novel in the same year.[65] Imagining an entire fantasy world existing beneath London, *Neverwhere* charts the adventures of a conventional citizen of 'London Above' – Richard Mayhew – as he 'disappears' when he meets Door, one of the inhabitants of 'London Below'. In a series of adventures both above and below London, culminating in his killing of a ferocious beast that haunts his dreams, Mayhew discovers a whole other London that cannot be seen by the majority of its inhabitants – a world that straddles the real and the fantastical. Throughout the novel, London's familiar names – for example Old Bailey; The Angel, Islington; and Blackfriars – are reimagined as mythic figures, often possessed with magical powers that infiltrate the mundane. In *Neverwhere*, connecting above and below is possible, but only for those who cannot be seen by those who live in the conventional world above. This acts as both a metaphor for society's 'unseen' – those, like the homeless, who tend to be ignored by the rest of us – and a call to move beyond one's everyday perceptions of the city, to see it anew. It is no accident that Richard Mayhew's name comes from the great chronicler of London's underworld in the mid-nineteenth century, Henry Mayhew, who explored the conditions of London's poorest citizens in his series of articles that would eventually be published as *London Labour and the London Poor* (1851).[66] In his fantastic voyage, the hero of *Neverwhere*, like his Victorian namesake, experiences a perceptual revolution, one that is profoundly personal but no less disruptive than the collective subversive forces imagined to be fermenting in the Paris underworld. For, at the end of the novel, Richard gives up his conventional life for good, walking through a magic hole in a mundane London wall back into the intoxicating darkness of the city's underworld.[67]

Neverwhere bears witness to a vision that seeks to enrich urban perception by bringing the city's hidden underground spaces – sewers, abandoned metro stations, vaults and catacombs – into an imaginative relationship with the mind, drawing on both the spatial characteristics of the underground itself and the rich and secretive histories that have accumulated in those spaces over time. In this sense, Gaiman's fantasy is not so far removed from the practices of those who venture into underground spaces as a form of recreation. A corollary to the illegal climbing of skyscrapers or other city heights touched on in Chapter Four, urban exploration below ground is centred on a desire to meld body and city – in Bradley Garrett's words, to 'decode the mysteries behind the urban metabolism' by actually entering into subterranean infrastructure itself.[68] What one finds underground are the city's veins and arteries – spaces that quite literally sustain urban life. The fact that we are not supposed to be in those spaces only adds to the sense of discovering some hidden truth beneath the city.

Many subterranean explorers leave traces of their visits to these clandestine spaces, as demonstrated dramatically in the enormous range of marks left by visitors over the last three centuries on the walls and ceilings of the Paris *carrières*, beautifully illustrated in the book *Paris Underground* (2005). These range from marks made by official visitors – inscriptions, surveyors' marks and directional signs – to those left by illegal explorers, including paintings, mosaics and sculpture (known as 'kata' art), sketches, graffiti tags, and even paper tracts. Unlike the above-ground world, where such ephemeral traces are often

Some of the
numerous artworks
created in the Paris
carrières.

erased, these multi-temporal histories remain as tangible presences
– testament to the underground as a site of preservation, of memories
materialized in a rich if bewildering tapestry of expression.

It is difficult to relate the informal and unplanned nature of such
traces to architectural practice, grounded as the latter is in organization
and control. What might be possible is for architects and urban planners to simply *allow* such spaces to continue to exist, in other words,
to leave them alone. This approach seems diametrically opposed to
the redevelopment plans introduced at the beginning of this chapter,
for example, turning abandoned underground railway stations into
new 'productive' spaces, whether swimming pools, skating parks or
art galleries. Yet designers might engage in a dialogue with underground spaces that seeks, like urban explorers, to bring those spaces
into view – to make an intervention that cuts through a city's levels
to create a new vertical perspective on urban space. This already
happens when subterranean sites in cities are deemed of historic
interest, particularly in ones that have ancient origins, such as Athens,
Mexico City or Rome, where past remnants are often located underground. For example, when the ruins of the Aztec Templo Mayor were

discovered below Mexico City, they were left open to view – a hole in the very heart of the city.[69] Another simple, but powerful, example of such an intervention is located in the city of Brescia in Italy. In July 2013 the group Brescia Underground were given permission by the city's municipal authorities to replace one of Brescia's manhole covers with a circular sheet of glass so that pedestrians could observe the flow of an ancient urban river beneath.[70]

In recent years, there has been a move by some municipal authorities to uncover underground rivers – a form of reverse urbanization that sees waterways 'daylighted' again. One example is the Saw Mill River in New York City, culverted in the 1930s but exposed again in 2011 as part of a redevelopment plan for the creation of the new Van der Donck Park.[71] Another is in Stockport, Greater Manchester, where, in 2015, the local council uncovered the historic Lancaster Bridge spanning the town's Merseyway Shopping Centre to reveal part of the river Mersey beneath, formerly hidden inside a 1930s culvert.[72] Finally, sometimes underground spaces are revealed by the actions of dedicated enthusiasts. This can be seen in the work currently being undertaken in Edge Hill, Liverpool, to open up the extraordinary network of tunnels dug by local resident Joseph Williamson and his hired workforce in the early nineteenth century.[73] Here, two groups of dedicated volunteers are painstakingly re-excavating the tunnels, a project that has already taken many years and which is opening up a dramatic series of spaces that are slowly being made accessible to the public. This excavation has no civic or commercial programme, rooted as it is in the enthusiasm of local residents; yet, in using virtually the same techniques as those that were employed to construct the tunnels nearly two centuries ago, the volunteers are connecting to the history of these spaces in a very personal and visceral way. They are choosing to reinhabit the city below themselves, using informal practices to achieve this.

In all of these cases, it is the underground spaces themselves that seem to offer a place in which human desires can be given expression.

Re-excavation of the Williamson Tunnels in Edge Hill, Liverpool, 2016.

In this they contrast sharply with the imagination of domed or bunker cities discussed earlier. Yet there are positive threads that might connect all three imaginative tropes explored here, ones that could inform future approaches to urban undergrounds. First, domes, bunkers and revolutionary underground spaces are all defined by *thresholds* – spaces that connect what is above to what is below and, as Brescia Underground's project demonstrates, those thresholds can be brought into the public realm rather than hidden from it. Second, all underground spaces invite an engagement with what is inside and what is outside – in other words, an awareness of interconnection, even if that awareness is achieved through its opposite, namely, incarceration. Here, future projects might use the idea of enclosure to flag up human vulnerability, not in order to condemn or evade it, but rather the reverse – to celebrate its liberating potential for *deeper* connections to be forged between what is inside and outside, above and below. Finally, the hidden nature of underground spaces – their dark recesses and frightening shadows – could be incorporated creatively into the urban fabric by emphasizing rather than erasing the differences between what is above and below. Here, inspiration could be taken from those who have already engaged with underground spaces – for example, homeless people seeking shelter, soldiers forced to inhabit bunkers, graffiti writers and urban explorers, street children hounded into sewers, or eccentrics compelled by strange desires to dig.[74] It might seem counterintuitive to bring the darkness of the underground into urban space – especially when urban development over the last few centuries has been concerned with precisely the opposite: to bring light and open-air into the 'dark' city. However, by allowing that darkness in, we may yet discover that the fears we possess about the underground are unreal and that those fears might then be embraced rather than rejected.

III
UNMADE CITIES

6
Ruined: Sprawl, Disaster, Entropy

Ruins are everywhere in cities. There is the constant churn of demolition and rebuilding that sees buildings torn down to be replaced by new ones, often simply because the new promises a higher return than the old. There are many structures that hang on once they've been abandoned – buildings that survive in dilapidation because no new use can be found for them. There are also much older ruins – remnants of the past that have been deliberately preserved or which have miraculously survived. Finally, even if we cannot see it, the built environment is always on the verge of ruin – only ceaseless maintenance of all the structures in our cities prevents this. Witness the emergence of cobbles from underneath the tarmac – the ruins of the past returning to remind us of the city's buried remains.

Ruin also comes to our cities in other ways. On an almost daily basis, we witness the horrors of violent urban destruction on screens and in newspapers, from the events of 9/11 that are, thanks to the live media coverage on that day, unforgettably burned into our collective unconscious, to more recent 'urbicide' in cities of the Middle East,[1] whether a result of civil war, religious extremism or the ongoing u.s.-led War on Terror. In addition, for the first time in many decades, the prospect of nuclear destruction has regained its power – arguably more likely now than it was even at the height of the Cold War. Much of this ruin imagery has fed into fiction, whether in recent (post-)apocalyptic cinema and television, increasingly sophisticated backdrops of video games, or the work of contemporary artists, as seen in the 'Ruin Lust' exhibition held at Tate Britain in 2014.[2] There is no doubt that how we imagine the ruin of cities impacts upon how we approach and plan for it in real life; yet, on the whole, architects and urban planners have been either reluctant or unable to make sense of these connections.

Ruins will also be part of our cities in the future. In a world dominated by the prospect of ever more dire threats to urban life – whether the catastrophic damage that will likely be wrought by climate change, wars and terrorism that deliberately target cities, or violence resulting from increasing social division – architects and urban planners have no choice but to develop a receptiveness towards destruction and ruin in the built environment.[3] Just as acceptance of one's own mortality can lead to a freer and more compassionate life, so the same in architecture might transform the built environment into something far more humane, rich and meaningful than it currently tends to be. In a world ruled by a form of global capitalism that seems hell-bent on continuing and accelerating its 'creative' destruction, there is an urgent need to foster a radically different approach to ruination, one that regards it as an inevitable product not just of capitalism, but rather of any society that fails to acknowledge and accept limits, vulnerabilities and endings.

Sprawl

As the American writer Rebecca Solnit has observed, 'a city – any city, every city – is the eradication, even the ruin, of the landscape from which it rose.'[4] Yet modern cities ruin on a far greater scale than their pre-modern counterparts. Until the nineteenth century, cities were, on the whole, compact built environments because their transport networks were defined by walking. The development of railways from the 1830s onwards, underground trains from the 1860s and electric trams from the 1880s were instrumental in the horizontal growth of cities that characterized nineteenth-century industrial conurbations like Manchester. For the first time, railways and trams allowed people in cities to live at a distance from where they worked, spawning the rapid growth of suburbs that mushroomed around formerly compact cities. In the early twentieth century, the mass production of auto-mobiles accelerated this process, resulting in the rapid development of vast suburban metropolitan areas, particularly in the United States.[5] Today, urban sprawl is resulting in the merging of already large cities into regional megalopolises, perhaps most notably in China's Pearl River Delta, currently witnessing the most rapid urban expansion in human history and the increasingly likely future agglomeration of Hong Kong (population, 7.4 million in 2018), Shenzhen (10.8 million) and Guangzhou (13 million).[6]

Given this tendency of cities to grow outwards, it is not surprising that the imagination of urban sprawl has dominated representations of future cities from the early twentieth century onwards, in both utopian and dystopian modes of conjecture. On the one hand, in avant-garde architectural projects like Frederick Kiesler's The City in Space (1925) and Constant's New Babylon (1956–74), sprawl is synonymous with a radically flexible and liberating form of urban life. In Kiesler's project, designed as an exhibit for the Exposition Internationale des Arts Décoratifs in Paris in 1925, a vast elastic city abolishes all distinctions between the rural and the urban, its buildings liberating inhabitants from the rigid architectural geometry of walls and floors by providing a continuous, intertwining and multi-level series of ramps.[7] Constant's later New Babylon project, which occupied the architect for nearly two decades, envisaged an anarchic and potentially planet-girdling city constructed by its own citizens in a continuous state of play.[8]

From the 1970s onwards, future sprawling cities tended to be envisaged as degraded environments marked by ecological meltdown, overpopulation and social collapse. Sprawling cities characterized the cyberpunk novels of the 1980s and '90s – for example, the con-tinuous Boston-Atlanta Sprawl that forms a key part of the urban

world of William Gibson's *Neuromancer* (1984) or the urban 'Glop' of Marge Piercy's novel *He, She and It* (1991). Gibson's imagined future mega-city is chock-full of the technological detritus of the past:

Plan of Constant's
New Babylon
as if built over
Amsterdam, c. 1963.

> the junk looked like it had grown there, a fungus of twisted
> metal and plastic . . . cooking itself down under the pressure
> of time, silent individual flakes settling to form a mulch, a
> crystalline essence of discarded technology, flowering secretly
> in the Sprawl's waste places.[9]

In dystopian cinema from the same era, the sprawl of future cities is often depicted as overpopulated and lawless. The future New York

The tower blocks of
Mega-City One in
Dredd (2012).

in *Soylent Green* (1973) is home to 40 million residents in a world
without fresh food, the monstrous city having polluted the countryside
to death. Similar to the Sprawl is Mega-City One in *Dredd* (2012), an
almost endless urban zone that extends from Florida to Ontario, with
somewhere between 100 and 800 million residents.[10] Characterized
by crime-infested super-blocks, Mega-City One survives only because
of the brutal tactics of its law enforcers, Judge Dredd being the most
effective.

It is but a short step from imagining such vast agglomerations of
cities to ones that envelop the whole world: planet-wide urban worlds
like Isaac Asimov's Trantor in his *Foundation* series of novels, or its
contemporary derivative Coruscant in the *Star Wars* prequel films,
a literal global city at the political heart of that franchise's fictional
empire. Unsurprisingly, at this scale, the city's human dimension
and any discernible sense of *genius loci* is swallowed up by its all-
encompassing vastness. No wonder then, that perhaps the most
memorable appearance of Coruscant is in a night-time chase sequence
in *Star Wars Episode II: Attack of the Clones* (2002), where the outsized
skyscrapers of the city become merely a spectacular stage-set for
CGI-enhanced action.

Just how such an inhuman city might affect the lives of its occupants is precisely the premise of J. G. Ballard's 1957 short story 'The

Concentration City'. Published at a time when technological optimism about the future city was still high, Ballard's story reflects the author's abiding interest in how a contraction of space might play out in cities of the near future.[11] Beginning with a series of terse verbal exchanges that provide an immediate sense of the scale of the city ('Millionth Street', 'Take a Redline elevator and go up a thousand levels to Plaza Terminal'), Ballard's story centres on engineer Franz's attempts to find some open space in the city in which to test a flying machine he dreams of building.[12] In a city in which space is subject to endless price wars, Franz's attempted escape proves fruitless – after travelling continuously on an express train for three weeks he realizes that the city is limitless, arriving back where he started from. Found guilty of a type of 'thought-crime', Franz is arrested and sent to a psychiatrist, who explains to him the absurdity of the idea of free space. In Ballard's nightmare urban world, both human beings and city space are reduced to pure economic units, resulting in the complete imprisonment of the city's citizens. Moreover, in a city without end, development becomes the same as destruction. On his journey Franz witnesses a vast cavity where part of the city had collapsed, killing millions; here, he sees thousands of engineers and demolition workers reconstructing the ruined city in order to increase the value of its chief commodity: space.[13]

In the 1980s, the emergence of cyberpunk as a recognized cultural genre – in music, film, fiction and graphic novels – challenged the pervasive sense of pessimism about the future of urban sprawl that clearly informed fictions like 'The Concentration City'. Cyberpunk grew out of an awareness of the future impact of the personal computer, which first appeared in the early 1980s. In almost all cases, cyberpunk fictions are based on speculative visions of how humans would be altered in a media-dominated and information-saturated age. With a distinct future-noir aesthetic fusing high technology with punk counterculture, bodies with machines (usually computers), and the virtual with the material, cyberpunk took the bleak, dystopian urban futures of the post-war period and injected them with a sense of sublime beauty and radical new social and cultural possibilities. Given its most prominent expression in Gibson's novel *Neuromancer* and in Ridley Scott's *Blade Runner*, cyberpunk saw the urban ruins of the future – whether the blighted and detritus-strewn Sprawl of *Neuromancer* or the industrial decay and rain-sodden bleakness of Los Angeles in *Blade Runner* – as places where select countercultural groups could flourish in the ruins. Hence the emphasis in many cyberpunk fictions on salvage as an important economy in future urban communities, such as the post-nuclear Los Angeles depicted in Richard Stanley's film *Hardware* (1990), where a lone female artist acquires parts for her highly desirable junk sculptures from a black-market economy of salvaged machine parts, although one piece of junk eventually turns out to be a self-constructing murderous robot. Even as the future cities imagined by cyberpunk are as dystopian and ruined as their forebears, they are not envisaged as terminal end-points for urban life but rather as starting points for something new which incorporates rather than erases ruins. This view of ruins tends to see them as a playground: 'blank canvases' in which to escape and thrive in the new virtual world of cyberspace. Such a cleaving of material and mental space often leads to the protagonists of cyberpunk favouring the ecstatic and responsibility-free world of cyberspace over any serious engagement in the material aspects of the cities in which they live.[14]

Another important way in which ruins function in cyberpunk cities is through the enfolding of new and old architectures, as seen most spectacularly in the retro- and high-tech fusions of a future Los Angeles in *Blade Runner*, where the city is defined by a pandemonium of architectural styles and of the juxtaposition of the archaic and the modern. The film's most iconic structure – the gargantuan and monolithic Tyrell Corporation building – resembles an outsized Aztec or Egyptian funerary structure, while the hyper-industrial cityscape that fills the screen in the opening shot recalls the steelworks of Teeside, where Ridley Scott grew up.[15] In this future Los Angeles, new architectural possibilities are suggested by the reinscribing of history on the modern city – a characteristic post-modernist reaction against modernism's forgetting of the past. Such history often makes itself present as ruins from the past. Thus in Tsutomu Nihei's manga *Blame!* (1998–2003), a former urban area of Hong Kong – Kowloon Walled City – is reimagined as the basis for a future cyberpunk city. Once the most densely populated urban area on Earth, Kowloon Walled City started as a self-governed settlement in the early twentieth century before expanding into an informal city by the 1950s and housing, at its maximum extent, 33,000 people within 2.8 hectares (6.9 acres) in largely self-built one-room-wide buildings of thirteen or fourteen storeys.[16] Demolished in 1994 in preparation for the British handover of Hong Kong to China in 1997 (and now an urban park), Kowloon Walled City has nevertheless lived on as an inspiration for those, like Nihei, who have gained from its chaotic structures intimations of a future city in which construction is incremental and autonomous. Perhaps if urban citizens were freed from the rules imposed on them by municipal authorities, they would create a city of bits, one in which future population growth would be contained not in clusters of mega-tall skyscrapers, but rather in an extraordinary organic assemblage of individual structures. Such a city would certainly be messy and

The future Los Angeles cityscape in the opening sequence of *Blade Runner* (1982).

chaotic – the very antithesis of Western urban life, which lays great stress on cleanliness and order. Yet many contemporary urban spaces are sterile precisely because they refuse to engage with what is old because it is cast as outdated. In learning to accept the mess of urban life, we can come to understand that the old always informs the new – that the two might be interwoven rather than separated.

The melding of old and new is a powerful undercurrent in the history of how architects have engaged with ruins.[17] In the eighteenth century, the Italian artist Giovanni Battista Piranesi both obsessively catalogued the ruins of ancient Rome and also used them imaginatively to construct his fantastic *capriccios* (imagined cityscapes comprised of clusters of ancient funerary monuments and other ruins) and *carceri* (vast prisons in which semi-ruined, monolithic architectural forms overwhelm diminutive figures).[18] Piranesi's work influenced a generation of architects who would go on to design and build structures deliberately designed to ruin like those of ancient Rome, so as to provide magnificent memorials in the future, an example being Joseph Gandy's bird's-eye view of architect John Soane's Bank of England as

Illustration from Tsutomu Nihei's manga *Blame! 1 Master Edition*, trans. Melissa Tanaka (2016), p. 251.

Joseph Gandy, bird's-eye view of the Bank of England in ruins, 1830, watercolour.

Haworth Tompkins, artist's studio built in the ruins of a former dovecote at Snape Maltings, Suffolk, 2013.

a future ruin, painted in 1830 at the request of Soane himself.[19] In more recent architectural practice, the ruins of the past tend to be more literally fused with the new. This is demonstrated in Britain in both the 2013 renovation of Astley Castle by Witherford Watson Mann to create a domestic property (the project winning the prestigious RIBA Stirling Prize) and an artist's studio that London architects Haworth Tompkins inserted into a ruined dovecote in 2010 in the village of Snape, Suffolk.[20] On a larger scale, in Cologne in 2010, architect Peter Zumthor created the Kolumba Museum, a modernist brick structure that seems to grow out of the remains of a Gothic church ruined by Allied bombs during the Second World War.[21] In all these cases, the weathered patinas of the ruins are reflected in the new materials; whether the rusting CorTen steel-clad box of the artist's studio, or the bare brick walls and floors of the new section of Astley Castle and the Kolumba Museum. Although aesthetically very different from cyberpunk visions of the fusion of old and new, these contemporary projects nevertheless demonstrate the same principle at work, namely of the incorporation, not eradication, of ruins into architecture. Even as these projects are only at the scale of individual (and rural) structures, they still provide a glimpse into what a city that builds *with* its ruins rather than erases them might look like in the future.

Disaster

Cities have always been haunted by the prospect of their own ruin, but increasingly so in the modern period, when the technology of warfare developed in such a way as to make possible the ruination of entire cities, culminating in what is still the most significant urban destruction in history, namely, the Allied aerial bombardments of the Second World War, which saw the decimation of many German and Japanese cities.[22] Throughout history, the imagination of urban destruction has taken many cultural forms: from the biblical stories of the demise of the Tower of Babel and Sodom and Gomorrah to confrontations with the past in Chinese *huaigu* poetry of the first millennium CE.[23] In the modern period in the West, imagined urban destruction often centred on aesthetic responses to natural disasters, such as the Lisbon earthquake of 1755,[24] and intimations of imperial decline as seen in Edward Gibbon's seminal text *The History of the Decline and Fall of the Roman Empire* (1776–88), as well as countless other mediations on empire in both European and North American contexts throughout the nineteenth and twentieth centuries and arguably with renewed force today in the United States.[25] Anxieties about the vulnerability of empire produced some of the first post-apocalyptic representations of future cities: from the 'last man' trope in fiction in the early nineteenth century, namely in Cousin de Grainville's *Le Dernier Homme* (1805) and Mary Shelley's *The Last Man* (1826), to pictorial images like Gustave Doré's engraving of London in ruins. These foundational texts and images would eventually feed into numerous literary and cinematic representations of future urban ruin, from H. G. Wells's novel *The War of the Worlds* (1898) – the first to imagine cities destroyed by aliens – to the *Terminator* series of films, which drew on more recent fears about the growing power of computers.

Despite their obvious power as fictions that either highlight prescient cultural anxieties or warn against destructive tendencies in urban life, in many of these post-disaster urban fictions, ruined future cities function as dramatic stage sets for tales of survival, usually centring on a 'hero' figure, almost always male.[26] Disaster may also produce ruins that play a more active role in urban life. In the aftermath of the Second World War, some of the many urban ruins produced by aerial bombing on both sides became designated as important sites of memory, the most notable examples in Britain and Germany being Coventry Cathedral and the Kaiser Wilhelm Memorial Church in Berlin.[27] When both churches were rebuilt in modernist styles in the 1950s, the half-ruined structures were incorporated into the new ensemble of buildings as memorials to the conflict. More indirect forms of memorialization can be seen in the ways in which some contemporary ruins are read as allegories of urban decline, perhaps most notably Michigan Central Station in Detroit, built in 1913 but abandoned since 1988 and featured in the opening scenes of Godfrey Reggio's 2002 film *Naqoyqatsi: Life as War*. Presented as a contemporary counterpart to the Tower of Babel, Michigan Central Station is employed in this film to challenge capitalist ideas of endless progress and, more generally, the folly of overreaching human ambition.

A more literal Tower of Babel appears in *Their Refinement of the Decline* (2014), one of Michael Kerbow's *Portents* series of paintings. Here, Bruegel's famous tower is reconfigured as a vast industrial structure, sprouting innumerable chimneys and dominating the city around it.[28] An obvious allegory of the destructive nature of industrial production and a warning about its possible future effects on the planet, this image of a dystopian urban future relies on exaggeration for its dramatic effect. It also pictures a ruin that is both constructive and destructive; the industrial tower, like its biblical namesake in Bruegel's painting, hovering uncertainly between a state of frenetic construction and catastrophic collapse. Whenever ruins become memorials they do so in the context of countering the conventional

idea of memorials as something *permanent*. By their very nature, ruins are transient; if they are memorials to anything it is to the transient nature of all things and the limited powers of humankind to counter this.[29]

Michael Kerbow, *Their Refinement of the Decline*, 2014, oil on canvas.

Buildings like Coventry Cathedral and the Kaiser Wilhelm Memorial Church are unusual examples of ruins that have been preserved and integrated into new buildings. But what might the physical fabric of a future city look like if *all* of its ruins were taken into its new buildings, that is, if nothing was erased? Architectural salvage might produce a startling aesthetics of bricolage, while an engagement with the formal qualities of ruins themselves might result in new architectural geometries. In many of the drawings produced by the

Deanna Petherbridge, *Umbria Rurale 1*, 2010, ink and wash on paper.

British artist Deanna Petherbridge, ruins enter into a dialogue with the representation and practice of architecture itself.[30] With their multiple perspectival angles and serial forms, works like *Umbria Rurale I* (2010) explore how ruins might be imaginatively reconstructed into new architectural assemblages. In the case of *Umbria Rurale I*, these ruins are defunct farm structures discovered by the artist in rural Italy that exist side-by-side with the new, the ruins in effect telling 'a history of agricultural evolution and obsolescence'.[31] In her delicate drawing, that history is condensed into a single structure – an angular bricolage of plastic piping, stone columns and weathered timber. In other works, such as 'Ribbon City' (1976), from her series *The City as Imago Mundi*, half-formed structures agglomerate into strange urban landscapes seemingly comprised of industrial cast-offs that emerge from threatening blocks of stone or concrete. Although Petherbridge's drawings resemble conventional architectural

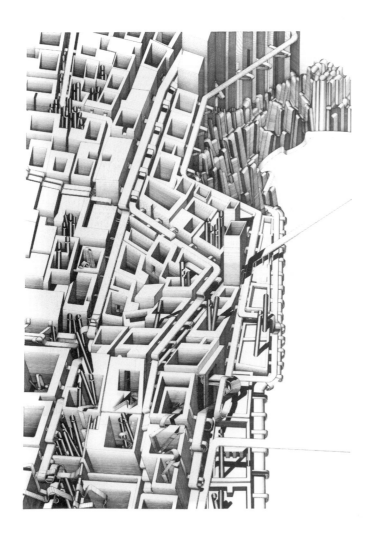

Deanna Petherbridge,
'Ribbon City', from
*The City as Imago
Mundi*, 1976,
ink on paper.

representations in their precision and use of orthographic projection,
they disorientate in their perspectival ambiguity and subvert the idea
of architecture as innately anthropomorphic. Yet what might at first
sight seem like an alienating and disturbing architecture is in fact the
result of trying to incorporate some sense of history into buildings
that is not merely anodyne heritage. As Petherbridge herself has stated,
her fractured, half-ruined, half-constructed forms are attempts to

represent 'the patterns of destruction and preservation' that infuse all buildings and cities.[32] In other words, they are ways of opening up untapped potentialities of architecture itself, of imagining a city that does not merely build a superficial image of itself and its history in its buildings but one that openly displays in its architecture the rich yet uncertain collisions of past, present and future.

If art has the potential to imagine new ways in which ruins might be incorporated into cities, then ruins themselves have also been seized on by artists to transform them. In virtually every city across the world, abandoned buildings become places in which illicit forms of art flourish, most visibly in the proliferation of graffiti tags and other visual motifs that cover the walls of many urban ruins. One city in particular, Detroit, has become synonymous with not only widespread urban ruination but the transformation of those ruins through creative practices.[33] With upwards of 80,000 abandoned buildings – the result of decades of endemic racial discrimination, industrial

Scott Hocking, *Ziggurat and Fisher Body 21*, site-specific installation 2007–9.

disinvestment and white flight to the suburbs – Detroit has, in recent years, seen an influx of young, mainly white, artists, writers and musicians who have been attracted to the city because of low property prices and rents.[34]

Detroit's ruins have seen an extraordinarily rich and varied engagement by artists, from ubiquitous street art and graffiti to site-specific installations and buildings incorporated into urban farms. Longstanding works include Tyree Guyton's Heidelberg Project, begun in 1986, in which abandoned homes in an impoverished majority-black area of the city have been literally overtaken by discarded objects, from rusting car parts to naked children's dolls.[35] More recent works in the city include a series of site-specific installations in some of Detroit's iconic ruins by local artist Scott Hocking, such as *Ziggurat and Fisher Body 21* (2007–9) in the vast Fisher Body Plant building, which used 6,201 of the building's wooden floor tiles to create a striking pyramid.[36] Although this work has been criticized by local art historian Dora Apel as glossing over the social and economic causes of Detroit's ruination, Hocking's installation nevertheless offers a striking example of built forms emerging from and within ruins.[37] His ziggurat may seem to belong to an archaic past, but its form emerged from the processes of ruination itself. Indeed, like many of Hocking's other sculptures, this work has already been lost to those processes, being deliberately destroyed by the building's owners. Just like Petherbridge's drawings, Hocking's installation flags up the significance of the long cycles of creation and destruction that have defined the history of cities in the modern period and long before.

In one of Sigmund Freud's last works, *Civilization and Its Discontents* (1930), he made an explicit analogy between the history of the city and that of the mind. For Freud, the mind, like the city, is a palimpsest where 'earlier phases of development [are] absorbed into the later ones, for which they supplied the material'.[38] In this reading, the mind can never be free of anything that has contributed to its formation, however traumatic or painful. Indeed, the basis of a well-integrated psyche lies precisely in an acceptance of past traumas that cannot be moved on from but need to be continually worked through. And if this is true for the city, then architects and urban planners have a duty to make visible those past traumas so that collective healing can be possible. What the ruins of Coventry Cathedral and the Kaiser Wilhelm Memorial Church, the drawings of Deanna Petherbridge and the installations of Scott Hocking collectively suggest, each in their own distinctive ways, is just how the memory of disaster might be preserved in built form in order to contribute to the healthy development and communal life of cities in the future.

Entropy

As mentioned above, if maintenance ceases, buildings inevitably start to decay. This tendency for all materials to degrade over time is known as entropy and is a fundamental part of the branch of physics known as thermodynamics, which measures the degree of disorder within any closed system. Entropy suggests that ruins are always present and also that ruin is a process rather than an object – a verb rather than a noun.

The American artist Robert Smithson was obsessed by entropy and his work has been key in influencing a generation of architects, artists and critics interested in future-oriented conceptions of ruins.[39] Smithson's 1967 article 'The Monuments of Passaic' saw him travel through the post-industrial landscape of New Jersey conjuring mythic timescapes out of the remains of half-constructed motorways, industrial detritus and empty car parks. In this article Smithson also coined the term 'ruins in reverse' to mean incomplete or abandoned structures; another way of describing these might be as new ruins.[40] Along with novelist J. G. Ballard and a host of subsequent artists, Smithson has forged fertile imaginative readings of new ruins. This is a particularly prescient issue; for, in the aftermath of the 2008 global financial crisis and the bankruptcy of many property developers, thousands of structures around the world – from individual buildings to entire cities – have been left incomplete: ruins in reverse whose futures are now radically uncertain.[41] With a characteristic visual lexicon of exposed breeze blocks, skeletal concrete frames, black rectangular holes waiting for windows, and concrete pillars sprouting tendrils of steel, new ruins do not conform to the conventional aesthetic of ruins – the slow decay of materials like stone, brick and timber that speaks of lost pasts; rather, they seem to be stuck in a frozen time in which past, present and future intermingle uncertainly. In a remarkably direct way, in their open display of such uncertainty, unfinished structures represent, albeit in extreme form, the condition found in most cities – that is, the constant churning of creation and destruction.

Entropic decay also represents a significant leitmotif in post-war science fiction novels, their future sprawling cities often overflowing with the discarded junk of the past. In Philip K. Dick's proto-cyberpunk novel *Do Androids Dream of Electric Sheep?*, published in 1968 and the basis for Scott's *Blade Runner*, a future San Francisco is a hollowed-out city, most of its population having escaped nuclear fallout on Earth by relocating to space colonies. In a suburban apartment complex inhabited by just one man – John Isidore – everything is slowly being taken over by what Isidore terms 'kipple' – the accumulated detritus of existence that will eventually consume everything. Isidore is given solace in his lonely existence in the otherwise abandoned apartment block by his contemplation of the building's future ruin, when 'everything within [it] would merge, would be faceless and identical, mere pudding-like kipple piled to the ceiling of each apartment. And, after that, the uncared-for building itself would settle into shapelessness.'[42] Dick's vision of a future city slowly succumbing to entropy is in stark contrast to *Blade Runner*'s translation of the novel's setting to a vibrant and overcrowded future Los Angeles; yet, in both novel and film, Isidore's apartment (J. F. Sebastian's in the film) remains a place of melancholic solace, the film using Sebastian's reanimated discarded toys as equivalents of Dick's kipple, with both providing comfort in that they foster the contemplation of timescales beyond the lifespan of the individual human.

Part of the pleasure of imagining future cities emptied of their inhabitants lies in the feeling of peace that comes with expanding how we normally think about time. But the imagined entropic decay of future cities also represents a threat to our sense of significance as both individuals and collectively as a species; one that feeds into the anxieties that underpin many cinematic visions of future cities, such as London in *28 Days Later* (2002) and New York in *I Am Legend* (2007), where the empty city hides monstrous threats, namely infected hordes of post-humans.[43] Empty cities may also serve as vehicles to voice anti-urban feeling, such as in Clifford D. Simak's 1944 story 'The City', in which the author promotes the values of his rural Wisconsin upbringing in imagining a future city abandoned by its inhabitants in favour of a more wholesome and politically autonomous pastoral existence.[44] In a similar vein, the future city in Charles Platt's novel *The Twilight of the City* (1974) falls victim to a global economic collapse which sees its descent into inter-factional warfare, the central protagonist eventually finding a new and more stable life in the countryside.

More ambivalent is J. G. Ballard's 'The Ultimate City' (1976), the longest of his many short stories, which sets a future Garden City – seemingly an ecological urban utopia run on renewable energy – against its defunct counterpart: a twentieth-century metropolis powered by petroleum that now lies in ruins. The story centres on the figure of Halloway, who forsakes the bucolic but puritanical life of Garden City in favour of the freedom and thrill of the metropolitan ruins, to which he escapes in order to repair its abandoned cars and restore electricity to its decaying buildings and street lights. Mustering an eccentric cohort of misfits to realize his dream of restarting the city, Halloway clearly feels a strong sense of nostalgia for the vaunting ambition of metropolitan life that came out of the technological utopianism of early modernist urban planning.[45] But Ballard's story is also a cautionary tale: as Halloway's plan unfolds and the city is reinhabited, so it quickly descends into violence, crime and chaos, recapitulating the same turn of events that led to the city's downfall in the first place.

What is unusual about Ballard's tale is the way in which it suggests the emergence of a post-urban world after the orgy of destruction has ended. Throughout the story, Halloway is attracted to the detritus left over from industrial technologies which created its own 'fierce and wayward beauty':

> Halloway was fascinated by the glimmering sheen of the metal-scummed canals, by the strange submarine melancholy of drowned cars looming up at him from abandoned lakes, by the brilliant colours of the garbage hills, by the glitter of a million cans embedded in a matrix of detergent packs and tinfoil, a kaleidoscope of everything that one could wear, eat and drink. He was fascinated by the cobalt clouds that drifted below the surface of the water, free at last of all plants and fish, the soft chemical billows interacting as they seeped from the sodden soil . . . He gazed raptly at the chalky white-ness of old china-clay tips, vivid as powdered ice, abandoned railyards with their moss-covered locomotives, the undimmed beauty of industrial wastes produced by skills and imagin-ations far richer than nature's, more splendid than any Arcadian meadow. Unlike nature, here there was no death.[46]

At once terrifying and exhilarating, Ballard's deliberately provocative invitation to find beauty in industrial wastes has its echo in Halloway's creative impulse to build new structures out of those wastes – whether pyramids of old television sets, aircraft parts, freight trains and missile launchers, or skyscrapers made out of abandoned cars stacked on top of each other. This aesthetic delight in industrial wastes would clearly appal those who are currently pushing for cities to become greener and cleaner; yet, in their startlingly alien forms and textures, Ballard's industrial wastes offer up a vision of something quite different: the possibility of a utopian reworking of industrial disaster rather than a repudiation of it.[47] Clearly Ballard was concerned that simply forsaking energy-guzzling cities in favour of greener alternatives would not solve all of humanity's problems, particularly the destructive impulses that lie at the heart of Halloway's desire to leave his eco-paradise.

The disturbing spectacle of industrial wastes that so delights Halloway can be seen as a highly prescient example of how we might relate more positively to the detritus of our own contemporary cities. As demonstrated by the colossal garbage vortexes in the world's oceans – created by the 8 million tonnes of discarded plastic that end up there every year – our urban wastes are fundamentally altering the ecosystem of the planet. Indeed, some estimate that, by 2050, there will be more plastic than fish in the world's oceans.[48] It may seem downright unethical to find beauty in these toxic wastes; yet Ballard suggests that we don't solve anything by merely discounting them from having any value, aesthetic or otherwise. For those plastics in our oceans share with the wastes in 'The Ultimate City' a permanence that means they will never die. When all natural life in the sea is gone, plastic will still remain as the 'new' nature that never perishes, affecting the earth's ecosystems for tens of thousands of years to come.

Such incorruptible wastes seem to defy the entropic principle that governs most conceptions of future ruined cities. These are often imagined as places in which nature returns, creating a verdant post-urban world without humans. Made popular by James Lovelock's influential Gaia hypothesis, first put forward in the 1970s,[49] the Earth is widely understood today as a self-regulating ecological system that will go on flourishing without us, hence the popularity of televisual and cinematic renderings of the world without humans, such as Animal Planet/Discovery Channel's joint production *The Future is Wild* (2002), the History Channel's *Life after People* (2008), National Geographic Channel's *Aftermath: Population Zero* (2008) and films like *I Am Legend* and *Oblivion* (2013).[50] In *Oblivion*, a future alien invasion has left the Earth ravaged by the after-effects of nuclear war and geological upheavals caused by the destruction of the Moon. More notable for its spectacular renderings of a ruined New York City than its derivative plot, the film provides startling images of the city's skyscrapers embedded in canyons, its sports stadiums and cultural buildings sunk into the ground, and, in one of the film's publicity posters, the Empire State Building engulfed by a waterfall, an image that directly recalls one of artist Tsunehisa Kimura's photomontages published in *Visual Scandals by Photomontage* in 1979. Although creating a spectacular fusion of the human and the non-human and providing a strong sense of how the ruins of the human world will inevitably interact with the nature that might engulf them in the future, the film nevertheless glosses over this interaction by presenting it in almost geological terms, as if the skyscrapers of New York have become the natural cliffs and canyons they have been so often compared with. The reality of any future collision of nature and cities will almost certainly look a lot messier and far less beautiful than *Oblivion*'s seductive vision.

An image from Tsunehisa Kimura's *Visual Scandals by Photomontage* (1979) compared with a publicity poster for the film *Oblivion* (2013).

More prescient in terms of contemporary awareness of the Anthropocene is Colm McCarthy's 2016 film *The Girl with All the Gifts*. In a future London where the human population has been decimated by a fungal infection that turns its victims into flesh-eating zombies, a group of survivors seek contact with Beacon, a large military base presumed to be a safe area. The group is led by Melanie – the girl of the film's title – an infected child who has developed some tolerance to the fungus so that she is able to partially resist her cannibalistic urges. Like many in the post-apocalyptic genre, the film's plot is well worn, the tired zombie trope being the most obviously derivative element of its narrative setup. Yet its portrayal of how human life might adapt to a catastrophic pandemic is a far cry from the reassuring 'hero' mould of similar films like *I Am Legend*. The post-apocalyptic London encountered by Melanie and the non-infected survivors is overgrown with both natural vegetation and a deadly plant that sprouts from the decomposing bodies of the infected humans. Spiralling up the Post Office Tower in a dense, vine-like formation, these plants support seed pods that threaten to create a new, far more deadlier, air-borne version of the infection that would undoubtedly wipe out all the remaining humans on Earth. The film concludes with Melanie forsaking her non-infected companions and setting light to the seed pods, thus ending the era of humanity but leaving behind a group of children who, like her, are infected but are also able to be civilized. Recalling the invasion of London by homicidal plants in John Wyndham's novel *The Day of the Triffids* (1951),[51] the film cleverly disrupts conventional notions of how the human and non-human might interact in a future ruined city.

Ruins present a whole host of potent metaphors that inspire and disturb in equal measure. In thinking through the implications of the city *as* a ruin – urbanization being an inevitable ruinous process in its own right – the city's destructive and constructive tendencies might be reconciled. Ruins might also be left alongside new constructions – or even housed within them – as a way of reflecting on this relationship; or the sprawling edges of cities, so often a kind of *terra incognita*

– might become sites on which to engage more intimately with the landscape which the city destroys. Ruins might also be reassessed as memorials, not so much the standard idea of a memorial as a permanent reminder of an event or person in a city's history, but rather as reminders of different, more painful histories, and even of the inevitable transience of what we often take to be permanent in our cities. Ruins might be lived in as architectural entities in their own right, even as they usually don't conform to what we would expect of habitable structures. Finally, the detritus produced by the city and its inhabitants might be reconfigured into something beautiful, if no doubt disturbingly so. Whether we like it or not, our wastes – inorganic and organic alike – are just as much part of what counts as nature today as that which we cultivate in our urban parks and gardens. Only by forging connections between these ruins and the world in which they sit can we begin to untangle and work with the nature we are all co-producing.

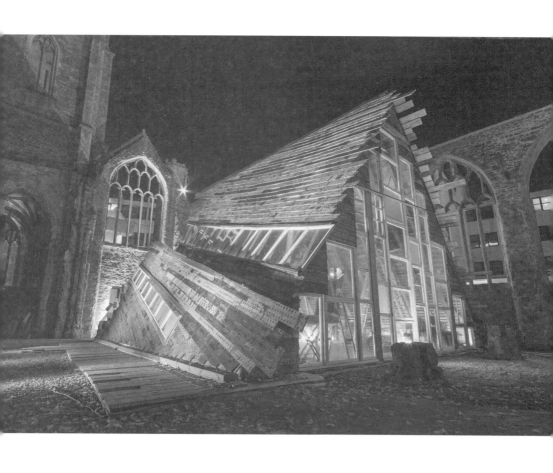

7
Remade: Salvaging What Remains

Between 29 October and 21 November 2015, the American artist Theaster Gates staged *Sanctum*, his first UK public project, in Bristol – as part of the cultural programme for the city's status as 2015 European Green Capital.[1] Housed inside a temporary structure made from salvaged materials scavenged from former places of industry and religious devotion in the city, Gates invited dozens of musicians and other artists across Bristol to stage a performance of music, sound and spoken word in the structure continuously for 24 days, or 576 hours.[2] By siting *Sanctum* inside the ruins of Bristol's Temple Church – a late medieval building bombed by the Luftwaffe in 1940, leaving just a ruined exterior – Gates turned buildings and materials deemed to be waste into art. As with his previous work in the blasted neighbourhoods of Chicago's south side, Gates's intervention in Bristol demonstrated his belief that ruins and waste must be accepted in order to be transformed, that is, integrated back into an urban life that more often than not consigns them to oblivion.[3] In this sense, *Sanctum* demonstrates a resolutely optimistic vision of salvage as a healing tool in cities where ruins are conventionally regarded as signs of death and decay.

Salvage can provide many alternative ways of engaging with the city. First, it can be thought of as a political practice – one that values the reuse of discarded materials in order to challenge capitalism's fundamental basis in the creation of ever-vaster quantities of waste. Second, it can be mobilized in political protests, as has already been

Theaster Gates, *Sanctum*, Bristol, 2015.

done in the Occupy demonstrations against the domination of global finance. Using salvaged materials to create temporary shelters and other living spaces challenges the increasingly draconian securitization of urban space across the world, particularly in the wake of many terrorist attacks in cities after 9/11 and the ensuing War on Terror.[4] Third, it can overturn the top-down elitist conception of architecture. Salvage means that users rather than architects will design and make their own buildings, perhaps drawing inspiration from the many millions of people who already do so in the vast informal settlements that encircle countless cities in the developing world. Finally, urban wastes of all kinds might be incorporated back into construction as a way of radically changing architecture's tendency to take more from the Earth than it gives. Integrating waste *into* architecture might produce future cities of rich potential that expand how we think about what cities are actually made out of.

So, how can we radically reconsider our attitudes towards that which we fear and often, by consequence, reject in our cities? And rejected materials represent only one aspect of this theme. It could be argued that the rejection of the social 'other' – whether framed in racial, ethnic or economic terms – is a far more pressing issue today in our cities than an embracing of their ruins, rubbish or waste. However, in starting with acceptance of those material things, we might take the steps that allow us to address larger social fears. Acceptance here is not to be confused with resignation or cynicism; on the contrary, it involves an active seeking out of what has been cast out in order to embrace it. Only with such acceptance can any genuine transformation begin. Furthermore, the radical acceptance and transformation of waste should not be confused with recycling; rather than feeding waste back into a capitalist system that is predicated on exploitation and destruction, we might instead produce 'valueless' products that will emerge outside the loops of circulation and accumulation.[5] Such products will likely look more like art than any marketable commodity, more like Gates's *Sanctum* in fact. For, in the wastes of our cities lie lost dreams – the ruined remains of past hopes for better futures. Even if our future cities end up as ruined wastelands – as countless post-apocalyptic fictions have imagined – they might still provide a basis on which to build more hopeful futures. Indeed, it might actually take such catastrophic ruination to finally spur us into action. As critic John Berger eloquently expressed: 'the promise is that again and again, from the garbage, the scattered feathers, the ashes and broken bodies, something new and beautiful may be born.'[6]

Salvage

Architectural salvage, also known as the creative reuse or 'upcycling' of building materials, is the process of transforming by-products, waste materials, and useless or unwanted products into new materials or products of better quality or for better environmental value. Salvage usually results in a distinct architectural aesthetic: distressed timber, carefully sandblasted old brick or stone, rusting metals. Becoming popular in the wake of neoliberal regeneration strategies beginning in the 1980s that saw the conversion of derelict former industrial premises in developed-world cities into high-end 'loft' living spaces,[7] the appeal of architectural salvage rests on a positive understanding of unwanted and often decaying materials and spaces as more 'authentic' than the brand new.[8] For aficionados of this kind of salvage, the patina of decay in a material signifies a visible form of history; yet it is a thoroughly aestheticized past, devoid of any references to social history which, particularly in the cases of former industrial buildings, include those former residents and workers displaced by disinvestment.

Reacting to this superficial reading of history, critic Evan Calder Williams has reclaimed salvage as a potent force in challenging capitalism's tendency to recast architectural leftovers as chic in order to make them valuable once again. He invents 'salvagepunk', a practice that rests on the idea that in the wastes of the world lie the shattered utopian dreams of the past, which are waiting to be unlocked once

Lebbeus Woods, 'Quake City', from *San Francisco: Inhabiting the Quake*, 1995, graphite and pastel on paper.

again. In this mode, what is constructed out of the material ruins of the past is not the valuable commodity that constitutes the shabby-chic aesthetic, but rather 'social relations [of] concrete attempts to move beyond capitalism'.[9] For Williams, in a world of salvagepunk, 'there is no new construction, just the occupation of other architectures.'[10] This startling definition implies that cities are essentially organic assemblages of constructions that never lose their past histories, even as demolition and redevelopment might appear to destroy them. Here, the future city is always being fashioned out of the ruins of the past; it's an agglomeration not just of material remains but also of social ones.

'Salvagepunk' is a term that might well be applied to the work of speculative architect Lebbeus Woods, who from the 1980s onwards produced a plethora of exquisite drawings that attempted to visualize just what an architecture based on salvage might look like. His 1993 publication *War and Architecture*, produced in response to the deliberate targeting of cities during the Bosnian War (1992–5), was a manifesto for the reconstruction of Sarajevo. Developing his notions of the 'scab' and 'scar', Woods envisaged the bomb-damaged buildings of Sarajevo being reconstructed from their ruined fragments, a process led by the citizens of the city themselves in order to create new 'freespaces' to foster a radically new social order free from hierarchical control.[11] Woods set his idea of salvage against the two tendencies that he saw as dominating responses to war-damaged cities: on the one hand, the careful restoration of damaged or destroyed structures (exemplified in the recent reconstruction of pre-Second-World-War Dresden); and, on the other, the modernist idea of the *tabula rasa* – starting afresh from a blank slate. In the mid-1990s Woods turned his attention to a different kind of destructive force in his series of projects intended to prepare the city of San Francisco for the 'Big One' – a hypothetical earthquake of magnitude 8+ that will almost certainly strike the city sometime in the near future.

In absolute opposition to the conventional policy of strengthening existing structures, Woods imagined a whole series of buildings that were constructed, transformed or even completed by earthquakes themselves – 'an architecture that uses earthquakes, converting to a human purpose the energies they release . . . an architecture that inhabits earthquakes, existing in their space and time'.[12] Woods's series of drawings pictured the elements of his new self-penned Seismicity. Shard Houses would be built on the stable pilings of piers on the west side of San Francisco Bay, made out of the 'scavenged shards of the industrial wasteland'. When the Big One strikes, the mud on which the Shard Houses rest would liquefy, turning the structures into floating homes. Meanwhile, Slip Houses would allow for the movement of the earth by sitting on a nearly frictionless silicon surface; while Wave Houses, built from ball-jointed frames, would flex and re-flex in the quake. Fault Houses would literally inhabit the San Andreas Fault, harnessing the energy of earthquakes to determine their forms; while Horizon Houses would turn, 'reorienting their forms and fixed interior spaces relative to the horizon'. Finally, Quake City

– a gigantic structure that Woods imagined straddling a redundant industrial dock – would be an architecture without a point of origin, one that had simply accumulated over the years, with each successive earthquake shifting its 'fragmented, irregular mass, reshuffling the plates that once might have been called floors, walls, or ceilings'.[13] All of these imagined structures are seemingly built from scavenged materials, whether discarded timber, corrugated iron and other sheet metal, or used pipes and other plastics. This turning away from conventional building materials is characteristic of Woods's approach – he wanted architecture to be made from below, assembled by its users rather than fabricated in advance by architects and builders. For Woods, architectural salvage wasn't just about creating a certain kind of aesthetic, a grandiose form of upcycling; rather, it deliberately shifted the power to build into the hands of users rather than architects – an anarchic architecture, or 'anarchitecture', as Woods himself described it.

In reality, self-built urban environments rarely look as beautiful as Woods's drawings suggest they might. Instead, they aggregate on the fringes of countless cities in developing countries across the world as insanitary informal housing largely borne out of desperation rather than hope. Who indeed would choose to live in a house built entirely from salvaged materials? Woods might imagine his salvaged houses as 'freespaces' created by citizens liberated from the shackles of authoritarian architectural modernism; yet he presupposes that people *would* choose a nomadic and free-spirited urban existence in favour of the comfort and security offered by the conventional home.

Woods's equating of salvage with freedom has its counterpart in another imagined future vision of San Francisco, post-Big One, namely in William Gibson's 'Bridge' trilogy of novels: *Virtual Light* (1993), *Idoru* (1996) and *All Tomorrow's Parties* (1999).[14] The Bridge that unites these novels is a reconstituted Bay Bridge, salvaged by thousands of squatters after the earthquake known as the Little Grande left it unstable and derelict. In contrast to the post-quake fate of San

Francisco's tallest building – the Transamerica Pyramid – which is held together by a steel brace, the Bay Bridge has mutated into a fantastic bricolage of salvaged materials:

> The integrity of its span was rigorous as the modern program itself, yet around this had grown another reality, intent upon its own agenda. This had occurred piecemeal, to no set plan, employing every imaginable technique and material. The result was something amorphous, startlingly organic. At night, illuminated by Christmas bulbs, by recycled neon, by torch-light, it possessed a queer medieval energy. By day, seen from a distance, it [seemed like] the ruin of England's Brighton Pier, as though viewed through some cracked kaleidoscope of vernacular style.[15]

A slum by any other estimation, Gibson's Bridge is unquestionably a utopian community very much in the spirit of Woods's drawings.[16] Throughout the course of the three novels, the social life and practical infrastructure of the Bridge is fleshed out in extraordinary detail. We are immersed in the everyday lives of those who live in the shack-like rooms; we learn about the improvised sewage and electricity supply networks; and we inhabit the heady micro-worlds of the countless bars, shops and clubs that fill the Bridge's interstitial spaces. Gibson is not describing an urban environment that can be planned, or per-haps even drawn in the way that Woods imagines it can be. Rather, there is no agenda, no underlying structure to the formation of the Bridge community: 'the place had just *grown*; it looked like one thing patched into the next, until the whole space was wrapped in this formless mass of *stuff*, no two pieces of it matched.'[17] Gibson contrasts this anarchic form of urban growth with that envisaged by the mega-corporations who are seeking to remake San Francisco into a self-sufficient luxury enclave for the super-wealthy. What is at stake here is not how cities are made, but who is entitled to make them.

Like Woods, Gibson asks us whether we truly do prefer to have our cities made for us by others, or whether we'd be willing to take matters into our own hands, joining with those who are already forced by necessity to do so.

For architect Jonathan Gales, architectural salvage begins in a very different place from Woods's or Gibson's damaged or derelict structures, namely in an imagined future when all architecture is in a state of incompletion. In his short film *Megalomania* (2014), made by Gales's animation studio Factory Fifteen, the whole of London has become a vast construction site, with all of its buildings caught in an arrested development that could result in either future decay or renewed development.[18] In this seemingly abandoned city, the London Eye has grown informal appendages very much like those seen constructed on Gibson's Bridge, while a giant skyscraper structure pictured at the end of the film is in fact an enormous assemblage of different construction elements: scaffolding, cranes, panels and a concrete frame. Inspired by the sudden collapse of the global construction industry in the wake of the 2007–8 financial crisis, which temporarily halted the building of now iconic buildings like London's Shard and

London under construction, from Jonathan Gales's short film *Megalomania* (2014).

Occupy site at
St Paul's Cathedral,
2011.

Dubai's Burj Khalifa, not to mention countless areas of new housing across Europe, *Megalomania* exaggerates the time-lag between a building's construction and completion in order to flag up how vulnerable architecture is to fluctuations in the flows of global capital.[19] In visualizing an entire city as a petrified construction site, the film asks if unfinished buildings might become the norm rather than the exception in our future cities and how we might go about salvaging their remains into something useful and inhabitable.

If Gales's vision has a direct political resonance in its call for urban citizens to reoccupy the ruins created by periodic crises in global capitalism, then the many structures created by the recent Occupy Movement provide us with some idea of what a future salvaged city might actually look like in reality. From 2011 onwards, a series of protests took place in many cities across the world that were characterized by the occupation of public spaces for sometimes weeks on end before the municipal authorities acted to disperse the protestors.[20] What resulted were temporary urban communities in cities such as New York and London defined by makeshift architectures: groups of tents being the most obvious but also including tables, chairs and even libraries made from salvaged timber and plastics, plus improvised sanitation networks to keep the sites and their inhabitants clean.[21] In the case of the Umbrella Movement in Hong Kong, which lasted for 79 days from September to December 2014, such practical forms of salvage were also accompanied by aesthetic ones, namely sculptural installations such as the 3-metre-high (10-ft) Umbrella Man made from salvaged wood and umbrellas, the latter used by protestors to shield themselves from police using tear gas and pepper spray.[22] In addition, a city bus abandoned during the protests was covered in Post-it notes bearing messages of defiance and hope, while improvised stairs made from salvaged palettes allowed protestors to circumvent roads and other barriers. In all of these cases, urban protests were invested with architectural elements that fostered a form of ephemeral and mobile construction borne out of salvage, one that could not be more different from a conventional urbanism that plans and implements static forms of development. The fluid and shapeshifting urbanism of the Occupy Movement suggests that flexible and responsive cities of the future might result from the coming together of the immateriality of social media and the material leftovers of capitalism – exactly the kind of salvagepunk envisaged by Williams, Woods and Gibson.

Slum

If architectural salvage has been understood by some as a potentially utopian form of construction, then for the billion-plus people that currently live in at least 200,000 informal settlements – often simply called 'slums' – in cities across the developing world, such constructions are something quite different: habitats of last resort that are created because of a desperate shortage of conventional housing in the rapidly urbanizing Global South.[23] Whatever their local names – *favelas* in Brazil, *barrios* in Colombia, *bustees* in India or *callejones* in Peru, to name but a few – these informal settlements are characterized by self-built housing, usually constructed illegally, as well as an almost total lack of basic urban infrastructure, such as sanitation, water supply and waste-disposal facilities. Informal settlements usually look startlingly different from planned areas of cities, so much so that some, like Dharavi – one of Asia's largest slums, located in the very centre of Mumbai – have become fixtures on tourists' itineraries. Dharavi's visibility also grew as a result of it featuring in Danny Boyle's cinematic tale of rags to riches, *Slumdog Millionaire* (2008), where it was cast in vivid terms as a place of both extraordinary vibrancy and unmitigated squalor. Where the edges of Dharavi meet the rest of the city, its self-built structures agglomerate into miniature skyscrapers of shacks – their countless wooden panels, corrugated metal sheets, brick walls and improvised windows and waste pipes creating a chaos of forms that are simultaneously fascinating and repellant.

Although some informal settlements like Dharavi are constructed in urban centres, most proliferate on the edges of cities, often encircling the formal urban core and, in the cases of cities such as Caracas, Kinshasa and Manila, far exceeding the reach of the latter in terms of population and extent. As urban critic Mike Davis has pointed out, if the predictions of the UN Urban Observatory are correct – that by

The edges of the Dharavi informal settlement in Mumbai.

2020, up to 50 per cent of the total population living in cities will be housed in informal settlements – then the cities of the future, particularly the new mega-cities across the developing world, will not be primarily made out of glass and steel but rather:

> crude brick, straw, recycled plastic, cement blocks, and scrap-wood. Instead of cities soaring upwards towards heaven, much of the twenty-first-century urban world squats in squalor, surrounded by pollution, excrement, and decay.[24]

A future Los Angeles as a vast informal city in *Elysium* (2013).

If critics like Davis are unapologetic in their condemnation of the political, economic and social reasons for such appalling urban conditions, then others have argued that informal settlements must be accepted as part of the new urban condition because they will likely grow to become an ever larger part of future cities, whether we like them or not.[25] According to the British journalist Justin McGuirk, even though an attitude of acceptance of slums has been cynically manipulated by the interests of global capitalism to argue for the withdrawal of state and municipal responsibility for housing the urban poor, informal settlements nevertheless demonstrate extraordinary creative resourcefulness in building 'their own self-regulating systems … tight-knit communities and proving a crucial device for accessing the opportunities that cities offer'.[26] For the current and future generation of architects and urban planners, the 'rehabilitation' of slums might mean learning how to integrate them into the city as a whole, 'creating connections and flows, the points of communication and inclusion that will dissolve the lines of exclusion and collision'.[27]

Indeed, one of the great values of dystopian depictions of future cities is in drawing attention to what might happen if those connections are severed, the divisions between rich and poor heightened rather than diminished. If the near-future cities depicted in the films *Soylent Green* (1973), *Robocop* (1987) and *Looper* (2012) picture American cities – respectively New York, Detroit and Kansas City – overrun with the informal dwellings of the destitute, then Los Angeles in *Elysium* (2013) becomes, by 2159, an entire slum-city, the formal city having been relocated to space in an advanced technological utopian habitat that orbits the decaying Earth. The future city visualized in *Elysium* is a mixture of the real – parts of the film were shot in the Iztapalapa informal settlement on the edge of Mexico City – and the imagined: CGI transforms the skyscrapers of Los Angeles's central business district into a bricolage of architectural informality not unlike Gibson's Bridge community in *Virtual Light*. With the departure of humanity's wealthy few, the most obvious architectural embodiments of its former power have been repurposed by the poor. As might be expected, the film ends with the heroic reconciliation of the elite space colony and proletarian Los Angeles, but never makes clear exactly how and why the connections were so brutally severed in the first place.

In a different vein, the casting of the future city as slum has formed part of Didier Madoc-Jones and Robert Graves's *Postcards from the Future* project, a series of digital images created by the artists in 2010 showing how a future London might adapt to rising sea levels and a vast influx of migrants.[28] In a number of the images, the artists suggest that current areas of the city – Trafalgar Square, Buckingham Palace and the skyscrapers of the City of London such as Norman Foster's 'Gherkin' – might be transformed by climate refugees into informal settlements, or 'shanty towns' as the artists term them. Although troubling in their orientalizing of the supposedly 'exotic' slums of the Global South, these images nevertheless create startling juxtapositions of the highly formal and exclusive city and its often unacknowledged other, ones that lead us to question just why they are so different in the first place.[29] Finally, in the American photographer Noah Addis's ongoing series *Future Cities*, the artist simply records in photographs the structures and infrastructures of informal communities across the world, including Dharavi in Mumbai, suggesting that these communities in themselves offer lessons as to what might constitute more responsible urban planning and sustainable development in the future.[30]

In recent years, some architects and urban planners have developed an activist approach towards slums that embraces rather than condemns them. Representing a fundamental shift away from a modernist emphasis on top-down planning and slum clearance, practices such as Elemental in Santiago de Chile and Urban Think Tank in Caracas have engaged in projects that model themselves on the informality they have come to value in their home cities and elsewhere. Beginning in 2003, Elemental, led by architect Alejandro Aravena, designed and built 93 homes in Iquique in northern Chile (the Quinta Monroy project) that were revolutionary in that each of the homes was only comprised of half of what was intended. Thus every one of the 93 plots was provided with a formal concrete structure, including a roof, kitchen and bathroom, and residents were then responsible for extending these structures into full houses.[31] What at first might seem a ruthless abdication of responsibility on the part of the architects has in fact, over time, produced a hybrid architecture that mixes both formal and informal elements, the concrete cores now supplemented by a colourful array of plywood, timber, plasterboard and other materials.

Elemental, Quinta
Monroy project,
Iquique, Chile.

Extending this idea further, the photographic constructions of Dionisio González – the *Favela* series (2004–7) – picture fantastic multi-storey hybrid constructions that have emerged out of the *favela* architecture of Brazil but which also incorporate more formal design elements that seem to have been inspired by the outrageous geometries evident in the work of architects Frank Gehry or Zaha Hadid.[32] González's photomontages question conventional perceptions of slums as chaotic assemblages of buildings that have no bearing on architectural design.[33] The stacked structures in these images, which bear a striking similarity to those actually built in Dharavi, force us to think about what a collision of the formal and informal might actually look like. They also provide a 'raw vision of the world's urban future when the continued global mixing of the Developed and Developing worlds begins to clash and architecturally blur, break down and ultimately reconstruct itself into something else'.[34]

One example of this collision of the formal and informal already heralds what this 'something else' might look like, namely the Torre David in Caracas. From September 2007 until July 2014, an unfinished

52-storey skyscraper in central Caracas was home to 3,000 squatters, who had taken over what were to be prime downtown office spaces and turned them into their own apartments, shops and other amenities. As documented by Urban Think Tank, who made a film and book about the squatters and also presented their work at the 2010 Venice Biennale,[35] the occupation of Torre David was a direct result of president Hugo Chávez's demagogic politics, which encouraged the appropriation of redundant property by the disadvantaged.[36] It was Chávez's untimely death in 2013 that resulted in a change of government and the eventual eviction of the Torre David squatters in 2014 (the skyscraper was subsequently renovated and returned to its original function as offices).[37]

The occupation began in 2007 with refugees from Caracas's *barrios* located on the edges of the city deciding to take their chances living in a city-centre building that had been left unfinished since the death of its developer in 1993; in Caracas, like most Latin American cities, the urban poor are generally denied city-centre housing, which has a dramatic effect upon their ability to access employment in the urban core. With only an open concrete frame and unfenced stairwells

Dionisio González,
Nova Heliopolis II,
2006.

completed, Torre David was initially far from habitable; yet, over the years, squatters refashioned it into homes using a mixture of breeze-blocks, bricks, bed-sheets, cardboard, plastic and newspapers to infill the spaces, creating a startling juxtaposition of the formal and informal, as seen in many photographs of the building. Justin McGuirk has compared Torre David to Le Corbusier's Dom-Ino House of 1914, in which the fledgling arch-modernist architect attempted (unsuccessfully) to make his fortune by selling two-storey concrete frames and letting buyers fill in their own walls.[38] In this reading, Torre David was an (accidental) flexible architecture, a model of building in which 'citizens . . . complete the city, its buildings' remaining 'as works in progress' and where the distinction between the informal and the formal dissolves.[39] Here, what was to have been a beacon of finance capital was temporarily turned into one of social capital – the characteristic vertical exclusivity of the skyscraper seen in Chapter Four subverted, for a time at least, into 'horizontal redistribution'.[40]

Urban Think Tank believes that the occupation of Torre David offers a powerful model of how architecture might become more flexible in the face of increasingly chaotic and unstable urban futures. Indeed, they have seen in the building a mirror of their own Growing House project for the Anglican Church in Caracas, begun in 2003 and completed in 2005.[41] Here, Urban Think Tank were asked to design a system of emergency housing for the parish but, given the lack of available land, they instead chose to construct a two-storey concrete frame over an existing building and allowed residents to build their own apartments within that frame.[42] They also provided community spaces, including a kindergarten, cafe, meeting hall and retail units. As stated by Urban Think Tank, the project 'imitates the incremental development of self-help housing, but introduces a safe framework for user-driven solutions'.[43]

In Britain, the architecture collaborative Assemble have integrated this concept of user involvement in a very different way in their work in Liverpool's Granby Four Streets neighbourhood, an area badly

Torre David, Caracas, Venezuela, 2008.

affected by the city's riots in 1981 and which had been earmarked for a redevelopment that was never implemented. Collaborating with residents to resist the demolition of the decaying Victorian terraces, Assemble intervened by refurbishing the streets, house-by-house, providing street furniture and organizing and supporting grassroots action such as a local market and workshop, where members buy and sell handmade housewares.[44] The result is an incremental approach to urban regeneration, one that contrasts sharply with most developer-led initiatives, where renovation and new construction lead to gentrification and the pricing-out of former residents. Life in the Victorian terraces of Liverpool may seem far removed from that of the urban poor in Torre David, yet the rationale between these two examples is the same: to allow the *users* of architecture to define what a building should become, the architect in effect becoming a facilitator rather than a dictator of form and function. Here, architecture becomes about inventiveness, adaptability and resourcefulness, where users are allowed to create the very 'freespaces' that Lebbeus Woods first proposed in the 1990s. Of course, neither Torre David nor the Granby Four Streets look anything like Woods's angular but beautiful drawings; but they nevertheless mirror their basis in the collision of the formal and informal, creating a messy aesthetic that would be anathema to an architectural modernist, but which reflects a utopian social vision that embraces rather than rejects precariousness as a vital aspect of urban life.[45]

Waste

Cities are quite literally built on top of their own wastes. As structures are demolished and rebuilt, roads resurfaced time and again, and new buildings constructed on top of the ground-down rubble of old ones, the urban surface literally rises up, meaning that very old cities like London contain beneath their surfaces a rich archaeology of their own compacted detritus – a 'ruins memory' in the words of Rebecca

Solnit.[46] In the contemporary period of consumer capitalism, wastes have proliferated to such an extent that some informal communities are quite literally built on them, as in the 'garbage slums' of Quarantina outside Beirut, Hillat Kusha outside Khartoum, Santa Cruz in Mexico City and the Dhapa dump on the outskirts of Kolkata.[47] These infamous places flag up not only the desperate plight of some of the world's poorest urban citizens but also the unimaginable quantities of waste being produced by cities across the world today: around 1.3 billion tonnes a year, rising to an estimated 2.2 billion tonnes by 2025.[48] While a push towards recycling from the 1980s onwards has dominated urban policy in the West, often leading to a sense of complacency about the larger effects of unbridled capitalist consumption, vast heaps of garbage proliferate in informal communities where municipal or private disposal is at best only removing part of the accumulating wastes.[49] Indeed, despite widespread recycling, much of the waste produced by the affluent (particularly hazardous is e-waste) ends up in these poorer communities, with the 34 wealthiest nations producing more solid waste than the other 164 combined.[50]

The growing problem of finding suitable landfill sites for urban wastes has led some architects to develop ways of incorporating them into buildings, in line with the logic of a future production based on a completely closed resource cycle put forward by such organizations as the Zero Waste International Alliance and the MacArthur Foundation. As documented in the book *Building from Waste*, these design strategies are highly varied and encompass five principal methods: first, densifying waste materials using a garbage press to compact them into building blocks; second, processing waste into new materials such as tiles, bricks or panels; third, transforming the molecular state of waste and mixing it with other components, an example being Nappy Roofing made from recycled sanitary products; fourth, creating products that are never thrown away, such as the UNITED BOTTLE, a plastic container that can be reused as a building component; and, fifth, harnessing elements of the process of decay to generate 'growing' architectures, such as Biorock discussed in Chapter One, bacteria-based self-healing concrete and Myco Foam, a material created from agricultural waste and fungal mycelium.[51]

Architect and entrepreneur Mitchell Joachim has taken this approach a step further in proposing the construction of entire sky-scrapers in New York out of the city's waste materials in his practice Terreform ONE's Rapid Re(f)use project.[52] As Joachim has observed, Manhattan's inhabitants currently discard enough paper products to fill a volume the size of the Empire State Building every two weeks; Rapid Re(f)use would collect this material and, with the assistance of automated 3D printers, rapidly process it into the building blocks of new skyscrapers.[53] These automatons would be based on existing techniques used in industrial waste compaction; but they also derive from a more unlikely source, namely the robotic trash collector seen in the Disney/Pixar animated film WALL-E (2008). In the film, a future Earth has been completely abandoned by its human population,

Terreform ONE,
Rapid Re(f)use
project, 2010.

the result of its decimation by the wastes produced by a voracious consumerism that has relocated to space colonies. In the future city depicted in the film – probably New York City – the eponymous WALL-E (a Waste Allocation Load Lifter: Earth-Class robot) is left alone to gather and compact the vast quantities of waste left behind by humanity, which have rendered the city, and the world beyond, uninhabitable. As well as collecting certain discarded materials that appeal to the robot's anthropocentric nostalgia and desire to collect and organize, WALL-E builds new skyscrapers out of the blocks of compacted waste, in effect creating a new skyline for the city as its old skyscrapers succumb to the processes of decay. As Joachim explained, the film was released at the same time as he was conceiving his Rapid Re(f)use project and it 'profoundly infused the research agenda' of his design team.[54] Yet in proposing a project that imagines the future city as one 'without an [exhaust] tail pipe', or the zero-waste closed cycle envisaged by the MacArthur Foundation, Joachim sidesteps the principal message of WALL-E: that unbridled consumerism may not be able to contain its wastes in the future, that the longed-for closed cycle is in fact a capitalist illusion.[55] As any physicist will tell you, there is no

Skyscrapers of waste in *WALL-E* (2008).

such thing as a perfect exchange of energy; something is always lost as waste in this process. Perhaps if we are to incorporate waste products into the architecture of the future, then the latter should also draw attention to the problematic status of the waste products themselves, namely, as the inevitable consequence of a fundamentally unsustainable ideology of accumulation that is predicated on creating waste that need not exist in the first place.

The stories that make up the collection *Metatropolis* (2009) approach the question of the wastes of capitalism by reimagining the relationship between the future city and nature, or between the artificial and the organic. In these stories, which were conceived collaboratively by five authors as part of a 'world-building' exercise to develop a shared vision of an urban future, capitalist modes of production and waste-generation are turned on their heads.[56] Thus in Jay Lake's story, the future city of Cascadiopolis lies hidden in the forests of Washington between Portland and Vancouver, and is partly built into the 'basalt bones of the Oregon Cascades' (the material remains of ancient volcanic activity) and partly strung between the trees. The city's citizens (a mixture of biotech engineers and third-generation hippies) practise radical ways of harvesting natural resources: for example, their lighting is engineered from firefly genomes, their power from water and compressed springs, their food from genetically modified fungus and vegetables grown on micro-holdings.[57]

In two of the other stories in *Metatropolis*, both set in a near-future Detroit, abandoned buildings are transformed into sites of organic production. The first, Tobias Buckell's 'Stochasti-city', sees derelict downtown skyscrapers occupied by radical environmentalists and turned into vertical urban farms: truly sustainable buildings that do not recycle their 'forefather's leftovers, or scrabble about for what [they] could get today', but rather create a radical intervention 'right on the foundations of the existing'.[58] In the second, Elizabeth Bear's story sees another abandoned building in Detroit turned into a self-sufficient community. Here, the inhabitants mine landfill sites and scrapyards for all of the materials needed for construction and the creation of a system of permaculture. By salvaging wastes, this fledgling community challenges the exploitation of natural resources in capitalist economies by forging a 'collective economy' of shared skills, or social instead of financial capital.[59] These stories demonstrate a far more radical approach to waste than Mitchell Joachim's proposed skyscraper built from recycled paper in that they posit new social and economic modes of production. They challenge not only how waste is produced in capitalist economies but also how the construction and inhabitation of the entire built environment must change in order to accommodate genuinely new approaches.

Far stranger in its reconceptualization of urban wastes is China Miéville's imaginary city of New Crobuzon in his 2000 novel *Perdido Street Station*, introduced in Chapter Three. New Crobuzon is a fantasy reimagining of London – a splicing of the Victorian and modern city overlaid with the informality of cities like Cairo or Mumbai.[60] It is filled with a populace comprising humans; an array of human-animal hybrids such as khepri (part-human, part-scarab beetle), garuda (part-eagle) and vodyanoi (part-frog); and 'remades', a horrific underclass of humans re-engineered by the authorities to incorporate machine, animal or other organic parts. Such extreme hybridity is also reflected in the built environment of New Crobuzon itself, particularly in the slum areas of the city, such as Dog Fenn, where buildings are put together seemingly at random – 'ladders left against a wall one day [would] become the stairwells to a new storey, thrown precariously between two dropping roofs.'[61] In the khepri-dominated area of Kinken, the larval offspring of these human/beetle hybrids live in seemingly conventional architect-designed houses, but transform them by burrowing through their walls 'oozing their phlegm-cement from their abdomens'; this ooze collects over time, 'linking buildings into a lumpy, congealed totality'.[62]

If wastes seem to meld with the architecture of New Crobuzon, then they also exist as an autonomous form of intelligence in the Griss

Twist rubbish dumps located on the edge of the city. Here, the novel's hero Isaac, together with his loyal band of friends, encounters the Construct Council, an artificial intelligence that has self-assembled out of the collective detritus of the city. The creature's body is made entirely from rubbish: a 'vast skeleton of industrial waste twenty-five feet from skull to toe'; its limbs formed from 'cast-off pieces of stolen engines'; the whole 'thrown together and powered without the intervention of human beings'.[63] In overseeing the final saving of the city from the threat of the monstrous bio-engineered slake-moths, the Construct Council connects New Crobuzon's hidden detritus back into the living networks of the city. Throughout the novel, Miéville posits hybridity as a potent force in connecting the city with what it would rather discard. In the words of Mr Motley, a crime lord who has transformed himself into the ultimate hybrid – a tour-de-force amalgam of human, animal and machine parts – 'this is what makes the world . . . Transition. The point where one thing becomes another. It is what makes you, the city, the world, what they are.'[64] In integrating society's cast-offs into the city itself – whether in its buildings or in the very bodies of its citizens – Miéville imagines a world without waste. However, the resulting urban world is not the ordered, efficient, closed-cycle sustainable city imagined by promoters of zero waste but rather the opposite: a disturbing and unholy mess where the distinction between what is waste and what is not has completely dissolved.

The emphasis on hybridity in Miéville's fantastic city keys in with the central theme explored here: connecting the city's cast-offs – whether abandoned buildings, informal communities, rubbish or wastes – with the urban milieu in which they are both produced and also expelled. With salvage, the waste materials of architecture form the basis of the building process itself, producing a transitory, mobile architecture that is able to inhabit the in-between spaces of the city – an 'anarchitecture' that is made on the hoof. Such an architecture may become a necessary element in cities of the future, especially given the multiple threats that urban dwellers will need to confront, be they climate change, terrorism and urban warfare, or what seems to be ever-increasing social division. Engaging with informal settlements that, even now, dominate some urban centres in the developing world can foster a more unified and less segregated form of urbanism. Even as this approach will undoubtedly result in more chaotic future cities, the payoff will be the creation of more socially just cities, surely of greater importance than any questions of aesthetics or order. Finally, integrating waste back into the city brings detritus back into relationship with the forces that both produce it and then cast it out. In short, connecting the city with its detritus implies a wholesale re-evaluation of both the nature and *history* of waste, revealing its often untold stories and integrating it back into the urban environment, despite the mess this will undoubtedly leave in its wake.

It is by connecting more things up in the city that a richer future urban life will emerge. There is no imagined city without a real one – the two are already connected because what can be imagined already exists in reality, whether in the past or the present. Yet, too often, it is assumed that these two worlds are set against each other – the imagination seen as either antagonistic to or compromised by the instrumental, the old idealism versus pragmatism debate. Yet there are always connections that can be made, if one is willing to make space for them to appear. This is not to suggest that the imaginative and the instrumental are or will be comfortable bedfellows; far from it, but conflict and contradiction need not result in disconnection. As we know from the conflicts that rend both our urban societies and our own minds, the way to reconciliation is *through* those conflicts rather than around them. Perhaps the most fruitful way of moving forward is to simply allow the full richness of the imagination to make itself present – to enter wholeheartedly into the immense possibilities it incubates and makes known. Then, all kinds of unforeseen connections become evident, allowing a further interweaving of the everyday and the fantastical.

Allowing the imagination to flourish and inform how we conceive of our cities will not likely be a comforting process. Indeed, the urban imagination seems to flourish most effectively when confronted by what seem to be unassailable threats, whether climate change, social division, warfare or waste. The kind of transformation we need to see in our future cities can only come about if we are willing to face up to the vulnerability of our present way of life in the face of these many threats. Perhaps only if we fundamentally *accept* the power of these threats on us, particularly in terms of how we imagine they might play out in the future, can we actually become more resilient to them. But first we must be willing to sit *with* those threats, allowing them to infuse our imaginations, however uncomfortable that process may be. By doing this, we will not be resigning ourselves to the inevitable or giving up any hope of a better future; rather, we will be choosing to work with the rich, strange and disturbing potentialities of our minds instead of against them. In a very real sense, if we do this we will enter into the same world that architects, artists and novelists inhabit: an exciting but often frightening world in which anything might be possible if we allow space enough for it to appear. It is precisely *that* connection which offers hope of better futures for our cities, because it will result in the visionary moving from the territory of the lone pioneer or eccentric genius into the hands of the many – a move that will release the power of the imagination into the everyday world, offering the hope of genuine transformation for us all.

REFERENCES

Introduction: Real and Imagined Future Cities

1 For the Beijing image, see Dina Spector, 'Blade Runner or Beijing', Business Insider, 23 January 2013, www.businessinsider.com.

2 See Stephen Graham, 'Vertical Noir: Histories of the Future in Urban Science Fiction', CITY, XX/3 (2016), p. 394.

3 See Brian Merchant, 'Dubai's First Sci-fi Film is a Reminder that Dubai Itself is Not Actually Science Fiction', Vice, 30 April 2013, https://motherboard.vice.com.

4 See Richard Kearney, Poetics of Imagining: Modern to Post-modern (Edinburgh, 1998).

5 Quoted in Arnold H. Modell, Imagination and the Meaningful Brain (Cambridge, MA, 2003), p. 126.

6 See Gaston Bachelard, On Poetic Imagination and Reverie, trans. Colette Gaudin (Putnam, CT, 2005).

7 See David L. Pike, Metropolis on the Styx: The Underworlds of Modern Urban Culture, 1800–2001 (Ithaca, NY, 2007), p. 36.

8 James Donald, 'This, Here, Now: Imagining the Modern City', in Imagining Cities: Scripts, Signs, Memory, ed. Sallie Westwood and John Williams (London, 1997), p. 184.

9 See Blair Kamin, 'Frank Lloyd Wright Influenced the Burj Khalifa? Here's What the Tower's Designers Say: That's a Tall Tale', Chicago Tribune, 14 January 2010, http://featuresblogs.chicagotribune.com.

10 See Witold Rybczynski, 'Dubai Debt: What the Burj Khalifa – the Tallest Building in the World – Owes to Frank Lloyd Wright', Slate, 13 January 2010, www.slate.com.

11 The term 'Anthropocene' was first coined by Paul Crutzen in his 2000 article in the Global Change Newsletter, 41 (May 2000), p. 17. Christophe Bonneuil and Jean-Baptiste Fressoz have provided a longer historical context for the emergence of this awareness in The Shock of the Anthropocene: The Earth, History and Us, trans. David Fernbach (London, 2017).

12 See Bruno Latour, 'Agency in the Time of the Anthropocene', *New Literary History*, xlv/1 (2014), p. 1.

13 World Health Organization, 'Global Health Observatory (gho): Urban Population Growth', 2014, www.who.int, accessed 20 August 2018.

14 Dipesh Chakrabarty, 'The Climate of History: Four Theses', *Critical Enquiry*, 35 (2009), pp. 197–223.

15 Kathryn Yusoff and Jennifer Gabrys, 'Climate Change and the Imagination', *Wiley Interdisciplinary Reviews: Climate Change*, ii/4 (2011), pp. 516–34.

16 Carl Abbott, *Imagining Urban Futures: Cities in Science Fiction and What We Might Learn from Them* (Middletown, ct, 2016).

17 Graham, 'Vertical Noir', p. 388.

18 Darko Suvin, 'On the Poetics of the Science Fiction Genre', *College English* (1972), pp. 372–82.

19 Graham, 'Vertical Noir', p. 395.

20 See, for example, Etienne Turpin, ed., *Architecture in the Anthropocene: Encounters among Design, Deep Time, Science and Philosophy* (Ann Arbor, mi, 2013).

21 See Andy Merrifield, *Magical Marxism: Subversive Politics and the Imagination* (London, 2011), p. 18.

22 Fredric Jameson, 'Future City', *New Left Review*, 21 (2003), p. 73.

23 Donald, 'This, Here, Now', p. 185.

24 See Félix Guattari, *The Three Ecologies*, trans. Ian Pindar and Paul Sutton [1989] (London and New Brunswick, nj, 2000).

1 Drowned: Postcards from the Future

1 Kim Stanley Robinson, *New York 2140* (London, 2017).

2 See the Intergovernmental Panel on Climate Change's *Climate Change 2013: The Physical Science Basis, Summary for Policymakers* (2014), www.ipcc.ch, accessed 20 August 2018.

3 See *Stern Review: The Economics of Climate Change* (2006), http://mudancasclimaticas.cptec.inpe.br/~rmclima/pdfs.

4 Kathryn Yusoff and Jennifer Gabrys, 'Climate Change and the Imagination', *Wiley Interdisciplinary Reviews: Climate Change*, ii/4 (2011), pp. 516–34.

5 See Mike Hulme, *Why We Disagree about Climate Change: Understanding Controversy, Inactivity and Opportunity* (Cambridge, 2009); and Amanda Machin, *Negotiating Climate Change: Radical Democracy and the Illusion of Consensus* (London and New York, 2013).

6 Harriet Bulkeley, *Cities and Climate Change* (London and New York, 2013), p. 143.

7 See Mark Pelling, *Adaptation to Climate Change: From Resilience to Transformation* (London and New York, 2011).

8 On the variety of ancient mythic floods, see John Withington, *Flood: Nature and Culture* (London, 2013), pp. 9–32.

9 Ibid., pp. 19–20.

10 The sunken cities off the coast of Alexandria were the subject of the exhibition *Sunken Cities: Egypt's Lost Worlds*, held at the British Museum, London, 19 May–27 November 2016.

11 See Darran Anderson, *Imaginary Cities* (London, 2015), pp. 198–205, on sunken cities in history.

12 Hannah Osborne, 'Sunken City of Igarata Begins to Emerge as Brazil's Drought Sees Water Levels Plummet', *International Business Times*, 6 February 2015, www.ibtimes.co.uk.

13 On the evolution and proliferation of climate change fiction, see Adam Trexler, *Anthropocene Fictions: The Novel in a Time of Climate Change* (Charlottesville, VA, 2015). I am grateful to Adam for directing me to a wealth of city-based climate change novels.

14 Ibid., pp. 83–4. See also Carl Abbott, *Imagining Urban Futures: Cities in Science Fiction and What We Might Learn From Them* (Middletown, CT, 2016), pp. 160–70.

15 See Matthew Gandy, 'The Drowned World: J. G. Ballard and the Politics of Catastrophe', *Space and Culture*, IX/1 (2006), p. 86. In a 2009 interview, Ballard himself recognized the novel's prescience in relation to post-Katrina New Orleans (see 'New Orleans: Gewalt ohne Ende', *Zeit Online*, 8 September 2005, www.zeit.de).

16 On literary drownings of London, see Paul Dobraszczyk, *The Dead City: Urban Ruins and the Spectacle of Decay* (London, 2017), pp. 43–52; and Matthew Gandy, *The Fabric of Space: Water, Modernity and the Urban Imagination* (Cambridge, MA, 2014), pp. 185–8.

17 See Simon Sellers and Dan O'Hara, *Extreme Metaphors: Collected Interviews, J. G. Ballard* (London, 2014), pp. 83, 90.

18 J. G. Ballard, *The Drowned World* [1962] (London, 2011), p. 19.

19 Ibid., pp. 63, 68.

20 Sensationalist non-fiction predictions of future climate change include Mark Lynas, *Six Degrees: Our Future on a Hotter Planet* (London, 2008), with its cover image showing London's Houses of Parliament engulfed in seawater; and Naomi Oreskes, *The Collapse of Civilization: A View from the Future* (New York, 2014).

21 Other notable examples of city-based climate change novels that use the flood-as-duration motif are Donna McMahon's *Dance of Knives* (2001), set in a flooded Vancouver; Kim Stanley Robinson's *Forty Signs of Rain* (2004), the first in his Science in the Capital trilogy and set in Washington, DC; Saci Lloyd's London-based *The Carbon Diaries 2015* (2009) and its 2010 sequel; and David Brin's *Existence* (2012), which takes place in the Huangpu estuary on the edge of a flooded Shanghai.

22 On the origins and development of the idea of the New Zealander, see David Skilton, 'Contemplating the Ruins of London: Macaulay's New Zealander and Others', *Literary London Journal: Interdisciplinary Studies in the Representation of London*, ii/1 (2004). On Doré's engraving see also Lynda Nead, *Victorian Babylon: People, Streets and Images in Nineteenth-century London* (London, 2000), pp. 212–15.

23 On deluge as disaster in the cinematic tradition, see Withington, *Flood*, pp. 107–16; and Max Page, *The City's End: Two Centuries of Fantasies, Fears, and Premonitions of New York's Destruction* (London and New York, 2008), pp. 74–6, 89–91, 196, 220–26.

24 On the series of flood maps issued by the Environment Agency in 2011, see 'Our Future Underwater: Terrifying New Pictures Reveal How Britain's Cities Could Be Devastated by Flood Water', *Mail Online*, 9 March 2011, www.dailymail.co.uk. Linn's series of sea-level-rise maps can be viewed at http://spatialities.com/category/sea-level-rise-maps, accessed 20 August 2018.

25 On Ronsiaux's series of images, see Nina Azzarello, 'Architecture under Water: Francois Ronsiaux Images Man's Habitat Post Ice Thaw', *Designboom*, 23 January 2015, www.designboom.com; on Lamm's, see Meredith Bennett-Smith, 'Nickolay Lamm's Sea Level Rise Images Depict What U.S. Cities Could Look Like in Future', *Huffington Post*, 4 November 2013, www.huffingtonpost.com.

26 On the utopian in Squint/Opera 2's images, see Gandy, *The Fabric of Space*, pp. 210–13; and Marcus Fairs, 'Flooded London by Squint/Opera', *Dezeen*, 18 June 2008, www.dezeen.com.

27 See Fairs, 'Flooded London'.

28 Maggie Gee, *The Flood* (London, 2004), p. 189; George Turner, *The Sea and Summer* (London, 1987), p. 298; Stephen Baxter, *Flood* (London, 2008), pp. 172, 244.

29 *Manifest Destiny* was first exhibited in 2004 at the Brooklyn Museum of Art, which had commissioned the work. It has subsequently been acquired by the Smithsonian American Art Museum in Washington, DC. For commentary on the painting, see Alexis Rockman, *Manifest Destiny* (New York, 2005); Linda Yablonsky, 'New York's Watery New

Grave', *New York Times*, 11 April 2004; and Page, *The City's End*,
pp. 226–8.

30 See Rockman, *Manifest Destiny*, p. 6.

31 Dipesh Chakrabarty, 'The Climate of History: Four Theses', *Critical Enquiry*, 35 (2009), p. 213.

32 On the Futurama exhibit, see Lawrence R. Samuel, *The End of the Innocence: The 1964–1965 New York World's Fair* (New York, 2007), pp. 106–9; on Jacques Rougerie and Edith Vignes' early work, see the special issue of *L'Architecture d'aujourd'hui,* 175 (1974), titled 'Habiter la Mer', ed. Jacques and Edith Rougerie.

33 See Jude Garvey, 'Sub Biosphere 2: Designs for a Self-sustainable Underwater World', *Gizmag*, 23 June 2010, www.gizmag.com.

34 For a response to the project, see Alexander Hespe and Alanna Howe, 'Venice Biennale: Ocean City', *Australian Design Review*, 26 (October 2010), www.australiandesignreview.com.

35 The proposal was first illustrated in Wolf Hilbertz, 'Towards Cybertecture', *Progressive Architecture* (May 1970), p. 103. Fallis's numerous drawings for the project were redrawn and published by Paul Cureton in his article 'Videre: Drawing and Evolutionary Architectures', *Materials. Architecture. Design. Environment*, VII/10 (2013), pp. 16–27.

36 See Wolf Hilbertz, et al., 'Electrodeposition of Minerals in Sea Water: Experiments and Applications', IEEE, *Journal of Oceanic Engineering*, IV/3 (1979), pp. 94–113.

37 See, for example, Ari Spenhoff, 'The Biorock Process: Picturing Reef Building with Electricity', Global Coral Reef Alliance, 2010, www.globalcoral.org.

38 See A. Agkathidis, *Biomorphic Structures: Architecture Inspired by Nature* (London, 2016); and Michael Pawlyn, *Biomimicry in Architecture* (London, 2016).

39 The talk was titled 'Architecture That Repairs Itself?', www.ted.com, July 2009.

40 See www.crab-studio.com/soak-city.html for the complete series of renderings of Soak City; and Peter Cook, 'Looking and Drawing', *Architectural Design*, 1 September 2013, pp. 86–7, for a description of the project.

41 See Cook's Veg House project from 1996, illustrated in Peter Cook, *Architecture Workbook: Design Through Motive* (Chichester, 2016), pp. 142–5.

42 Tim Ingold, *Making: Anthropology, Archaeology, Art and Architecture* (London, 2013), p. 21.

2 Floating: Water and Urban Utopias

1 See Philip E. Steinberg, Elizabeth A. Nyman and Mauro J. Caraccioli, 'Atlas Swam: Freedom, Capital and Floating Sovereignties in the Seasteading Vision', in Ricarda Vidal and Ingo Cornils, eds, *Alternative Worlds: Blue-sky Thinking since 1900* (Oxford, 2014), pp. 76–7.

2 On artificial islands, see M. Jackson and V. Della Dora, '"Dreams So Big Only the Sea Can Hold Them": Manmade Islands as Anxious Spaces, Cultural Icons, and Travelling Visions', *Environment and Planning A*, 41 (2009), pp. 86–104. On Dubai's artificial islands, see Alessandro Petti, 'Dubai Offshore Urbanism', in Michel Dehaene and Lieven De Cauter, eds, *Heterotopia and the City: Public Space in a Postcivil Society* (London and New York, 2008), pp. 287–95; and Mike Davis, 'Sand, Fear and Money in Dubai', in *Evil Paradises: Dreamworlds of Neoliberalism*, ed. Mike Davis and Daniel Betrand Monk (New York, 2007), pp. 52–66.

3 On the development of marine structures for oil extraction and other utilitarian and military floating structures, see C. M. Wang and B. T. Wang, *Large Floating Structures: Technological Advances* (London, 2015).

4 On Tange's Tokyo Bay project and other marine cities proposed by the Japanese Metabolist architects, see Zhongjie Lin, *Kenzo Tange and the Metabolist Movement* (London, 2010), pp. 133–71; and Mieke Schalk, 'The Architecture of Metabolism: Inventing a Culture of Resilience', *Arts*, 3 (2014), pp. 286–90.

5 On the series of inhabited platforms known as the Oil Rocks see Geoff Manaugh, 'Oil Rocks', BLDGBLOG, 1 September 2009, www.bldgblog.com; and Marc Wolfensberger's film *Oil Rocks: City above the Sea* (2009). Although in a dilapidated condition today, the Oil Rocks are still inhabited and used to extract oil from the Caspian Sea.

6 On Fuller's schemes for floating cities, see Martin Pawley, *Buckminster Fuller* (London, 1990), pp. 157–62. On Triton City in particular, see Triton Foundation Staff, 'An American Prototype Floating Community', *Build International*, IV/3 (1971).

7 See Sandra Kaji O'Grady and Peter Raisbeck, 'Prototype Cities in the Sea', *Journal of Architecture*, X/4 (2005), p. 444.

8 Their early proposals, including Thallasopolis I, were featured in a special issue of *Architecture d'aujourd'hui*, 'Habiter la Mer', 175, ed. Jacques and Edith Rougerie (1974).

9 On the 2015 marine research centre, see the website of Jacques Rougerie at www.rougerie.com.

10 On Kikutake's Aquapolis, see the special edition of *Japan Architect*, '"International Ocean Exposition", Okinawa, Japan, 1975', 50 (1975).

11 O'Grady and Raisbeck, 'Prototype Cities', p. 444.

12 On the agenda of the Seasteading Institute, see their website at www.seasteading.org.

13 On the recent renewal of interest in Seasteading, see China Miéville, 'Floating Utopias: Freedom and Unfreedom of the Seas', in Davis and Monk, *Evil Paradises*, pp. 251–61; O'Grady and Raisbeck, 'Prototype Cities', pp. 454–8; and Steinberg, Nyman and Caraccioli, 'Atlas Swam'.

14 Since Bates's death in 2012, Sealand has continued to be owned by his son Michael. After setting up a pirate radio station on the former naval fort of Roughs Tower, Bates declared it to be a sovereign nation in September 1967. For an entertaining, if biased, history of Sealand, see Michael Bates, *Principality of Sealand: Holding the Fort* (Sealand, 2015).

15 See Miéville, 'Floating Utopias', pp. 241–2. For up-to-date information on the Freedom Ship, see the project's website at http://freedomship.com. Other examples include The World, a permanent residency cruise liner operated by ResidenSea Inc., and the SeaCode venture, launched in 2005 in California to secure a cruise ship to house tech-based innovation. See Philip E. Steinberg, 'Liquid Urbanity: Re-engineering the City in a Post-terrestrial World', in *Engineering Earth: The Impact of Mega-engineering Projects*, ed. Stanley D. Brunn (London, 2011), pp. 2113–22.

16 O'Grady and Raisbeck, 'Prototype Cities', pp. 455–6. For up-to-date information on New Utopia, see the project's website at www.new-utopia.com.

17 For the design competition brief, see www.seasteading.org/architectural-design-contest, accessed 20 August 2018.

18 See www.seasteading.org/architectural-design-contest/artisanopolis, accessed 20 August 2018.

19 Miéville, 'Floating Utopias', p. 251.

20 Quoted in Kyle Denuccio, 'Silicon Valley is Letting Go of its Techie Island Fantasies', *Wired*, 16 May 2015, www.wired.com.

21 See Peter Linebaugh and Marcus Redicker's *The Many-headed Hydra: Sailors, Slaves, Commoners and the Hidden History of the Revolutionary Atlantic* (London, 2002).

22 See John Vidal, 'The World's Largest Cruise Ship and Its Supersized Pollution Problem', *The Guardian*, 21 May 2016, www.theguardian.com.

23 On the houseboats of Amsterdam, see Jowi Schmitz and Friso Spoelstra, *Boat People of Amsterdam* (Lemniscaat, 2013).

24 Lloyd Kropp, *The Drift* (London, 1969), p. 23.

25 Ibid., p. 113.

26 Ibid., p. 250.

27 Miéville referenced Kropp's novel in his article 'Floating Utopias'.

28 On the utopian politics of Miéville's Armada, see Christopher Kendrick, 'Monster Realism and Uneven Development in China Miéville's *The Scar*', *Extrapolations*, L/2 (2009), pp. 258–75; and Sherryl Vint, 'Possible Fictions: Blochian Hope in *The Scar*', *Extrapolations*, L/2 (2009), pp. 276–92.

29 China Miéville, *The Scar* (London, 2002), p. 100.

30 Ibid., pp. 95–6.

31 Ibid., pp. 96, 103.

32 *The Scar* was the second book in Miéville's Bas-Lag trilogy, the name of his invented world; the others were *Perdido Street Station* (2000) and *Iron Council* (2004), both set in New Crobuzon.

33 Miéville, *The Scar*, p. 101.

34 Ibid., p. 104.

35 On Hollein's photo-collages, see Liane Lefaivre, 'Everything Is Architecture: Multiple Hans Hollein and the Art of Crossing Over,' *Harvard Design Magazine*, 18 (2003), pp. 1–5. The Port of London Authority project was awarded a RIBA President's Medal in 2010; details of the project can be found at www.presidentsmedals.com.

36 On Lau's project, see Geoff Manaugh, 'Flooded London 2030', BLDGBLOG, 30 June 2010, www.bldgblog.com.

37 On the IJburg development, see Koen Olthuis and David Keuning, *Float! Building on Water to Combat Urban Congestion and Climate Change* (London, 2010), pp. 45–7; and Catherine Slessor, 'Floating Houses, the Netherlands, by Marlies Rohmer Architects and Planners', *Architectural Review*, 27 June 2013, www.architectural-review.com. On the relationship between the IJburg community and other floating structures, see Nick Foster, 'Architecture: Floating Home Designs That Rock The Boat', *Financial Times*, 21 February 2014, www.ft.com. As Foster demonstrates, precedents for the IJburg development include 484 floating dwellings in Richardson Bay, Sausalito, California, which has developed as a bohemian community since the 1960s.

38 On the Waterpod project during its period afloat, see Melena Ryzik, 'Life, Art and Chickens Afloat in the Harbor', *New York Times*, 13 August 2009, www.nytimes.com; and Christopher Turner, 'A Floating Island of Sustainability', *Nature*, 461 (21 September 2009), available at www.nature.com. A history of the Waterpod project by Mattingly can be found at www.thewaterpod.org.

39 See Mary Mattingly, 'A Floating World', *The Waterpod Project*, www.thewaterpod.org/concept.html, accessed 20 August 2018.

40 On the Flock House project, see the website of the artist at www.marymattingly.com.

41 See Mary Mattingly, 'WetLand Project', *Wet-land*, www.wet-land.org/home.html, accessed 20 August 2018.

42 Ibid.

43 Kathryn Yusoff and Jennifer Gabrys, 'Climate Change and the Imagination', *Wiley Interdisciplinary Reviews: Climate Change*, II/4 (2011), p. 524.

44 See Peter Anker, 'The Closed World of Ecological Architecture', *Journal of Architecture*, 10 (2005), pp. 527–52.

45 See Mattingly's history of the Waterpod project at www.thewaterpod.org.

46 Turner's residency on the Maunsell forts is documented in Stephen Turner, *Seafort* (Ramsgate, 2006).

47 On the Exbury Egg project, see www.exburyegg.org.

48 The online diaries can be viewed at www.seafort.org/blog/index.html (the Seafort project) and https://exburyegg.me/beadles-blog (the Exbury Egg).

49 On the history of the Maunsell seaforts, see Frank R. Turner, *The Maunsell Sea Forts: The World War Two Sea Forts of the Thames and Mersey Estuaries* (1995).

50 Turner, *Seafort*, p. 85.

51 Details on the work of Project Redsand can be found at www.project-redsand.com. I am grateful to the Project for organizing public visits to the Maunsell seaforts, one of which I joined on 29 May 2016.

52 Details of the proposal can be found at http://arosarchitects.com/project/redsand-forts.

3 Airborne: Architecture and the Dream of Flight

1 'Airlander 10: Maiden Flight at Last for Longest Aircraft', BBC *News*, 17 August 2016, www.bbc.co.uk/news. More details about the *Airlander 10* can be found at www.hybridairvehicles.com.

2 'Airlander 10: Longest Aircraft Damaged during Flight', BBC *News*, 24 August 2016, www.bbc.co.uk/news.

3 Steven Connor, *The Matter of Air: Science and the Art of the Ethereal* (London, 2010), p. 31.

4 A useful introduction to the history and evolution of climate science is Spencer R. Weart, *The Discovery of Global Warming* (Boston, MA, 2008).

5 Gaston Bachelard, *Air and Dreams: An Essay on the Imagination of Movement*, trans. Edith R. Farrell and C. Frederick Farrell [1943] (Dallas, TX, 1988), p. 33.

6 Ibid., p. 29.

7 Ibid., p. 21.

8 Luce Irigaray, *The Forgetting of Air in Martin Heidegger*, trans. Mary Beth Mader (Dallas, TX, 1999), p. 8. See also Mark Dorrian, 'Utopia on Ice: The Climate as Commodity Form', in *Architecture in the Anthropocene: Encounters among Design, Deep Time, Science and Philosophy*, ed. Etienne Turpin (Ann Arbor, MI, 2013), p. 149.

9 Steven Connor, 'Building Breathing Space', lecture presented at the Bartlett School of Architecture, University College London, 3 March 2004, available at www.stevenconnor.com.

10 Ibid.

11 See, for example, Arvind Krishan and Nick Baker, *Climate Responsive Architecture: A Design Handbook for Energy Efficient Buildings* (London, 1999).

12 See Amy Kulper and Diane Periton, 'Introduction: Explicating City Air', *Journal of Architecture*, XIX/2 (2014), p. 162.

13 See Dorrian, 'Utopia on Ice'.

14 On the British contexts, see Tom Crook, *Governing Systems: Modernity and the Making of Public Health in England, 1830–1910* (Los Angeles, CA, 2016); on the French, see Alain Corbin, *The Foul and the Fragrant: Odor and the French Social Imagination* (London, 1994).

15 See Peter Sloterdijk, *In the World Interior of Capital: Towards a Philosophical Theory of Globalization*, trans. Wieland Hoban (London, 2013).

16 See David Gissen, *Manhattan Atmospheres: Architecture, the Interior Environment, and Urban Crisis* (Minneapolis, MN, 2014).

17 On the significance of the aerial view in modernist urban planning, see Nathalie Roseau, 'The City Seen from the Aeroplane: Distorted Reflections and Urban Futures', in *Seeing from Above: The Aerial View in Visual Culture*, ed. Mark Dorrian and Frederic Pusin (London, 2013), pp. 210–26; and Anthony Vidler, 'Photourbanism: Planning the City from Above and from Below', in *A Companion to the City*, ed. Gary Bridge and Sophie Watson (Oxford, 2002), pp. 35–45.

18 On tower blocks and streets in the sky, see Joe Moran, 'Imagining the Street in Postwar Britain', *Urban History*, XXXIX/1 (2012), pp. 166–86.

19 A recent example being Matthew E. Kahn and Siqi Zheng, *Blue Skies over Beijing: Economic Growth and the Environment in China* (New York, 2016).

20 On Hong Kong's skywalks, see Stephen Graham, *Vertical: The City from Satellites to Bunkers* (London, 2016), pp. 233–6.

21 On the Cloud Citizen scheme, see Evan Rawn, '"Cloud Citizen" Awarded Joint Top Honors in Shenzhen Bay Super City Competition', *ArchDaily*, 21 September 2014, www.archdaily.com.

22 See Connor, *The Matter of Air*, p. 10.

23 Jonathan Swift, *Gulliver's Travels* [1726] (Richmond, VA, 2009), pp. 126, 128.

24 Ibid., p. 131.

25 Gulliver does indeed compare the Laputan way of thinking with 'most of the mathematicians he has met in Europe' (p. 132).

26 See James Blish, *Cities in Flight* [1955–62] (London, 2010). The intergalactic flying island of Manhattan provides the focus for the first book, *Earthman, Come Home* (1955).

27 See Dani Cavallaro, *The Anime Art of Hayao Miyazaki* (London, 2006), pp. 58–63.

28 See Luke Cuddy, ed., *BioShock and Philosophy: Irrational Game, Rational Book* (Chichester, 2015).

29 See the online video 'BIOSHOCK INFINITE: Ken Levine Discusses Columbia, Elizabeth, and Religion', www.youtube.com, posted 13 December 2012.

30 On Krutikov's flying city, see Selim Omarovich Khan-Magomedov, *Georgii Krutikov: The Flying City and Beyond*, trans. Christina Lodder (Barcelona, 2015).

31 See Mike Crang, 'Urban Morphology and the Shaping of the Transmissible City', *CITY*, XLIII/3 (2000), pp. 310–13.

32 Karsten Harries, 'Fantastic Architecture: Lessons of Laputa and the Unbearable Lightness of Our Architecture', *Journal of Aesthetics and Art Criticism*, LXIX/1 (2011), pp. 57, 60.

33 On the Multiplicity project see www.johnwardlearchitects.com.

34 'Clive Wilkinson Suggests "Carpet Bombing" London with a Co-working Office in the Sky', *Dezeen*, 16 December 2015, www.dezeen.com.

35 On the earliest hot-air balloons and their cultural reception, see Charles C. Gillespie, *The Montgolfier Brothers and the Invention of Aviation, 1783–1784* (Princeton, NJ, 1983).

36 The scheme was published by Robertson as *La Minerva, an Aerial Vessel Destined for Discoveries, and Proposed to All the Academies of Europe, by Robertson, Physicist* (Vienna, 1804; repr. Paris, 1820).

37 See Fulgence Marion, *Wonderful Balloon Ascents; or, The Conquest of the Skies: A History of Balloons and Balloon Voyages* (New York, 1870), p. 133.

38 See Alfred Robida, *The Twentieth Century*, trans. Philippe Willems
    (Middletown, CT, 2004). The other illustrated novels were *La Guerre
    au Vingtième Siècle* (War in the Twentieth Century), published in 1887;
    and *La Vie Électrique* (The Electric Life), published in 1890.

39 On the history of airships, see Daniel G. Ridley-Kitts, *Military, Naval
    and Civil Airships since 1783: The History and Development of the Dirigible
    Airship in Peace and War* (London, 2012).

40 Philippe Willems, 'A Stereoscopic Vision of the Future: Albert
    Robida's *Twentieth Century*', *Science Fiction Studies*, XXVI/3 (1999),
    p. 371.

41 Ibid., p. 357.

42 On the use of German Zeppelins in the First World War, see Douglas
    H. Robinson, *The Zeppelin in Combat: A History of the German Naval
    Airship Division, 1912–18* (London, 2004). On aerial bombing in the
    Second World War, see Kenneth Hewitt, 'Place Annihilation: Area
    Bombing and the Fate of Urban Places', *Annals of the Association
    of American Geographers*, LXXIII/2 (1983), pp. 257–84.

43 See Julien Nembrini et al., 'Mascarillons: Flying Swarm Intelligence
    for Architectural Research', *Proceedings of the Swarm Intelligence
    Symposium*, SIS 2005 (June 2015), pp. 225–32. The military applications
    of such technology are included in Ying Tan and Zhong-Yang Zhen,
    'Research Advance in Swarm Robotics', *Defence Technology*, IX/1 (2013),
    pp. 18–39.

44 Cynthia J. Miller, 'Airships East, Zeppelins West: Steampunk's
    Fantastic Frontiers', in *Steaming into the Victorian Future: A Steampunk
    Anthology*, ed. Julie Anne Taddeo and Cynthia J. Millers (London,
    2014), pp. 145–61. Other prominent examples of airships in Steampunk
    fictions include Joe R. Lansdale's novel *Zeppelins West* (2001) and
    Alan Moore and Kevin O'Neill's illustrated series *The League
    of Extraordinary Gentleman* (1999), adapted into a film in 1999.

45 China Miéville, *Perdido Street Station* (London, 2000), p. 77.

46 See Sean Topham, *Blowup: Inflatable Art, Architecture, and Design*
    (London, 2002), p. 21. Other histories of inflatable structures include
    Marc Dessauce, ed., *The Inflatable Moment: Pneumatics and Protest
    in '68* (New York, 1999); Jacobo Krauel, *Inflatable Art, Architecture
    and Design* (London, 2014); and William McLean and Pete Silver,
    Air Structures (Form + Technique) (London, 2015).

47 On Ant Farm's inflatable structures, see Constance M. Lewallen and
    Steve Seid, *Ant Farm, 1968–1978* (Los Angeles, CA, 2004), pp. 2, 13,
    15–19, 43; on Archigram's see Simon Sadler, *Archigram: Architecture
    without Architecture* (Cambridge, MA, 2005), pp. 113–14, 129, 171, 186;

on the Utopie Group and the 'Structures gonflables' exhibition, see
Dessauce, *The Inflatable Moment*.

48 See Dessauce, *The Inflatable Moment*, pp. 25, 80–96. The architectural
critic Reyner Banham reflected on the obsession with inflatables in
his article 'Monumental Wind-bags', *New Society*, xi/290 (1968),
pp. 569–70.

49 See Topham, *Blowup*, p. 72.

50 Archigram's Instant City project (*c.* 1968–70) – a mobile segment
of urban life carried by balloons and airships – already signified the
future direction of inflatable structures. On their use in popular music
concerts by the designer Mark Fisher, a former pupil of Archigram at
London's Architectural Association, see Eric Holding, *Mark Fisher:
Staged Architecture* (London, 1999).

51 On the design concept, see 'Ark Nova by Arata Isozaki and Anish
Kapoor', *Dezeen*, 23 September 2011, www.dezeen.com.

52 Mike Chino, 'High-flying Algae Airships are Self-sufficient Airborne
Cities', *Inhabitat*, 5 October 2010, http://inhabitat.com. See http://
vincent.callebaut.org for details of the scheme.

53 See Samuel Medina, 'A City in the Sky: An Urban Space that Floats
in the Clouds', *CityLab*, 18 November 2011, www.citylab.com. See
http://tiagobarros.pt/Passing-Cloud for details of the project.

54 See http://tiagobarros.pt/Passing-Cloud.

55 See Saraceno's statement at http://tomassaraceno.com/about.
Book-length studies of Saraceno's work include Meredith Malone,
ed., *Tomás Saraceno: Cloud-Specific* (Chicago, il, 2014); Juliane Von
Herz et al., *Tomás Saraceno: Cloud Cities/Air-Port-City* (Berlin, 2011);
and Sara Arrhenius and Helena Granström, *Tomás Saraceno: 14 Billions*
(Berlin, 2011).

56 The catalogue *Tomás Saraceno: Cloud Cities* (2011) was published on
the occasion of the exhibition 'Cloud Cities' at the Nationalgalerie
at Hamburger Bahnhof-Museum fur Gegenwart, Berlin, and the
installation *In Orbit* at Kunstsammlung Nordrhein-Westfalen,
Düsseldorf.

57 The 'Cloud City' exhibition ran from 15 May to 4 November 2012
at the Metropolitan Museum of Art, New York. See Roberta Smith,
'Climbing into the Future, or Just into an Artist's Whimsy: Tomás
Saraceno's "Cloud City," on the Met's Roof', *New York Times*,
25 May 2012, www.nytimes.com.

58 On the ongoing progress of *Museo Aero Solar* see the project's blog
at https://museoaerosolar.wordpress.com. See also Tomás Saraceno,
Sasha Engelmann and Bronislaw Szerszynski, 'Becoming Aerosolar:

From Solar Sculptures to Cloud Cities', in *Art in the Anthropocene: Encounters among Aesthetics, Politics, Environments and Epistemologies*, ed. Heather Davis and Etienne Turpin (London, 2015), pp. 57–62.

59 On the *Becoming Aerosolar* project, see http://tomassaraceno.com. See also Sasha Engelmann, Bronislaw Szerszynski and Derek McCormack, 'Becoming Aerosolar and the Politics of Elemental Association', in *Tomás Saraceno: Becoming Aerosolar* (Vienna, 2015), pp. 63–80.

60 See *Tomás Saraceno: Cloud Cities*, exh. cat., Hamburger Bahnhof (Berlin, 2011), for some of these drawings.

61 See the artist's website at www.aerocene.com.

62 Quoted in Moritz Wesseler, 'Cloud Cities', in *Tomás Saraceno: Cloud Cities*, p. 94.

63 Ant Farm published 2,000 copies of their *Inflatocookbook* in 1970, which included cut-out diagrams and technical information on how to make inflatable structures (available to download at http://alumni.media.mit.edu/~bcroy/inflato-splitpages-small.pdf, accessed 20 August 2018). Saraceno has continued this tradition with his Aerocene Explorer, 'a tethered-flight starter kit, which will enable anyone to personally launch their own Aerocene solar sculpture and explore the skies' (see www.aerocene.com).

64 Engelmann, Szerszynski and McCormack, 'Becoming Aerosolar', p. 71.

65 Bruno Latour, 'Some Experiments in Art and Politics', *e-flux*, XXIII/3 (2011), www.e-flux.com/journal.

66 On the 2009 Venice Biennale exhibit, see http://tomassaraceno.com.

67 'Latour', 'Some Experiments in Art and Politics', n.p.

68 See David Pinder, 'Cities: Moving, Plugging in, Floating, Dissolving', in *Geographies of Mobilities: Practices, Spaces, Subjects*, ed. Tim Cresswell and Peter Merriman (Farnham, 2011), pp. 182–3.

69 See Nigel Clark, 'Turbulent Prospects: Sustaining Urbanism on a Dynamic Planet', in *Urban Futures: Critical Commentaries on Shaping the City*, ed. Malcolm Miles and Tim Hall (London and New York, 2003), pp. 182–93.

4 Skyscraper: From Icons to Experience

1 On speculative architectural visions of vertical cities, see Stephen Graham, *Vertical: The City from Satellites to Bunkers* (London, 2016), pp. 223–6; on the same in science fiction novels, see Carl Abbott, *Imagining Urban Futures: Cities in Science Fiction and What We Might Learn from Them* (Middletown, CT, 2016), pp. 28–43; and in science

fiction films, see Donato Totaro, 'The Vertical Topography of the Science Fiction Film', *Off Screen*, xiv/8 (2010), http://offscreen.com.

2   Updates about the occupancy of the Shard can be found at the building's website, www.the-shard.com.

3   See www.the-shard.com.

4   On the increasing concentration of skyscrapers in China and the Middle East, see Leslie Sklair, *The Icon Project: Architecture, Cities and Capitalist Globalisation* (Oxford, 2016).

5   See the 'Skyscraper Center', part of the website of the Council on Tall Buildings and Urban Habitat, at www.skyscrapercenter.com/buildings.

6   See Graham, *Vertical*. See also Andrew Harris, 'Vertical Urbanisms: Opening Up Geographies of the Three-dimensional City', *Progress in Human Geography*, xxxix/5 (2016), pp. 601–20, and Stuart Elden, 'Secure the Volume: Vertical Geopolitics and the Depth of Power', *Political Geography*, 34 (2013), pp. 35–51.

7   See Graham, *Vertical*, p. ix, and Donald McNeill, 'Skyscraper Geography', *Progress in Human Geography*, xxix/1 (2001), p. 44.

8   See Paul Haacke, 'The Vertical Turn: Topographies of Metropolitan Modernism', PhD thesis, University of California, Berkeley, 2011, p. 189, available at escholarship.org.

9   See Paul Dobraszczyk, 'City Reading: The Design and Use of Nineteenth-century London Guidebooks', *Journal of Design History*, xxv/2 (2012), pp. 123–44.

10 The literature on the development of skyscraper construction is vast and riven with opposing opinions as to what constituted the first building of this type. A useful overview of this literature is provided in Thomas van Leeuwen, *The Skyward Trend of Thought: The Metaphysics of the American Skyscraper* (Cambridge, ma, 1988). Studies of more recent skyscraper architecture include Eric Höweler and William Pedersen, *Skyscraper: Designs of the Recent Past for the Near Future* (London, 2003); Scott Johnson, *Tall Building: Imagining the Skyscraper* (New York, 2008); and Adrian Smith and Judith Dupré, *Skyscrapers: A History of the World's Most Extraordinary Buildings* (London, 2013).

11 On the association of New York's early skyscrapers with Babylon, see Leeuwen, *The Skyward Trend of Thought*, pp. 11–13, 39–41; Darran Anderson, *Imaginary Cities* (London, 2015), pp. 125–32; and Katherine Schonfield and Julian Williams, 'Elevated Territories', in *City Levels*, ed. Ally Ireson and Nick Barley (Basel, 2000), pp. 29–30.

12 Quoted in Leeuwen, *The Skyward Trend of Thought*, p. 13.

13 Ibid.

14 Ibid., pp. 11–13, 33–4.

15 Hugh Ferriss, *The Metropolis of Tomorrow* (New York, 1929), p. 62.

16 McNeill, 'Skyscraper Geography', p. 45. On the complex symbolism
    of the Petronas Towers, see Tim Bunnell, 'From Above and Below:
    The Petronas Towers and/in Contesting Visions of Development in
    Contemporary Malaysia', *Singapore Journal of Tropical Geography*, xx/1
    (1999), pp. 1–23.

17 See Javier Quintana, 'Making the Future Real', in *eVolo: Skyscrapers of
    the Future*, vol. II, ed. Paul Aldridge, Noemi Deville, Anna Solt and Jung
    Su Lee (New York, 2010), p. 37.

18 See Witold Rybczynski, 'Dubai Debt: What the Burj Khalifa – the
    Tallest Building in the World – Owes to Frank Lloyd Wright', *Slate*,
    13 January 2010, www.slate.com.

19 See Howard Watson, *The Shard: The Vision of Irvine Sellar*
    (London, 2017).

20 Maria Kaika, 'Autistic Architecture: The Fall of the Icon and the Rise
    of the Serial Object', *Environment and Planning D: Society and Space*,
    29 (2011), p. 985.

21 Ibid., p. 986.

22 Ibid., p. 976.

23 On the mediatic skyscraper, see McNeill, 'Skyscraper Geography',
    p. 47. Höweler and Pedersen identify the mediatic skyscraper as
    a contemporary trend in *Skyscraper: Designs of the Recent Past for
    the Near Future*, pp. 158–75.

24 Max Page, *The City's End: Two Centuries of Fantasies, Fears, and
    Premonitions of New York's Destruction* (London and New York, 2008).
    On the destruction of 9/11 and its imagined precedents, particularly
    Wells's *The War in the Air*, see Mike Davis, 'The Flames of New York',
    in Davis, *Dead Cities and Other Tales* (New York, 2002), pp. 1–20.

25 On *The World Inside*, see Abbott, *Imagining Urban Futures*, pp. 37–40.

26 The literature on modernist mass-housing projects is enormous, the
    best introduction perhaps being Alison Ravetz, *Council Housing and
    Culture: The History of a Social Experiment* (London, 2001). The most
    important architectural studies are Florian Urban, *Tower and Slab:
    Histories of Global Mass Housing* (London, 2011), and, in Britain, Miles
    Glendinning, *Tower Block: Modern Public Housing in England, Scotland,
    Wales and Northern Ireland* (London and New Haven, CT, 1994).
    On the demolition of Pruitt-Igoe, see Chad Friedrichs's 2012 film
    The Pruitt-Igoe Myth.

27 Graham, *Vertical*, p. 184.

28 On *High-Rise* as social critique, see Lucy Hewitt and Stephen Graham,
    'Vertical Cities: Representations of Urban Verticality in Twentieth-

century Science Fiction Literature', *Urban Studies*, LII/5 (2015), pp. 928–32.

29 Alastair Reynolds, *Terminal World* (London, 2011), p. 86.

30 Ibid., pp. 190, 297.

31 On seeing London from above in the nineteenth century, see Lynda Nead, *Victorian Babylon: People, Streets and Images in Nineteenth-century London* (London, 2000), pp. 21–6. On the panorama, see Stephan Oettermann, *The Panorama: History of a Mass Medium* (New York, 1997).

32 See Isabelle Fraser, 'What London's Future Skyline Will Look Like – All 436 Skyscrapers', *The Telegraph*, 9 March 2016, www.telegraph.co.uk.

33 See Michel de Certeau, 'Walking in the City', in *The Practice of Everyday Life*, trans. Steven Rendall (Los Angeles, CA, 1984), pp. 91–110. De Certeau uses the experience of the viewing platform of the former World Trade Center to frame his argument (p. 91).

34 Katherine Schonfield and Julian Williams, 'Elevated Territories', in *City Levels*, ed. Ireson and Barley, p. 43.

35 On early images of multi-level cities, see Graham, *Vertical*, pp. 220–26.

36 On urban futurism and early science fiction cinema, see James Chapman and Nicholas J. Cull, *Projecting Tomorrow: Science Fiction and Popular Culture* (London, 2013), pp. 13–42.

37 On elevated urban transportation systems, see Graham, *Vertical*, pp. 224–39; on pedestrian skybridges, see Antony Wood, 'Pavements in the Sky: The Skybridge in Tall Buildings', *arq: Architectural Research Quarterly*, VII/3–4 (2003), pp. 325–32.

38 On King and Wong's concept, see Kenneth King and Kellogg Wong, *Vertical City: A Solution for Sustainable Living* (n.p., 2015).

39 See Robert Gifford, 'The Consequences of Living in High-rise Buildings', *Architectural Science Review*, L/1 (2007), pp. 1–16.

40 See Mike Davis, *City of Quartz: Excavating the Future in Los Angeles* (London, 1990), p. 368.

41 See Will Self, 'Isenshard', in *The Future of the Skyscraper*, ed. Phillip Nobel (New York, 2015), pp. 71–2.

42 See, for example, 'Shanghai Tower Climb – in Pictures', *The Guardian*, 13 February 2014, which documents the 650-m (2,133-ft) ascent of the Shanghai Tower by Russian urban explorers Vadim Makhorov and Vitaliy Raskalov.

43 Bradley Garrett, *Explore Everything: Place-hacking the City* (London, 2013), pp. 80–91. See also Bradley Garrett, Alexander Moss and Scott Cadman, *London Rising: Illicit Photos from the City's Heights* (London, 2016).

44 See Theo Kindynis, 'Urban Exploration: From Subterranea to Spectacle', *British Journal of Criminology*, LVII/4 (2017), pp. 982–1001.

45 On Florian's Vertical City, see www.moma.org.

46 K. W. Jeter, *Farewell Horizontal* (London, 1989), p. 95.

47 See Clare Sponsler, 'Beyond the Ruins: The Geopolitics of Urban Decay and Cybernetic Play', *Science Fiction Studies*, XX/2 (1993), pp. 257–9.

48 Ibid., p. 253.

49 See Helen Roxburgh, 'Inside Shanghai Tower: China's Tallest Skyscraper Claims to Be the World's Greenest', *The Guardian*, 23 August 2016, www.theguardian.com.

50 Graham, *Vertical*, pp. 369–81.

51 On 'vanity' space in skyscrapers, see Sophie Warnes, 'Vanity Height: How Much Space in Skyscrapers Is Unoccupiable?', *The Guardian*, 3 February 2017, www.theguardian.com.

52 See Jean-Marie Huriot, 'Towers of Power', *Metropolitiques*, 25 January 2012, www.metropolitiques.eu. See also Lloyd Alter, 'It's Time to Dump the Tired Argument that Density and Height are Green and Sustainable', *Treehugger*, 3 January 2014, www.treehugger.com.

53 See Leeuwen, *The Skyward Trend of Thought*, pp. 79–143.

54 The most strident articulation of the relationship between architectural modernism, the skyscraper and nature remains Le Corbusier, *The City of Tomorrow and Its Planning* [1927] (New York, 1987), especially p. 280.

55 Yeang's publications include *Designing with Nature: The Ecological Basis for Architectural Design* (London, 1995); *The Green Skyscraper: The Basis for Designing Sustainable Intensive Buildings* (London, 1999); *Reinventing the Skyscraper: A Vertical Theory of Urban Design* (London, 2002); and *Ecodesign: A Manual for Ecological Design* (London, 2008).

56 On the Roof-Roof House, see Robert Powell, *Rethinking the Skyscraper: The Complete Architecture of Ken Yeang* (London, 1999), pp. 115–21; and Sara Hart, *Eco-Architecture: The Work of Ken Yeang* (London, 2011), pp. 26–37.

57 On Menara Mesiniaga, see Powell, *Rethinking the Skyscraper*, pp. 41–8; and Hart, *Eco-Architecture*, pp. 56–68.

58 On Boeri's vertical forest designs, see the website of the architect at www.stefanoboeriarchitetti.net.

59 Ibid.

60 See the website of the magazine at www.evolo.us for more information about the annual competitions.

61 Mathias Henning, 'Skyscraper Competitions', in *eVolo*, ed. Aldridge
    et al., p. 99.
62 For example, Eric Vergne's Vertical Farm skyscraper, in *eVolo*,
    ed. Aldridge et al., pp. 106–9.
63 For example, the 2009 winning entry, Kyu Ho Chun, Kenta Fukunishi
    and JaeYoung Lee's Neo Arc project, in *eVolo*, ed. Aldridge et al.,
    pp. 100–102.
64 For example, Daniel Widrid's Adaptive Tower System project, in
    Aldridge et al., eds, *eVolo*, pp. 183–5.
65 See Aldridge et al., eds, *eVolo*, pp. 181–2.
66 Ibid., pp. 186–7.
67 Ibid., pp. 145–7.
68 Ibid., pp. 171–2.
69 Graham, *Vertical*, p. 128.
70 See Aldridge et al., eds, *eVolo*, pp. 123–5.
71 On the BIQ House, see 'BIQ: Smart Material Houses', at
    www.iba-hamburg.de/en/nc/projects, accessed 20 August 2018.

5 Underground: Security and Revolution

1 Edward Bulwer-Lytton, *The Coming Race* [1871] (Santa Barbara, CA,
   1979), pp. 2–3.
2 See David Pike, *Subterranean Cities: The World beneath Paris and
   London, 1800–1945* (Ithaca, NY, 2005), p. 77.
3 Quoted in Anon., *The Brunels' Tunnel* (London, 2006), p. 11.
4 See Christopher Beanland, 'Meet the Men Transforming London
   Underground's Derelict Stations', *The Independent*, 24 September 2014,
   www.independent.co.uk.
5 See Eric Larson, 'Underground Cities: The Next Frontier Might
   be Underneath Your Feet', *Mashable*, 21 February 2014,
   http://mashable.com.
6 See Ye Ming, 'A Million People Live in These Underground
   Nuclear Bunkers', *National Geographic*, 16 February 2017, www.
   nationalgeographic.com.
7 See Paul Dobraszczyk, Carlos López Galviz and Bradley L. Garrett,
   eds, *Global Undergrounds: Exploring Cities Within* (London, 2016).
8 On 3D mapping, see Gavin Bridge, 'Territory, Now in 3D!', *Political
   Geography*, 34 (2013), pp. 55–7.
9 On Fourier's utopian communities and arcades, see Walter Benjamin,
   The Arcades Project, trans. Howard Eiland and Kevin McLaughlin
   (Cambridge, MA, 1999), p. 5; On Paxton's 'Great Victorian Way'

project from 1855, see Parliamentary Papers 1854–5 (415),
Report from the Select Committee on Metropolitan Communications,
23 July 1855. On the development of arcades, see Johann
F. Geist, *Arcades: The History of a Building Type* (Cambridge,
MA, 1985).

10 On iron-and-glass buildings in the nineteenth century, particularly
greenhouses and exhibition buildings, see Georg Kholmaier and
Barna von Sartory, *Houses of Glass: A Nineteenth-century Building
Type* (Cambridge, MA, 1991).

11 On visitors' responses to the Crystal Palace, see Isobel Armstrong,
Victorian Glassworlds: Glass Culture and the Imagination, 1830–1880
(Oxford, 2008), pp. 142–52.

12 *Household Words*, 3 May 1851, p. 122.

13 Quoted in Sigfried Giedion, *Space, Time and Architecture: The Growth
of a New Tradition* (Cambridge, MA, 1967), pp. 253–4.

14 See Lewis Mumford, *Technics and Civilisation* (San Diego, CA, 1934),
pp. 69–70.

15 See Robert Poole, *Earthrise: How Man First Saw the Earth* (London
and New Haven, CT, 2010).

16 On the emerging environmental consciousness and its political
effects, see Otis L. Graham, *Environmental Politics and Policy,
1960s–1990s* (Philadelphia, PA, 2000).

17 Douglas Murphy, *Last Futures: Nature, Technology and the End
of Architecture* (London, 2016), p. 3.

18 On Fuller's geodesic domes, see Martin Pawley, *Buckminster Fuller*
(London, 1990), p. 16. On the 1967 Montreal Biosphere, see David
Langdon, 'AD Classics: Montreal Biosphere/Buckminster Fuller',
Archdaily, 25 November 2014, www.archdaily.com.

19 On the work of Otto, see Winifried Nerdinger, *Frei Otto, Complete
Works: Lightweight Construction* (Basel, 2005). On the 1967 German
Pavilion, see David Langdon, 'AD Classics: German Pavilion,
Expo '67 / Frei Otto and Rolf Gutbrod', *Archdaily*, 27 April 2015,
www.archdaily.com.

20 See Murphy, *Last Futures*, pp. 120–21. On Drop City, see Mark
Matthews, *Droppers: America's First Hippie Commune, Drop City*
(Oklahoma City, OK, 2010), and John Curl's memoir *Memories of Drop
City: The First Hippie Commune of the 1960s and the Summer of Love*
(Lincoln, NE, 2007).

21 Murphy, *Last Futures*, p. 120.

22 Gaston Bachelard, *The Poetics of Space*, trans. Maria Jolas (Boston, MA,
1994), pp. 258–9.

23 See Alan Prendergast, 'Drop City, America's Boldest, Most Far-out
    Commune, Left a Surprising Legacy', *Westword*, 27 May 2015,
    www.westword.com.

24 On *Logan's Run*, see Murphy, *Last Futures*, p. 196; Donato Totaro,
    'The Vertical Topography of the Science Fiction Film', *Screen*, XIV/8
    (2010), available at http://offscreen.com; and James Chapman and
    Nicholas J. Cull, *Projecting Tomorrow: Science Fiction and Popular
    Culture* (London, 2013), pp. 147–58.

25 E. M. Forster, 'The Machine Stops' (1909), in *Collected Short Stories*
    (London, 1989), pp. 109–46. See also Carl Abbott, *Imagining Urban
    Futures: Cities in Science Fiction and What We Might Learn from Them*
    (Middletown, CT, 2016), p. 103.

26 Arthur C. Clarke, *The City and the Stars* [1956] (London, 2001).
    See also Abbott, *Imagining Urban Futures*, pp. 106–8.

27 Isaac Asimov, *The Caves of Steel* [1953] (London, 1997), p. 23.

28 See Abbott, *Imagining Urban Futures*, p. 104.

29 See Mark Dorrian, 'Utopia on Ice: The Climate as Commodity
    Form', in *Architecture in the Anthropocene: Encounters among Design,
    Deep Time, Science and Philosophy*, ed. Etienne Turpin (Ann Arbor,
    MI, 2013), p. 148.

30 Richard Buckminster Fuller, *Utopia or Oblivion: The Prospects for
    Humanity* [1969] (London, 1973), p. 353.

31 Frederick Pohl, *The Years of the City* (New York, 1984).

32 See Murphy, *Last Futures*, pp. 185–95. On the intricacies of the
    project, see Rebecca Reider, *Dreaming the Biosphere: The Theater
    of All Possibilities* (Santa Fe, NM, 2010).

33 Murphy, *Last Futures*, p. 194.

34 On the designs for Google's new headquarters, see Ricard Nieva,
    'Google Unveils Plans for Futuristic New Headquarters', CNET,
    27 February 2015, www.cnet.com/uk/news.

35 Murphy, *Last Futures*, p. 221.

36 On the Sunny Mountain Ski Dome, see Dorrian, 'Utopia on Ice'.
    On the domed shopping mall, see Brian Merchant, 'Dubai's Climate-
    controlled City is a Dystopia Waiting to Happen', *Motherboard*,
    9 July 2014, https://motherboard.vice.com.

37 Merchant, 'Dubai's Climate-controlled City'.

38 As seen in Peter Sloterdijk's trilogy of books *Sphären* (Spheres),
    published in German from 1998 to 2004 by Suhrkamp Verlag KG, and
    translated into English from 2011 to 2016.

39 Rosalind Williams, *Notes on the Underground: An Essay on Technology,
    Society, and the Imagination* (Cambridge, MA, 2008), p. 212.

40 See 'Sietch Nevada', Matsys Design, 2009, http://matsysdesign.com.

41 Luke Bennett, 'The Bunker Metaphor, Materiality and Management',
    Culture and Organization, xvii/2 (2011), pp. 155–73. See also Luke
    Bennett, ed., *In the Ruins of the Cold War Bunker: Affect, Materiality
    and Meaning-making* (London, 2017).

42 On Cappadocia's underground structures, see Ömer Ayden and Reşat
    Ulusay, 'Geotechnical and Geoenvironmental Characteristics of
    Man-made Underground Spaces in Cappadocia, Turkey', *Engineering
    Geology*, xc/3 (2003), pp. 245–72.

43 See Paul Virilio, *Bunker Archaeology* [1967] (Princeton, NJ, 1994).

44 On Cold War nuclear bunkers in cities across the world, see
    Dobraszczyk, Galviz and Garrett, eds, *Global Undergrounds,*
    pp. 117–19 (Prague), 121–3 (Stockholm), 124–6 (Shanghai), 159–61
    (Kinmen and Matsu); on the USA, see Tom Vanderbilt, *Survival City:
    Adventures among the Atomic Ruins of America* (Chicago, IL, 2010).
    On the Beijing Cold War shelters, see Ming, 'A Million People'.

45 For a description of Newman's scheme, see Alison Sky and Michelle
    Stone, *Unbuilt America* (New York, 1976), p. 192.

46 See M. Gane, 'Paul Virilio's Bunker Theorising', *Theory, Culture
    and Society*, 16 (1999), p. 90.

47 Mordecai Roshwald, *Level 7* (New York, 1959), p. 111.

48 Hugh Howey, *Wool* (London, 2013), p. 131.

49 On *City of Ember*, see Abbott, *Imagining Urban Futures*, pp. 97–9.

50 Ibid., pp. 111–12.

51 Harlan Ellison, *A Boy and His Dog* (New York, 1969), p. 234.

52 '"Depthscrapers" Defy Earthquakes', *Everyday Science and Mechanics*,
    November 1931, pp. 646, 708.

53 See Ivor Richards, *Groundscrapers and Depthscrapers of Hamza and
    Yeang* (London, 2001).

54 See 'Plans for Futuristic Underground "Skyscraper" beneath Mexico
    City's Zócalo', *Once and Future Mexico*, 26 November 2011, https://
    onceandfuturemexico.wordpress.com.

55 See Jess Zimmerman, 'Can We Turn Mining Pits into Underground
    Cities?', *Grist*, 19 October 2011, http://grist.org.

56 Angus Carlyle, 'Beneath Ground', in *City Levels*, ed. Ally Ireson
    and Nick Barley (Basel, 2000), pp. 100–101.

57 See Eric Nakajima, 'Liquefactower: The Sinking City/Honorable
    Mention, 2014 Skyscraper Competition', *eVolo*, www.evolo.us.

58 See Pike, *Subterranean Cities*, pp. 107–29; and also 'As above, so below:
    Paris Catacombs', in *Global Undergrounds*, ed. Dobraszczyk, Galviz
    and Garrett, pp. 197–9.

59 On the history and development of the *carrières*, see Caroline Archer and Alexandre Parre, *Paris Underground* (New York, 2005).

60 See Pike, *Subterranean Cities*, pp. 107–29.

61 Victor Hugo, *Les Misérables*, trans. Norman Denny [1862] (London, 1988), p. 619.

62 On the Situationist International, see McKenzie Wark, *The Beach beneath the Street: The Everyday Life and Glorious Times of the Situationist International* (London, 2015).

63 Pike, *Subterranean Cities*, p. 188. Luc Besson's later film *Subway* (1985) also charts the lives of a group of misfits living in spaces beneath Paris.

64 On the vertical structure of future London in *The Sleeper Awakes*, see Lucy Hewitt and Stephen Graham, 'Vertical Cities: Representations of Urban Verticality in Twentieth-century Science Fiction Literature', *Urban Studies*, LII/5 (2015), pp. 927–9, and Stephen Graham, 'Vertical Noir: Histories of the Future in Urban Science Fiction', *CITY*, XX/3 (2016), pp. 384–5.

65 See Gaiman's introduction to *Neverwhere* [1996] (London, 2005).

66 Henry Mayhew's reports on London's underclasses were first published as articles in the newspaper *The Morning Chronicle* in 1848–9, and then published in book form in 1851 as *London Labour and the London Poor*.

67 Gaiman, *Neverwhere*, pp. 371–2.

68 Bradley Garrett, *Explore Everything: Place-hacking the City* (London, 2013), p. 121.

69 See Dhan Zunino Singh, 'Under Kingdom: The Layers of Mexico City', in *Global Undergrounds*, ed. Dobraszczyk, Galviz and Garrett, pp. 37–9.

70 See www.bresciaunderground.com/english. On the work of Brescia Underground see Caroline Bâcle, 'Buried Waterways: Brescia Underground', in *Global Undergrounds*, ed. Dobraszczyk, Galviz and Garrett, pp. 223–7, and the film *Lost Rivers* (dir. Caroline Bâcle, 2012).

71 See Caroline Bâcle, 'Reverse Modernization: Saw Mill River, New York City', in *Global Undergrounds*, ed. Dobraszczyk, Galviz and Garrett, pp. 167–9.

72 See Alex Scapens, 'Historic Stockport Bridge Set to Be Revealed for the First Time in 78 Years', *Manchester Evening News*, 5 February 2015, www.manchestereveningnews.co.uk.

73 See Paul Dobraszczyk, 'Absurd Space: Williamson Tunnels, Liverpool', in *Global Undergrounds*, ed. Dobraszczyk, Galviz and Garrett, pp. 41–3. On the history of the tunnels and their role as a tourist attraction, see the website of the Williamson Tunnels Heritage

Centre, www.williamsontunnels.co.uk, and the Friends of
Williamson Tunnels, www.williamsontunnels.com. Williamson's
life has been dramatized in David Clensy's book *The Mole of Edge
Hill* (Liverpool, 2006).
74 Carlyle, 'Beneath Ground', p. 113.

6 Ruined: Sprawl, Disaster, Entropy

1 'Urbicide' was a term first coined by urban theorist Marshall Berman
in 'Falling Towers: City Life after Urbicide', in D. Crow, ed., *Geography
and Identity: Exploring and Living Geopolitics of Identity* (Washington,
DC, 1996), pp. 172–92.
2 Examples of apocalyptic destruction in post-9/11 cinema are legion
and in 2016 alone included *Pandemic*, *The Girl with All the Gifts*, *The
5th Wave*, *The Worthy* and *Resident Evil: The Final Chapter*. Examples
of post-apocalyptic computer games include *The Last of Us* (2013–)
and the *Fallout* series (1997–). On the *Ruin Lust* exhibition, see Brian
Dillon, *Ruin Lust: Artists' Fascination with Ruins, from Turner to the
Present Day* (London, 2014).
3 See Stephen Cairns and Jane Jacobs, *Buildings Must Die: A Perverse
View of Architecture* (Cambridge, MA, 2014), pp. 1–2.
4 Rebecca Solnit, 'The Ruins Memory' (2006), in *Storming the Gates
of Paradise: Landscape for Politics* (Berkeley, CA, 2007), p. 352.
5 On the history of urban sprawl, see Robert Bruegmann, *Sprawl:
A Compact History* (Chicago, IL, 2005), and David C. Soule, *Urban
Sprawl: A Comprehensive Reference Guide* (Westport, CT, 2005).
6 See Eric Hilare and Nick Van Mead, 'The Great Leap Upward:
China's Pearl River Delta, Then and Now', *The Guardian*, 10 May 2016,
www.theguardian.com.
7 On Kiesler's work, see Stephen J. Phillips, *Elastic Architecture:
Frederick Kiesler and Design Research in the First Age of Robotic Culture*
(Cambridge, MA, 2017).
8 On New Babylon, see Trudy Nieuwenhuys, Laura Stamps, Willemijn
Stokvis and Mark Wigley, *Constant: New Babylon* (Berlin, 2016)
9 William Gibson, *Neuromancer* [1984] (London, 1995), pp. 62, 90–91.
10 On Mega-City One, see Abbott, *Imagining Urban Futures*, p. 63, and
Darran Anderson, *Imaginary Cities* (London, 2015), pp. 82–3.
11 See Andrzej Gasiorek, *J. G. Ballard* (Manchester, 2005), pp. 101–3.
Other notable writings by Ballard about future urban life include
the short stories 'The Overloaded Man' (1961), 'Billennium' (1961),
'The Subliminal Man' (1963) and 'The Ultimate City' (1976), as well

as the novels *The Drowned World* (1962), *The Burning World* (1964), *High-Rise* (1975) and *Hello America* (1981).

12   J. G. Ballard, 'The Concentration City' (1957), in *The Complete Short Stories of J. G. Ballard* (London and New York, 2010), p. 23. See also Gasiorek, *J. G. Ballard*, pp. 101–3, and Abbott, *Imagining Urban Futures*, p. 153.

13   Ballard, 'The Concentration City', pp. 27–8.

14   Clare Sponsler, 'Beyond the Ruins: The Geopolitics of Urban Decay and Cybernetic Play', *Science Fiction Studies*, xx/2 (1993), p. 262.

15   See Tsutomu Nihei, *Blame! Master Edition* (New York, 2016). The graphic novel was originally published in Japan by Kodansha as a ten-volume edition from 1998 to 2003.

16   On Kowloon Walled City, see Ian Lambot and Greg Girard, *City of Darkness: Life in Kowloon Walled City* (London, 1993).

17   See Robert Harbison, *Ruins and Fragments: Tales of Loss and Rediscovery* (London, 2015).

18   On the work of Piranesi, see Luigi Ficacci, ed., *Piranesi: The Complete Etchings* (London, 2016).

19   On Piranesi's influence on Soane, see John Wilton-Ely and Helen Dorey, eds, *Piranesi, Paestum and Soane* (London, 2013).

20   On the Astley Castle project, see Amy Frearson, 'Astley Castle Renovation wins RIBA Stirling Prize 2013', *Dezeen*, 26 September 2013, www.dezeen.com; on the dovecote project, see Chris Barnes, 'The Dovecote Studio by Haworth Tompkins', *Dezeen*, 14 February 2010, www.dezeen.com.

21   See Karen Cliento, 'Kolumba Museum', *Archdaily*, 6 August 2010, www.archdaily.com.

22   On the development of aerial warfare and its impact on cities, see Kenneth Hewitt, 'Place Annihilation: Area Bombing and the Fate of Urban Places', *Annals of the Association of American Geographers*, LXXIII/2 (1983), pp. 257–84.

23   On the Chinese tradition of contemplating ruined cities, see Wu Hung, *A Story of Ruins: Presence and Absence in Chinese Art and Visual Culture* (London, 2012), pp. 18–19.

24   See Alexander Regier, 'Foundational Ruins: The Lisbon Earthquake and the Sublime', in *Ruins of Modernity*, ed. Julia Hell and Andreas Schonle (Durham, NC, and London, 2010), pp. 357–74.

25   On the British context, see David Skilton, 'Contemplating the Ruins of London: Macaulay's New Zealander and Others', *Literary London Journal: Interdisciplinary Studies in the Representation of London*, II/1 (2004); on the American context, see Nick Yablon, *Untimely Ruins:*

An Archaeology of American Urban Modernity (Chicago, IL, 2009), pp. 147–52.

26 On the emergence of the 'hero' trope in post-apocalyptic cinema, see Mick Broderick, 'Surviving Armageddon: Beyond the Imagination of Disaster', *Science Fiction Studies*, XX/3 (1993), pp. 362–82.

27 On Coventry Cathedral, see Louise Campbell, *Coventry Cathedral: Art and Architecture in Post-war Britain* (Oxford, 1996); on the Kaiser Wilhelm Memorial Church and other war ruins in Germany, see Rudy Koshar, *From Monuments to Traces: Artifacts of German Memory, 1870–1990* (Los Angeles, CA, 2000).

28 The full range of paintings in the *Portents* series can be viewed at the artist's website at http://michaelkerbow.com.

29 Solnit, 'The Ruins Memory', p. 351.

30 See Gill Perry et al., *Deanna Petherbridge: Drawings and Dialogue* (London, 2016). The catalogue was published on the occasion of a major exhibition of Petherbridge's works at the Whitworth Art Gallery, Manchester, 2 December 2016–4 June 2017.

31 Deanna Petherbridge, 'The Impossibility of Landscape', in Perry et al., *Deanna Petherbridge*, p. 101.

32 Cited in Martin Clayton, 'Petherbridge and the Art of the Past', in Perry et al., *Deanne Petherbridge*, p. 67.

33 On artists' engagement with ruins in Detroit, see Paul Dobraszczyk, *The Dead City: Urban Ruins and the Spectacle of Decay* (London, 2017), pp. 149–88; Dora Apel, *Beautiful Terrible Ruins: Detroit and the Anxiety of Decline* (New Brunswick, NJ, 2015), pp. 101–12; Michel Arnaud, *Detroit: The Dream Is Now* (Detroit, MI, 2017); and Julie Pincus and Nichole Christian, *Canvas Detroit* (Detroit, MI, 2014).

34 The most compelling account of the decline of Detroit is Thomas Sugrue's *The Origins of the Urban Crisis: Race and Inequality in Postwar Detroit* (New York, 1996).

35 On the history of the Heidelberg Project, see www.heidelberg.org.

36 On Hocking's work, see the website of the artist at http://scotthocking. com; a special issue of the journal *Detroit Research*, 1 (2014); and Dobraszczyk, *The Dead City*, pp. 180–83.

37 See, for example, Apel, *Beautiful Terrible Ruins*, p. 106.

38 Sigmund Freud, *Civilization and Its Discontents* [1930], trans. David McLintock (London, 2002), p. 9.

39 See Dillon, 'Introduction', *Ruin Lust*, p. 14.

40 The article, which also included Smithson's photographs, was originally published as 'The Monuments of Passaic', *Artforum* (December 1967), pp. 52–7.

41 See Dobraszczyk, *The Dead City*, pp. 189–213, for an investigation
    of new ruins in Spain, Britain and Italy.

42 Philip K. Dick, *Do Androids Dream of Electric Sheep?* [1968] (London,
    1972), p. 20.

43 See Anirban Kapil Baishya, 'Trauma, Post-apocalyptic Science Fiction
    and the Post-human', *Wide Screen*, III/1 (2011), pp. 1–25.

44 See Abbott, *Imagining Urban Futures*, pp. 121–2.

45 See Gasiorek, *J. G. Ballard*, p. 129.

46 J. G. Ballard, 'The Ultimate City' (1978), in Ballard, *The Complete Short
    Stories*, p. 915.

47 See Gasiorek, *J. G. Ballard*, p. 133.

48 Graeme Wearden, 'More Plastic Than Fish in the Sea by 2050, Says
    Ellen MacArthur', *The Guardian*, 19 January 2016, www.theguardian.
    com.

49 See James Lovelock, 'Gaia as Seen through the Atmosphere',
    Atmospheric Environment, 6 (1972), pp. 579–80.

50 On the television programmes, see Mark S. Jendrysik, 'Back to the
    Garden: New Visions of Posthuman Futures', *Utopian Studies*, XXII/1
    (2011), pp. 34–51. On *Life after People*, see Christine Cornea, 'Post-
    apocalyptic Narrative and Environmental Documentary: The Case
    of "Life after People"', in *Dramatising Disaster: Character, Event,
    Representation*, ed. Christine Cornea and Rhys Owain Thomas
    (Cambridge, 2013), pp. 151–66.

51 On ruined London and nature in *The Day of the Triffids*, see
    Dobraszczyk, *The Dead City*, pp. 29–32.

7 Remade: Salvaging What Remains

1 See 'Theaster Gates: Sanctum/2015, Situations', www.situations.org.
   uk.

2 See Mark Brown, 'U.S. Artist Theaster Gates to help Bristol Hear
   Itself in First UK Public Project', *The Guardian*, 20 July 2015, www.
   theguardian.com.

3 On Gates's wider work, see Carol Becker and Achim Borchardt-Hume,
   Theaster Gates (London, 2015).

4 See, for example, Stephen Graham, *Cities Under Siege: The New Military
   Urbanism* (London, 2011).

5 Evan Calder Williams, *Combined and Uneven Apocalypse*
   (Winchester, 2011), p. 41.

6 John Berger, 'Rumor', preface to Latife Tekin, *Berji Kristin:
   Tales from the Garbage Hills* (London, 2014), p. 8.

7 See, for example, Sharon Zukin's classic account of the early regeneration of areas of New York City in *Loft Living: Culture and Capital in Urban Change* (New York, 1989).

8 See, for example, Sharon Zukin, *Naked City: The Death and Life of Authentic Urban Places* (Oxford, 2011).

9 Calder Williams, *Combined and Uneven Apocalypse*, p. 42.

10 Ibid., p. 15.

11 Lebbeus Woods, *War and Architecture* (New York, 1993).

12 See Lebbeus Woods, 'Radical Reconstruction', in Woods, *Radical Reconstruction* (New York, 2004), p. 21.

13 Ibid.

14 On the work of Gibson, see Dani Cavallaro, *Cyberpunk and Cyberculture: Science Fiction and the Work of William Gibson* (New Brunswick, NJ, 2000).

15 William Gibson, *Virtual Light* [1993] (London, 1994), p. 58.

16 See Carl Abbott, *Imagining Urban Futures: Cities in Science Fiction and What We Might Learn from Them* (Middletown, CT, 2016), pp. 217–20, and Michael Beehler, 'Architecture and the Virtual West in William Gibson's San Francisco', in *Postwestern Cultures: Literature, Theory, Space*, ed. Susan Kollin (2007), pp. 82–95.

17 Gibson, *Virtual Light*, p. 163.

18 See Amy Frearson, 'Megalomania by Jonathan Gales', *Dezeen*, 7 March 2012, www.dezeen.com.

19 On architectural incompletion as ruins, see Paul Dobraszczyk, *The Dead City: Urban Ruins and the Spectacle of Decay* (London, 2017), pp. 189–213.

20 On the Occupy Movement, see Noam Chomsky, *Occupy* (London, 2012); and David Harvey, *Rebel Cities: From the Right to the City to the Urban Revolution* (London, 2013).

21 On Occupy New York and architecture, see Reinhold Martin, 'Occupy: What Architecture Can Do', *Places Journal* (November 2011), https://doi.org/10.22269/111107.

22 On architecture and the Umbrella Movement, see Anthony Ko, 'Subverting Everyday: The Umbrella Movement of Hong Kong', unpublished essay, Bartlett School of Architecture, UCL, 2016. See also Jason Y. Ng, *Umbrellas in Bloom: Hong Kong's Occupy Movement* (London, 2016), and Francis L. F. Lee, *Media, Mobilization and the Umbrella Movement* (London, 2016).

23 Sources on informal cities are numerous, but two fine overviews of their global prevalence can be found in Mike Davis, *Planet*

of Slums (London, 2006), and Robert Neuwirth, *Shadow Cities: A Billion Squatters, a New Urban World* (London, 2004).

24 Davis, *Planet of Slums*, p. 19.

25 See John Turner, *Housing by People* (London, 1976); Robert Fichter, ed., *Freedom to Build: Dweller Control of the Housing Process* (New York, 1972), and Justin McGuirk, *Radical Cities: Across Latin America in Search of a New Architecture* (London, 2015).

26 McGuirk, *Radical Cities*, p. 25.

27 Ibid., p. 26.

28 Graves and Madoc-Jones's image can be found at www.london-futures. com/2010/10/18/hello-world, accessed 21 August 2018. The series of digital images were presented as large-scale back-lit transparencies in the exhibition *Postcards from the Future* at the Museum of London, October 2010–March 2011.

29 On this orientalizing tendency in the *Postcards from the Future* series, see Andrew Baldwin, 'Premediation and White Affect: Climate Change and Migration in Cultural Perspective', *Transactions of the Institute of British Geographers*, XLI/1 (2015), pp. 78–90.

30 On the photographic series, see the artist's website, www.noahaddis. com. See also Alessandro Imbriaco, Noah Addis and Aaron Rothman, 'Makeshift Metropolis', *Places Journal* (June 2001), https://doi. org/10.22269/140602.

31 See McGuirk, *Radical Cities*, pp. 80–98. Elemental have also subsequently tested the idea of building half-houses in Constitución in Chile (after the 2010 earthquake); Monterrey, Mexico; Guatemala and Peru. For a short film about the Quinta Monroy project, see Elemental's website at www.elementalchile.cl.

32 For the complete series of images, see the artist's website at www.dionisiogonzalez.es.

33 Bryan Finoki, 'Squatter Imaginaries', *Subtopia* (28 November 2007), http://subtopia.blogspot.co.uk.

34 Ibid.

35 The book is Alfredo Brillembourg and Hubert Klumpner, eds, *Torre David: Informal Vertical Communities* (Zurich, 2012); the film is *Torre David* (2013; available at http://u-tt.com/film/torre-david-film, accessed 21 August 2018). Other films include *Venezuela's Tower of Dreams* made by BBC journalist Olly Lambert in 2014.

36 See McGuirk, *Radical Cities*, pp. 179–80.

37 See Virginia Lopez, 'Caracas's Tower of David Squatters Finally Face Relocation after 8 Years', *The Guardian*, 23 July 2014, www.theguardian.com.

38 McGuirk, *Radical Cities*, p. 202.

39 Ibid., p. 203.

40 Ibid., p. 206.

41 On the growing house project, see Urban Think Tank's website at http://u-tt.com.

42 See McGuirk, *Radical Cities*, pp. 201–2.

43 See http://u-tt.com/project/anglican-church, accessed 21 August 2018.

44 See Nate Berg, 'From Theater Gates to Assemble: Is There an Art to Urban Regeneration?', *The Guardian*, 3 November 2015, www.theguardian.com.

45 McGuirk, *Radical Cities*, p. 205.

46 Rebecca Solnit, 'The Ruins Memory' (2006), in *Storming the Gates of Paradise: Landscape for Politics* (Berkeley, CA, 2007), pp. 351–70.

47 See Davis, *Planet of Slums*, p. 47.

48 See Dirk E. Hebel, Marta H. Wisniewska and Felix Heisel, *Building from Wastes: Recovered Materials in Architecture and Construction* (Basel, 2014).

49 See Davis, *Planet of Slums*, pp. 33–169. See also Alejandro Bahamón and Maria Camila Sanjinés, *Rematerial: From Waste to Architecture* (London, 2010).

50 Hebel, Wisniewska and Heisel, *Building from Wastes*, p. 7.

51 Ibid., pp. 33–169.

52 On the Rapid Re(f)use project, see the website of Terreform ONE at www.archinode.com.

53 See Mitchell Joachim, 'City and Refuse: Self-reliant Systems and Urban Terrains', in Hebel, Wisniewska and Heisel, *Building from Wastes*, pp. 22–3.

54 Ibid., p. 23.

55 On WALL-E, see Christopher Todd Anderson , 'Post-Apocalyptic Nostalgia: WALL-E, Garbage, and American Ambivalence toward Manufactured Goods', *Lit: Literature Interpretation Theory*, XXIII/3 (2012), pp. 267–82; and Hugh McNaughton, 'Distinctive Consumption and Popular Anti-consumerism: The Case of *Wall*E*', *Continuum*, XXVI/5 (2012), pp. 753–66.

56 John Scalzi, ed., *Metatropolis* (New York, 2009), pp. 9–11.

57 Jay Lake, 'In the Forests of the Night', in *Metatropolis*, ed. Scalzi, pp. 13–77.

58 Tobias S. Buckell, 'Stochasti-city', in *Metatropolis*, ed. Scalzi, p. 127.

59 Elizabeth Bear, 'The Red in the Sky Is Our Blood', in *Metatropolis*, ed. Scalzi, p. 165.

60 See Abbott, *Imagining Urban Futures*, p. 211.

61 China Miéville, *Perdido Street Station* (London, 2000), p. 157.
62 Ibid., pp. 255–6.
63 Ibid., pp. 547–8.
64 Ibid., p. 51. See also Joan Gordon, 'Hybridity, Heterotopia, and Mateship in China Miéville's *Perdido Street Station*', *Science Fiction Studies*, xxx/3 (2003), pp. 456–76.

BIBLIOGRAPHY

Abbott, Carl, *Imagining Urban Futures: Cities in Science Fiction and What We Might Learn From Them* (Middletown, CT, 2016)

Anderson, Darran, *Imaginary Cities* (London, 2015)

Asimov, Isaac, *The Caves of Steel* [1953] (London, 1997)

Bachelard, Gaston, *On Poetic Imagination and Reverie*, trans. Colette Gaudin (Putnam, CT, 2005)

Ballard, J. G., *The Complete Short Stories of J. G. Ballard* (London and New York, 2010)

—, *The Drowned World* (London, 1964)

Brayer, Marie Ange, et al., *Future City: Experiment and Utopia in Architecture, 1956–2006* (London, 2007)

Broderick, Mick, 'Surviving Armageddon: Beyond the Imagination of Disaster', *Science Fiction Studies*, XX/3 (1993), pp. 362–82

Brook, Daniel, *A History of Future Cities* (London, 2014)

Cairns, Stephen, and Jane Jacobs, *Buildings Must Die: A Perverse View of Architecture* (Cambridge, MA, 2014)

Chakrabarty, Dipesh, 'The Climate of History: Four Theses', *Critical Enquiry*, XXXV/2 (2009), pp. 197–223

Chapman, James, and Nicholas J. Cull, *Projecting Tomorrow: Science Fiction and Popular Culture* (London, 2013)

Connor, Steven, *The Matter of Air: Science and the Art of the Ethereal* (London, 2010)

Cook, Peter, *Architecture Workbook: Design through Motive* (Chichester, 2016)

Davis, Mike, *Dead Cities and Other Tales* (New York, 2002)

Dobraszczyk, Paul, *The Dead City: Urban Ruins and the Spectacle of Decay* (London, 2017)

—, Carlos López Galviz and Bradley L. Garrett, eds, *Global Undergrounds: Exploring Cities Within* (London, 2016)

Ferriss, Hugh, *The Metropolis of Tomorrow* (New York, 1929)

Gasiorek, Andrzej, *J. G. Ballard* (Manchester, 2005)

Gibson, William, *Virtual Light* (London, 1994)

Graham, Steven, *Vertical: The City from Satellites to Bunkers* (London, 2016)

Hebel, Dirk E., Marta H. Wisniewska and Felix Heisel, *Building from Wastes: Recovered Materials in Architecture and Construction* (Basel, 2014)

Howey, Hugh, *Wool* (London, 2013)

Jeter, K. W., *Farewell Horizontal* (London, 1989)

Kearney, Richard, *Poetics of Imagining: Modern to Post-modern* (Edinburgh, 1998)

Kropp, Lloyd, *The Drift* (London, 1969)

Leeuwen, Thomas van, *The Skyward Trend of Thought: The Metaphysics of the American Skyscraper* (Cambridge, MA, 1988)

McGuirk, Justin, *Radical Cities: Across Latin America in Search of a New Architecture* (London, 2015)

Malone, Meredith, ed., *Tomás Saraceno: Cloud-specific* (Chicago, IL, 2014)

Miéville, China, *Perdido Street Station* (London, 2000)

—, *The Scar* (London, 2002)

Murphy, Douglas, *Last Futures: Nature, Technology and the End of Architecture* (London, 2016)

Nobel, Phillip, ed., *The Future of the Skyscraper* (New York, 2015)

O'Grady, Sandra Kaji, and Peter Raisbeck, 'Prototype Cities in the Sea', *Journal of Architecture*, X/4 (2005), pp. 443–61

Olthuis, Koen, and David Keuning, *Float! Building on Water to Combat Urban Congestion and Climate Change* (London, 2010)

Page, Max, *The City's End: Two Centuries of Fantasies, Fears, and Premonitions of New York's Destruction* (London and New York, 2008)

Pawley, Martin, *Buckminster Fuller* (London, 1990)

Pike, David L., *Subterranean Cities: The World beneath Paris and London, 1800–1945* (Ithaca, NY, 2005)

Reynolds, Alastair, *Terminal World* (London, 2011)

Robida, Alfred, *The Twentieth Century*, trans. Philippe Willems (Middletown, CT, 2004)

Robinson, Kim Stanley, *New York 2140* (London, 2017)

Sklair, Leslie, *The Icon Project: Architecture, Cities and Capitalist Globalisation* (Oxford, 2016)

Spiller, Neil, *Visionary Architecture: Blueprints of the Modern Imagination* (London, 2007)

Topham, Sean, *Blowup: Inflatable Art, Architecture, and Design* (London, 2002)

Trexler, Adam, *Anthropocene Fictions: The Novel in a Time of Climate Change* (Charlottesville, VA, 2015)

Turner, Stephen, *Seafort* (Ramsgate, 2006)

Vidal, Ricarda, and Ingo Cornils, eds, *Alternative Worlds: Blue-sky Thinking since 1900* (Oxford, 2014)

Virilio, Paul, *Bunker Archaeology* (Princeton, NJ, 1994)

Williams, Evan Calder, *Combined and Uneven Apocalypse* (Winchester, 2011)

Woods, Lebbeus, *Radical Reconstruction: Lebbeus Woods* (New York, 2004)

Yusoff, Kathryn, and Jennifer Gabrys, 'Climate Change and the Imagination', *Wiley Interdisciplinary Reviews: Climate Change*, 11/4 (2011), pp. 516–34

ACKNOWLEDGEMENTS

I was able to begin the research for this project as a result of being awarded
an Independent Scholar Research Fellowship in 2016 from the Independent
Social Research Foundation, to whom I'm immensely thankful. I'm grateful
to Ben Hayes, formerly at Reaktion, who kickstarted the book, and to Vivian
Constantinopoulos, who took on the project. Grateful thanks also to the
Bartlett School of Architecture for providing funding for permissions fees for
some of the images, through their Architecture Research Fund. Many people
have been generous in providing images for the book and I am particularly
grateful to Iwan Baan, Tiago Barros, Luke Crowley, Paul Cureton, John Dent,
the Estate of Lebbeus Woods, Bradley L. Garrett, Dionisio González, Scott
Hocking, Mitchell Joachim, Michael Kerbow, Andrew Kudless, Anthony Lau,
Jeffery Linn, Max McClure, Mary Mattingly, Eric Nakajima, Cristobal Palma,
Deanna Petherbridge, Gavin Robotham, Alexis Rockman, the San Francisco
Museum of Modern Art, Squint/Opera, Studio Tomás Saraceno, Stefan Shaw,
Vertical Inc. and Philip Vile.

The research and writing was greatly influenced by my ongoing teaching
at the Bartlett in London, an extraordinarily creative institution which I am
privileged to be part of. I'm grateful to all of my students for inspiring and
challenging me to think outside my academic comfort zone, and particularly to Richard Breen and Anthony Ko for taking the time to talk through
their final-year design projects with me. The work was also enriched by the
symposium *Unmoored Cities: Radical Urban Futures and Climate Catastrophes*,
which I co-organized with UCL Urban Lab, Robin Wilson and Barbara Penner
in May 2018. Thanks to the Bartlett for funding this event through their
Architecture Projects Fund and to Ben Campkin and Jordan Rowe at UCL
Urban Lab, Barbara Penner, and all the speakers who contributed to this
event: CJ Lim, Viktoria Walldin, Rob La Frenais, Sasha Engelmann, Thandi
Loewenson, Maggie Gee, Rachel Armstrong, Jennifer Gabrys, Robin Wilson,
Matthew Butcher, Shaun Murray, Dean Sully, Penelope Haralambidou and
Jonathan Hill.

An earlier version of Chapter One was published as 'Sunken Cities: Climate Change, Urban Futures and the Imagination of Submergence', *International Journal of Urban and Regional Research*, XLI/6 (2017), pp. 868–87. Bits and pieces of Chapter Five were garnered from my contributions to *Global Undergrounds: Exploring Cities Within* (London, 2016); while parts of Chapters Six and Seven were developed from material first published in *The Dead City: Urban Ruins and the Spectacle of Decay* (London, 2017).

Finally, my thanks to Lisa and Isla, both of whom bore patiently my many anxieties over this project and sustained me throughout in countless other ways. My father first introduced me to the world of architecture and has never been less than supportive of my research and writing, even though I chose not to follow in his footsteps and become an architect myself. In light of his encouragement and inspiration, it is to him that I dedicate this book.

PHOTO ACKNOWLEDGEMENTS

The author and publishers wish to express their thanks to the below sources of illustrative material and/or permission to reproduce it. Every effort has been made to contact copyright holders; should there be any we have been unable to reach or to whom inaccurate acknowledgements have been made please contact the publishers, and full adjustments will be made to any subsequent printings.

Courtesy AFP Photo/Lucerne Festival Arknova 2013: p. 94; courtesy Iwan Baan: p. 212; courtesy Tiago Barros: p. 96; courtesy CRAB Studio: p. 47; courtesy Luke Crowley: p. 57; courtesy Paul Cureton: pp. 44–5; photo Paul Dobraszczyk: pp. 66, 723, 120–21, 164, 203; from *Everyday Science and Mechanics*, 11/12 (November 1931): p. 157; from Hugh Ferriss, *The Metropolis of Tomorrow* (New York, 1929): p. 111; courtesy Bradley L. Garrett: p. 163; courtesy the Gemeentemuseum Den Haag: p. 171; courtesy John Gollings: p. 43; courtesy Dionisio González: p. 211; courtesy Scott Hocking: p. 184; from Blanchard Jerrold, *London: A Pilgrimage* (London, 1872): p. 32; courtesy Mitchell Joachim, Terreform ONE: p. 216; courtesy Michael Kerbow: p. 181; from Moses King, *King's Views of New York* (New York, 1911): p. 123; courtesy Andrew Kudless/ Matsys: p. 151; courtesy Anthony Lau: pp. 62–3; courtesy Jeffrey Linn: p. 33; courtesy Max McClure: p. 194; courtesy Mary Mattingly: p. 69; courtesy Eric Nakajima: p. 158; © Tsutomu Nihei and courtesy Kodansha Ltd: p. 176; courtesy Christobal Palma: p. 210; courtesy the artist (© Deanna Petherbridge): pp. 182 (photo Anna Arca Photography, London), 183 (photo John Bodkin, Dawkinscolour, London); Pixabay: pp. 112 (photo smarko), 130 (photo zhang-junming); from 'G.E. Robertson' [Étienne-Gaspart Robert], *La Minerve, Vaisseau Aërien Destiné aux Découvertes, et proposé à toutes les Académies de l'Europe; par le Physicien Robertson, Ci-devant Professeur à l'Ecole Centrale du Département de l'Ourte, de la Societé Galvanique, de celle d'Émulation de Liége, et de celle pour l'Encouragement des Sciences et Arts de Hambourg* (Paris, 1820): p. 89; courtesy Alexis Rockman: pp. 36–7; San Francisco Museum of Modern

INDEX